STRATEGIES OF THE SILENT IN
MEDIEVAL ENGLISH LITERATURE

STRATEGIES OF THE SILENT IN MEDIEVAL ENGLISH LITERATURE

Edwin D. Craun

THE PENNSYLVANIA STATE UNIVERSITY PRESS
UNIVERSITY PARK, PENNSYLVANIA

Library of Congress Cataloging-in-Publication Data

Names: Craun, Edwin D. author
Title: Strategies of the silent in medieval English literature / Edwin D. Craun.
Description: University Park, Pennsylvania : The Pennsylvania State University Press, 2025. | Includes bibliographical references and index.
Summary: "Explores how key figures in major Middle English texts use silence strategically in public life. Drawing on Latin traditions, it examines how rulers, advisors, dissidents, outcasts, and seekers employ silence to govern, maintain power, resist oppression, protect themselves, or learn, highlighting its complex social and political functions"— Provided by publisher.
Identifiers: LCCN 2025006896 | ISBN 9780271099910 hardback | ISBN 9780271099941 paperback
Subjects: LCSH: English literature—Middle English, 1100–1500—History and criticism | Silence in literature | Politics and literature | LCGFT: Literary criticism
Classification: LCC PR275.S55 C73 2025 | DDC 820.9/353—dc23/eng/20250521
LC record available at https://lccn.loc.gov/2025006896

Copyright © 2025 Edwin D. Craun
All rights reserved
Printed in the United States of America
Published by The Pennsylvania State University Press,
University Park, PA 16802–1003

The Pennsylvania State University Press is a member of the Association of University Presses.

It is the policy of The Pennsylvania State University Press to use acid-free paper. Publications on uncoated stock satisfy the minimum requirements of American National Standard for Information Sciences—Permanence of Paper for Printed Library Material, ANSI Z39.48–1992.

*In memory of
Eleanor Woodworth Craun,
my mother, and
Prof. Sidney M. B. Coulling
and Dean William J. Watt,
colleagues and mentors,
all of whom knew the value and
limitations of silence in public*

CONTENTS

Acknowledgments | ix
Editorial Practices, Translations, and Abbreviations | x

Introduction: Reading the Riddles of Public Silences | 1

1 Why Public Silences Matter: Albertano da Brescia and Clerical Texts | 14

2 The Art of Political Silence: The Prudent King of Hoccleve's *Regiment of Princes* | 30

3 Corrupt Political Silences: *Mum and the Sothsegger* | 45

4 Patient Silences Under Interrogation: Jesus in the York Cycle and William Thorpe | 69

5 The Limitations of Silence in Social Life: Thomas Hoccleve's "My Complaint" and "Dialogue" | 100

6 Wise Silences in the Life of Learning: Will and the Philosophers in *Piers Plowman* | 123

Postscript: Literary Invention, Power Differentials, and Ethical Multiplicity | 150

Notes | 155
Bibliography | 176
Index | 189

ACKNOWLEDGMENTS

A monograph written in retirement during the COVID years, when scholarly colleagues were enmeshed in the toils of online teaching and conferences were in abeyance, needs few acknowledgments, yet those few are all the heartier. Michael Kuczynski cheered me on after reading several chapters, and Katharine Breen, as an editor of *The Yearbook of Langland Studies*, had earlier advised me astutely as I set about revising much of chapter 6, as had two anonymous readers for the journal. That version was published as "A Taciturn Will" in *YLS* 33 (2019): 43–67. I was greatly indebted during the COVID years to the librarians of Washington and Lee University, especially Elizabeth Teaff, Shana Shutler, and Laura Hewett, who hunted down books for me in the stacks and on Interlibrary Loan and then left them in bundles outside the locked library doors.

I am indebted to the following institutions for access, before and after the COVID years, to manuscripts in their keeping: the Weston Library of the Bodleian (chiefly), the British Library; the Worcester Cathedral Library; the Bibliothèque municipale de Lyon; the Provost and Fellows of Oriel College, Oxford; the Master and Fellows of University College, Oxford; and the Master and Fellows of Trinity College, Cambridge.

At two stages, the resourceful Louise Uffelman helped to prepare the files for submission to the Pennsylvania State University Press. Its executive editor, Ellie Goodman, manifested interest in this monograph from the start, and its two anonymous readers suggested many ways to expand the range of Middle English texts and make my arguments more assertive.

As with all my research and writing over nearly fifty years, my primary debt is to my loving, resourceful, and tolerant wife, Marlys Jean, who not only kept the home fires burning (quite literally since we heated with wood) but had a far more demanding life than I as a psychiatric social worker engaged in delivering public mental health services in rural counties on the fringes of Appalachia.

EDITORIAL PRACTICES, TRANSLATIONS, AND ABBREVIATIONS

Whether in my transcriptions from manuscripts or in passages taken from editions, I retain Middle English thorn and yogh, as well as Middle English spelling, and, with Latin texts, I use *v* for the consonant, *u* for the vowel. In Latin and Middle English transcriptions, I add modern punctuation and capitalization, and I expand contractions. I give the names of medieval writers, except Thomas Aquinas, in their vernaculars, not in Latin for some and in English for others or in a mix of the two (Guillaume Peyraut, not William Peraldus). In translating the Vulgate, I rely on the Douai version, modernizing slightly. All other translations are mine. I use the following abbreviations:

CCCM	Corpus Christianorum. Continuatio Mediaevalis
CCSL	Corpus Christianorum Scriptorum Latinorum
DMLB	*Dictionary of Medieval Latin from British Sources*
EETS	Early English Text Society
LCL	Loeb Classical Library
MED	*Middle English Dictionary*
PL	Patrologia Latina
SAC	*Studies in the Age of Chaucer*
YLS	*The Yearbook of Langland Studies*

INTRODUCTION

Reading the Riddles of Public Silences

"A certain philosopher, asked whether he was staying silent because he lacked words or because he was foolish, responded to those talking: 'No foolish person is able to stay silent'" (Philosophus quidam aliis loquentibus et, interrogatus utrum propter inopiam verborum aut quia stultus esset taceret, respondit: "Nemo stultus tacere potest").[1] John of Mirfield (d. 1407), an Augustinian canon attached as chaplain to St. Bartholomew's Hospital, Smithfield, recalls this anecdote as he knits together an entry on silence in his late fourteenth-century *Florarium Bartholomei* (An anthology from Bartholomew's), a vast compendium, by topic, of moral and medical material copied well down into the fifteenth century. In the anecdote, someone's silence in a social situation puzzles and disturbs at least one of the speakers. Although unsure of what to make of it, he proposes two causes: lack of eloquence or stupidity, the elastic word *stultus* suggesting social ineptitude, fatuity, lack of consideration, and/or mental limitation. The wise man's pithy rejoinder negates both possibilities. Its brevity indicates rhetorical skill; its acuity, considered social analysis derived from experience. Moreover, by choosing not to argue against his interrogator, which might entail verbal confrontation and a fair amount of speech, he displays, as his silence has, a considered choice to be taciturn, to prefer silence or brief and infrequent utterances to loquacity. As John of Mirfield and other moral writers of the late thirteenth and fourteenth centuries tell this anecdote, silence elicits a precipitous but "knowing" response: it can only be due to deficiency, mental or social. Yet the reply indicates the very opposite: silence while others are speaking may spring from strength of mind and character. However, as a sign, just as words are, silence may be misconstrued readily, especially by the loquacious, as in John's anecdote. Of what, in any given situation, is silence a sign?

The philosopher of this anecdote cagily uses the social situation in which he finds himself, his companions' loquacity, and his questioner's presumptuous reading of his silence as an occasion to provoke the talkers to think about both silence and speech. His very terseness forces his auditors to puzzle out what his reply might mean and apply its significance to themselves. Is he simply defending himself from a false interpretation of his silence? (I'm not a fool because fools can't stay silent.) Is he impugning his questioner? (You're a fool because you're unable to keep your dicey conjectures to yourself.) Is he indicating that the loquacity of all the speakers discloses that each one of them is *stultus*: socially obtuse, fatuous, or lacking a quick wit? Or is he suggesting that wisdom entails knowing the value of silence and learning when and how to practice it, even in company? However his auditors might interpret his rejoinder, it may enable them to see silence, and to see speech, in a new light, reconsidering why others might remain silent, whether they possess the powers to interpret the silences of others, and even perhaps whether silence is a response to what they are saying. He has turned the tables on his interrogator, becoming the wise one, the one who takes control of a situation and makes a statement that will be remembered.

Silence, of course, is necessary for conversation itself to take place. Erving Goffman, a pioneer of Conversation Analysis, notes that potential speakers routinely remain silent for a time out of deference to others so that they may speak or continue to speak.[2] Beyond this basic function, silence, like speech, is a mode of communication with many functions, as modern theorists of communication insist. Indeed, strategically using silence while others are speaking may further the silent one's communicative purposes.[3] It may influence the course of speech in political, forensic, and social situations: in debate, consultation, trials, verbal assaults, and casual conversation. It may enable people to accomplish what they desire: listening to discern the character and motives of those who are speaking, learning from speakers, preserving integrity, implying certainty or superiority, ducking hostility, cloaking feelings or thoughts, preserving secrets, seizing others' attention, shunning conflict with the powerful. Silence for them is not simply an act of restraint. It is a good that offers opportunities to the person who chooses it. Yet what silence means in any given situation, what the silent are communicating with the sign of silence, let alone what they are trying to achieve with it, is difficult to fathom because of its many functions. Does a silence indicate agreement or disagreement with what is being said? Does the person lack sufficient information to talk on the topic, or are they pondering carefully what to say? Are they bored or raptly attentive? Are they excluding themselves from a conversation they consider beneath them, even reprehensible, or are they concerned about avoiding saying anything that might hurt a speaker? These are some of the twenty potential meanings for a silence compiled by the sociolinguist Richard L. Johannesen, a list he considers far from exhaustive.[4]

Voluntary silences that may puzzle other characters and demand considered interpretation from readers and audiences punctuate at crucial points a wide range of late Middle English texts: dramatic, petitionary, satiric, autobiographical, visionary, dialogic, instructional, and advisory. Some silences, like that of John of Mirfield's wise man, provoke others present to come up with causes, revealing their own thoughts, feelings, emotions (culturally scripted and performed feelings), intentions, and cultural presuppositions.[5] Thus, they set up a contrast in ways of life that invites ethical reflection and, perhaps, judgment by other characters and by readers or auditors. The Caiaphas, Anna, Pilate, and Herod of the York cycle of biblical plays are baffled by the silences and rare riddling utterances of the Jesus they attempt to interrogate. Yet they are also eager to interpret them. That contemporary high priest (in the eyes of Wycliffites) Archbishop Thomas Arundel interrogates the suspected heretic William Thorpe, only to be confronted by a mosaic of passionate speech and silences he does not readily grasp. In *Mum and the Sothsegger*, by contrast, Mum is all too ready to disclose why he stays silent in certain political, ecclesiastical, and legal situations. Yet his advocacy of the strategic silences that achieve his purposes is contested by other figures, constructing a conflict over opposed ethics of the place of silence in political life that invites readers to adjudicate their worth. In Thomas Hoccleve's "My Complaint" and "Dialogue," Thomas, the figure for the poet, considers the failed strategies of silence that he adopted in order to convey to others that his social conduct was no longer shattered by the "wilde infirmitee" of his past. Why have others misconstrued his silences as signs of mental illness? What might convince them that his feelings, emotions, and thoughts are no longer disordered? In other texts, like the third dream in *Piers Plowman*, silence escapes the attention of modern readers, occluding profound shifts in feelings, emotions, thoughts, and speech. If we neglect to puzzle out the reasons for these silences, interpreting them as we do the poem's passionate debates, we can miss why Will the Dreamer adopts different ways of achieving his purposes, even how he does so. Even when an advisory text, like Hoccleve's *Regiment of Princes*, advocates prudent practices of silence, the political strategies and political capital created by silence may elude modern readers.

How can we interpret such silences, let alone weigh their social and ethical worth, when silence has so many functions and the texts themselves display how readily figures misconstrue what impels others to renounce speech? Silence while others are talking is, of course, not a thing in itself, as Tiziana Suarez-Nani reminds us. It depends on the speech surrounding it, whether it negates that or simply stands apart from it.[6] For the Polish sociolinguist Adam Jaworski, a voluntary silence must be interpreted within the linguistic web in which it occurs: "the same interpretive processes apply to someone remaining meaningfully silent in discourse as to their speaking."[7] Just as auditors who wish to speak are dependent on adjacent speech acts in the order in which they occur, so are observers of silences in political and social situations. Just as an auditor must infer from another's speech its genesis and illocutionary force (Does it deny, threaten, insult, or warn?), so must readers, although narrators may give them cues. To examine how potential speakers can make such assessments of speech acts, sociolinguists have adopted ethnographical principles that we can convert into questions for readers encountering silences in late medieval texts. What is the genre of speech at work when a figure refrains from speaking, and what are its conventions? The meaning of silence in a philosophical debate (if, for example, John of Mirfield's *philosophus* were in the midst of philosophers) might be quite different from that in a trial, casual conversation, or even a theological disputation. What is the setting? If a noblewoman is under lock and key in her bedroom, her silence in her lover's presence might signify something very different from her silence when they are dining in her father's hall. What are the political, forensic, or social roles of the participants, vocal and silent? What differences in power are created by these roles? A judge's silence might very well signify something quite different from the accused's silence. Within social roles, rank matters. A squire of low degree's silence before an earl's daughter he loves might convey something quite different than if he were of her social rank or higher. Given their roles and ranks, what does their society expect of them in such an exchange?[8] The amount an unmarried woman might speak to a man while walking down a street was governed by cultural prescriptions. Beyond these questions involving social context and the power relations it establishes, sociolinguists, like historians of emotions, invite us to ask tactical or attitudinal questions. What stance toward the speakers is the taciturn person conveying? Respect, hostility, disapproval, alienation, or one or more of many other stances?[9] And, given how society describes—indeed, constructs—emotions for the silent one's community, what emotions are they expressing by that stance? Anger? Fear? Despair? Love? All of these questions about silence recognize that a silence, like an act of speech, is a social performance, one dependent on the presence of speech.[10] That speech, of course, is fluid, as Conversation Analysis insists, for speakers constantly shift their footing by changing the kind or framework of the conversation, their stance, and even the self they are projecting within their social roles.[11]

As these questions indicate, a society's norms governing both speech and silence become crucial for readers who come across, and take account of, silence in medieval narratives and plays. Such norms, as writers indicate, shape literary figures and implied readers, providing them with a moral language, tools for ethical reflection, and, to some extent, an identity shared to some degree with their society in general and to some degree with the differentiated social groups in which they are embedded. I am adopting the position of Seyla Benhabib and, behind her, of Hans-Georg Gadamer in his philosophical hermeneutics: that agents are embedded in communities that develop in them habits of practical reason and ethical understandings that they apply in specific situations.[12]

The most fruitful way to grasp how such norms construct silences in late medieval English narratives, plays, lyrics, and mirrors for princes is to examine instructional moral texts of several genres in circulation in England from the mid-thirteenth century to the late fifteenth: treatises on the ethics of speech; collections of *exempla* for preachers; treatises of advice for rulers and counselors; basic school texts; collections of wise sayings; alphabetized pastoral *distinctiones* with entries on silence or, more often, taciturnity as the inclination to stay silent. (The high number of entries on "Silencium" or "Taciturnitas" in these preaching aids is particularly striking because so many collections peter out about halfway through the alphabet after affording a large amount of space to the early letters.)[13] Largely unedited and unprinted, these texts offer guidance on the ethics of silence, giving norms and strategies for their societies as a whole and for specific social groups. They set forth the general circumstances that determine if it may be beneficial (*utilis*) to withhold speech, not only for the silent one but also for other persons, present or not (*bona* or *discreta* [thoughtfully determined] *taciturnitas*). They also spell out the circumstances under which it may be destructive (*mala* [evil], *indiscreta*, or *nimia* [excessive] *taciturnitas*). These texts are constructed from several cultural and ethical traditions, especially from Roman popular morality and Stoic texts as transmitted in late antique and early medieval collections of sayings and anecdotes (*dicta et facta*), from Jewish wisdom literature as learned from the Christian Bible, and from patristic texts, most often the writings of Pope Gregory I. Take for an example our anecdote about the wise man, as found in John of Mirfield's *distinctio* "De silencio." The writings of ancient wise men teach us, John claims at the outset, that no one can be fully virtuous or wise without moderating speech, that is, governing the tongue with an eye to certain norms (*modi*). This claim he confirms first with over twenty authoritative sayings (*sententiae*) attributed to Solomon, Sirach (Ben Sira), the apostle James, "Seneca" (really the Roman mime Publilius Syrus), several ancient philosophers, and the school text *Disticha Catonis*. Then he recalls several anecdotes from the *Vitae patrum* (Lives of the Fathers) about the arduous, sustained discipline that makes such control possible. Considerably more briefly, John turns to the dangers of excessive, evil, and thoughtless (*indiscreta*) taciturnity in one social group: clerics required to teach, preach, and correct the conduct of those who are committed to their charge. There he quotes just a few biblical and patristic *sententiae*. In a closing section, marked by a *paragraphus* (¶) in British Library MS. Royal 7.F.XI, he states a comprehensive, balanced practice of silence: the mouth ought to be so carefully guarded that it neither rejects life-giving teaching nor speaks freely what is ruinously destructive: "Ponenda est ergo ori custodia ut nec vitalem edificacionem clausum dampnet nec letalis pernicies liberum sociatur egressum." To develop this, he gives our anecdote, adding to the presumptuous question (really a statement like so many "questions" after a lecture) and to the wise man's reply a second question and the wise man's reply to that. The new speaker reacts to the wise man's dictum that the foolish cannot remain silent. "Cui alter ergo: 'Cur solus tu linguam cohibes?' 'Quia,' inquit, 'dixisse me aliquando penituit; tacuisse numquam.'"[14] (Then, another said to him: "Why are only you restraining the tongue?" "Because," he said, "to have spoken has grieved me sometimes; to have kept silence, never.") Careful not to construe the silence himself, this second speaker comprehends that this silence, alone as it is amid the conversation, is a deliberate act of restraint. And the wise man's will to avoid the regret, even loss, that speech can precipitate is then reinforced immediately outside the anecdote by a well-known saying from the *Disticha Catonis*, which is embedded in a Middle English political satire we will take up in chapter 3: "Nam nulli tacuisse nocet; nocet esse locutum" (To have kept silence harms no one; to have spoken harms).[15] Thus, John converts the wise man's answer into an explicit preference for taciturnity as the inclination to keep silent in order to avoid harming anyone within, or even outside of, the immediate social circle.

As John of Mirfield's *distinctio* reveals, moral writers supply their contemporaries (and those who follow) with both classical and scriptural authoritative material, the one reinforcing the other. With this material, they develop measures by which people may discern in specific situations whether speech should be avoided or embraced. Thus, they may learn to moderate their tongue, governing it by a *moderamen*, a means of control. Often formulated in terms of the consequences of speech and of silence, beneficial or destructive, these *modi* usually promote a self-protective ethic of caution, of initially restraining the tongue until the situation, the other speakers, one's own emotional state, and the likely consequences of speaking (or not) have been assessed. Beyond this realm of practical rationality, moral writers also formulate norms in terms of potential speakers' wills: of what they desire and what they detest, of what they are pursuing and what they are avoiding, and so, in part, of what emotions are assisting them in achieving what they seek.[16] Intention, as always, matters in medieval moral thought. What ends do people have in mind when they choose to be silent? What do they seek to accomplish with their silences? Although moral writers often generalize about the will, emotions, and intentions, they may also apply general norms to the conduct of certain social groups. Clerical writers insist that the love of their fellow humans should guide all who consider speaking or remaining silent. Yet they also specifically condemn any cleric who, out of fear, remains silent when he could rebuke the sins of the rich and powerful, especially those in his pastoral care. Although all Christians were bound by charity (and by canon law) to rebuke sinful conduct in others in order to amend their fellows (the practice of fraternal correction), clerics were especially reprehensible for such silences because of their *officium*, their chosen position in life that obligates them to teach and correct others.[17] Finally, moral writers look to the consequences of acts of silence. What benefits or destructive effects do they bring for the agent, for others, for the community? A royal adviser's silence cloaking his own thinking from a rival at court would have very different consequences from his silence about a course of action against a national enemy that is decided on, but not yet executed, by the royal council and the king. Thus, the fundamental questions that are used, along with circumstances, to evaluate the moral nature and gravity of any act, including any speech act (Is that killing homicide or necessary self-defense? Are those words slander or just idle talk?) also apply to silence.[18] Silence is as much a moral act requiring ethical reflection as speech. That is why moral writers, like the English compiler of the widely distributed *De lingua* (On the tongue; ca. 1290), often append chapters on silence to treatises on the sins of the tongue or on virtuous speech.

Exempla, like pithy *sententiae*, are staples of late medieval moral writing, presenting readers with specific situations, as John of Mirfield's historical anecdote does, in which characters choose to remain silent while others are speaking and expecting them to speak. When *modi* are developed in moral texts by exempla, another ethical element often emerges as central: the figure's virtues and/or vices. As a desirable *habitus* (perhaps best translated as "disposition" or "condition") formed over time by social norms, examples, and repeated actions, a virtue helps to maintain stability or consistency in conduct, a quality that, J. D. Burnley has noted, was valued greatly in late medieval culture.[19] Virtues give people direction and strength as they try to deal with situations that are difficult to manage and, often, even difficult to assess. John Gower's Genius urges Amans to acquire patience so that he will be able to hold his tongue rather than vent his spur-of-the-moment feelings in the sort of angry speech that has been alienating his lady.[20] Socrates, Genius tells Amans by way of example, was so given to patience that when his quarrelsome wife insulted him repeatedly and then threatened to dump cold water on his head, "he al softe / Sat stille and noght a word ansuered." After she furiously spilled the water all over him, he, "which wolde noght forsake / His patience," commented mildly that she was simply bestowing wind and rain on him in accordance with the season.[21] Although exemplary figures, like Gower's Socrates, could choose to act contrary to their virtuous (or vicious) disposition, virtue or vice is a powerful force in moving them toward silence.

By considering only voluntary silences, such as that of Socrates or John of Mirfield's wise man, this book obviously excludes the tongue-tied, those whom *De lingua* describes as deprived of speech by a weighty ligature binding the tongue, and the coerced, like those bound to silence by penance.[22] It also omits those figures for whom silence has become obligatory, even if they chose the social role that dictates it, like the religious within their enclosures and confessors (when it comes to what they have heard in confession). Moreover, by examining silences amid the flow of conversation, the book excludes the silences of rapt mystics. Oddly enough, such nonpolitical and nonsocial silences have interested medieval historians of all types more than voluntary ones have. In addition, voluntary silences in one mode of vernacular narratives are also excluded: romances with figures who disguise their identity and cloak their love, even sometimes from the one they love. Almost without exception—even including penitential romances like *Guy of Warwick*—they do not draw on the learned classical and biblical tradition of moral thought about the strategies and ethics of silence in public life. Although I plan to write about the silences of lovers, especially women, I will do it elsewhere.

This book begins with the role of silence in the craft of governing, then moves to the practice of coercive power exercised by religious authorities, in conjunction with the state, against dissidents, who find in silence strategies for resistance and refusal. In these institutional contexts, silence becomes a successful strategy for power, for influence, and for resistance when it springs from settled habits of virtue, like the prudence of a ruler or advisers and the patience of a religious dissident. Their virtues give them deep resources, powers of restraint, consistency (and, therefore, integrity), and time for reflection in fraught and shifting situations. Coercion and asymmetrical power also shape social relations when an individual is seen by a defined group to violate its norms. As in inquisitorial dialogues, silence may be accompanied, even generated, by a fear of missteps that might worsen the deviant's isolated and seemingly helpless position. Finally, this book turns to the social relations between an eager and passionate inquirer and authoritative figures who advocate a philosophical wisdom that values taciturnity in those who are seeking a good life. In the verbal exchanges of education, as in those of a court or social cohort, unequal power relations operate, though the scope of punitive threat may seem more limited. For this reason, silence remains a powerful strategy for obtaining what is desired even when self-protection is not its end.

In this framework moving from the most public situation to the least, each set of vernacular texts is prefaced by an analysis of prescriptive Latin moral writing that deals with the types of taciturnity and silence explored in the vernacular literature, developing the virtues and emotions central to the strategies of the silent. Chapter 1 presents the major sources of discourse on taciturnity: the conduits from antiquity to the thirteenth century, Albertano da Brescia's *De arte loquendi et tacendi* (On the craft of speaking and keeping silent), and the clergy's moral writing from the thirteenth to the fifteenth centuries. Albertano argues that taciturnity is a craft that forestalls violence and promotes prosperity in communal life, all the while advancing the individual citizen. Although his arguments for the benefits of silence rely on a tapestry of Roman, Jewish, and Christian texts, he builds up a barebones practical framework for using initial circumspect silence to assess any speaking situation within civic life. More than *De arte*, clerical texts develop prudence as the virtue that makes taciturnity valuable, indeed, even possible. Not only does it foresee the likely outcomes of speaking or staying silent, but, if it is governed by love, it ensures that those outcomes will benefit others. While clerics share Albertano's sense of the multiple benefits of both initial taciturnity and sustained silence, they distrust even more than he the unrestrained feelings and emotions that drive hasty and excessive speech, the source of violence, self-sabotage, and failed projects.

Prescriptive moral writing on taciturnity and silence in general shapes poems considering ways in which the early Lancastrians can govern effectively in a time of popular unrest, especially ways in which they can gather reliable and comprehensive counsel. In chapter 2, I consider how Thomas Hoccleve's *Regiment of Princes* advises Prince Henry (soon to be Henry V) to practice taciturnity as a practical cautionary strategy, derived largely from Albertano's and the clerics' textual amalgam, that will both build up his own reputation and advance the welfare of the realm. Guided by the virtue of prudence, the habit of examining the past in order to make decisions with an eye to their outcomes, taciturnity can avert rash speech in political situations, preventing disaffection, enmity, and strife at court and, more broadly, throughout the realm. Taciturnity becomes exemplary political conduct. Chapter 3 takes up how the evil twin of prudent taciturnity found more than a foothold at the Lancastrian court in the eyes of Hoccleve and, especially, the Wycliffite author of the satire *Mum and the Sothsegger*. Both poets mock royal advisers, lay as well as clerical, for clinging so desperately to status and reward that they hide popular discontent from the king and refuse to question his destructive designs. I contend that when this self-interested silence is justified in *Mum* by appeals to Roman popular morality, it opens up fissures in the amalgam of classical and of Jewish and Christian materials shaping why moral writers promote taciturnity. In *Mum*, shaped by a long moral tradition of unmasking evil taciturnity and given point by John Wyclif's apocalyptic denunciation of culpably silent ecclesiastics, self-interested silence permeates all institutions, vitiating good governance, working against the welfare of others and the kingdom as a whole.

The four interrogation pageants of the York cycle create a brilliant, lively, and sustained contrast between a patiently silent Jesus and the four violent, manipulative, arrogant, and angry questioners. All of them, I argue in chapter 4, attempt to construe Jesus's baffling and infuriating silences in their own terms as arising from trickery, incapacity, or impotent awe in the face of their greatness. In my reading, they are wholly given over to language as a tool for enforcing hierarchal rule, using threats, boasts, and demotic insults to delegitimize and marginalize the silent Jesus, just as they do the bystanders in their courts. In these ways, I conclude, the York citizens are invited not only to detest the genres of speech the powerful use to intimidate and subject but also to discern the value of patient silence in adversity, especially that caused by corrupt and oppressive political and ecclesiastical authorities. It has the power to resist, to refuse to acknowledge corrupt institutions, to subvert inquisitorial ploys, to shun retaliatory speech, to preserve one's integrity, and to help realize one's purposes. Yet how can mere humans imitate the patient silence of Jesus, divine as well as human? After glancing at the surprising silences of Margery Kempe, chapter 4 ends by examining how the Wycliffite William Thorpe chooses when to use silence to resist his interrogators and when to contest their charges in order to avoid the evil taciturnity condemned by Wyclif.

Although chapter 5 shifts to social situations from institutional ones, it retains a focus on silence as a strategy for dealing with oppressive power. Thomas in Hoccleve's "My Complaint" has been cast out of his close urban social cohort of government clerks and is dogged by the hostile scrutiny of former companions who suspect that his former mental illness has returned and will disrupt their tightly policed norms of sociability. He is paralyzed by fear, an emotion that in moral writing may either obviate a good outcome by its overwhelming images of a terrible future or assist agents in acting for their own benefit. Hoccleve uses this situation to probe more fully and deeply than any other late medieval English writer why initially appealing silences fail to benefit oppressed figures. Out of fear lest he worsen his isolation, Thomas retreats from conversation altogether, aiming to escape his former cohort's misjudgments and slights. Yet he comes to realize that silence has debilitating limits. As an ambiguous sign, it may be misconstrued as a sign of illness, while, as moral texts warn, it only aggravates his sorrows. Finally, Thomas, I argue, finds a way out of the prison house of silence by grasping that his writing can become a confession of faith in a redemptive God, whose mutable natural world has brought him healing as well as suffering, as it has done and will do to others.

In contrast with Hoccleve's Thomas moving away from silences of limited efficacy and oppressive weight, Will in the third dream in *Piers Plowman* moves from impulsive speech to embrace taciturnity within the social process of learning from authoritative figures. Moral discourse on taciturnity, I argue in chapter 6, informs the final episodes of this dream, leading Will the Dreamer to grasp how essential taciturnity is for learning wisdom and acquiring knowledge. Moral sayings from Greek philosophers prescribing for their pupils and from Jewish wisdom literature help Will to understand how his own reckless and adversarial speech, directed toward an authoritative figure who could enlighten him, has blocked the way to learning what constitutes a life worth living and has inflicted injuries and losses on him. More importantly, Will learns from his experience and his wise instructor Imaginitif to embrace verbal restraint and attentive listening, rather than angry disputation, as a means to learn from others what he passionately desires to know.

Quite by chance, I began writing about culpable and destructive self-interested silences in political life during the first impeachment trial of President Donald Trump, in which some holders of public office and presidential advisers refused even to appear as witnesses and some of those who did invoked the self-protective right to remain silent. Chapter 4, on patient silence while suffering seemingly overwhelming adversity, occupied the first five months of the COVID-19 pandemic, during which so many people were cut off from others even as they were gutted by a little understood and possibly fatal virus. I began writing about silence generated by fears of a threatening future during the strangely and violently contested aftermath of the US presidential campaign of 2020. Also by chance, thirty-five years ago, I began a book-length study of deviant speech in late medieval English literature (*Lies, Slander, and Obscenity in Medieval English Literature*) while public figures were being interrogated by Congress over lying during the Iran-Contra affair. Fifteen years later, I wrote much of *Ethics and Power in Medieval English Reformist Writing*, a study of what constituted effective social critique in late medieval England, during protests over the Second Iraq War. We are sometimes told (Are we not?) that medieval studies has little to do with our pressing problems and public debates. As a literary historian, I offer unapologetically this third monograph (a trilogy!) on the ethics of communication in medieval moral, narrative, and dramatic literature. Public silences then, as now, have strategies and consequences, dimensions that medieval imaginative writers explore subtly yet analytically in order to provoke ethical reflection and pragmatic action.

CHAPTER 1

WHY PUBLIC SILENCES MATTER
Albertano da Brescia and Clerical Texts

The third distich of the *Disticha Catonis*, that fundamental text used to teach English schoolboys Latin, English composition, conduct, and morality, presents silence as the proper initial stance, the default position, in all arenas of public life: "Virtutem primam esse puta compescere linguam: / Proximus ille deo est, qui scit ratione tacere." As the somewhat expanded Northern translation of this distich reads:

> Þe first vertew, me suete [sweet] sone dere,
> Is to daunte [bring under control] þe tunge and stere;
> For alwei next to God is he,
> Þat wel with resoun stille kan be.[1]

Taciturnity is the greatest of all virtues, claims the author of a thirteenth-century commentary on the *Disticha* preserved in Bodleian Library, MS Canon Latin Classical 72. Reason, he continues, teaches us when to speak and when to stay silent, using prudence, which makes distinctions between situations with very cautious circumspection. When we hold our tongues for the purpose of living well or not committing evil, we draw near to God. These "teaching points" he confirms with sayings from Ovid's *Ars amatoria*, Pope Gregory the Great, the encyclopedist Isidore of

Seville, and the book of Proverbs.[2] Why did Christian *grammatici*, Richard Hazelton asked some time ago, keep the *Disticha* as an early reader in schools, given that its precepts are self-centered and opportunistic, based on a "cynical, calculating view of human motives"? To answer his question, he turned to commentaries like this on the *Disticha*, discovering that they explicate the distiches by glossing them with verses from the Jewish wisdom books included in the Vulgate—and, I would add, with passages from patristic writers. In fact, he discovered that this commentary, like others, states that the subject matter of "Cato" ("materia Catonis") is the four cardinal virtues, which direct one to lead an honest life, to avoid going astray, and even to reach eternal life.[3]

In and of itself, the *Disticha* conveys what Teresa Morgan categorizes as Roman popular morality, a common set of norms that circulated widely throughout Roman society, often percolating down from philosophers to its lowest social levels. This body of practical morality is grounded in a strong sense of natural necessity, of human limitations, and of the sheer difficulty of human life. Roman *gnomai* and historical exempla, many attributed to the wise and learned (*sapientes* or *philosophi*), plus proverbs and fables, presented two courses of action. To act against human limitations and the course of the world as humans have observed it over time is pointless or even impossible, leading to disastrous consequences; to act in accordance with both yields good consequences, usually prosperity and social stature. In this unabashedly self-interested ethic, the results determine whether people evaluate an act as good or evil. To know how to use foresight to assess potential outcomes is to be wise; to repeat one's mistakes or those of others, especially by rushing into things, is to be foolish.[4] Silence in the *Disticha*, as in Roman popular morality in general, becomes key in assessing situations and so in forestalling any harm to oneself and to allies or friends. To restrain speech while others are speaking freely enables one to observe their characters: "Perspicito cuncta tacitus, quid quisque loquatur: / Sermo hominum mores et celat et indicat idem" (Keeping silent, examine all things thoroughly, what each person speaks; / The speech of people both hides their character and also reveals it).[5] Such silent circumspection prevents precipitous, unguarded words that might lead to conflict and even violence, might endanger the social standing and reputation of speakers or others, and might disclose their counsel, their partially or fully formed plans of action. While the *Disticha* presents speech as potentially harmful, silence harms no one:

"Nam nulli tacuisse nocet, nocet esse locutum," a line that will echo down through this chapter, the next two, and the last.[6]

This popular morality was transmitted to thirteenth-century and later writers by other collections of wise sayings from late antiquity and the following centuries, as well as by the *Disticha*, compiled in the fourth century. The maxims collected under the name of the Roman mime Publilius Syrus, known and admired in the first and second centuries, survive in an astonishing 156 medieval manuscripts, while sayings and anecdotes from the *Facta et dicta memorabilia* (Memorable deeds and sayings) of the first-century anthologist Valerius Maximus are widely retailed in medieval texts. Other collections of sayings from antiquity were assembled during the early and high Middle Ages, like the tenth-century one wrongly attributed by its nineteenth-century editor to Caecilius Balbus, which contains a section on *taciturnitas*, or the late twelfth-century *Florilegium morale Oxoniensis*, scattered with exhortations to practice silence from Ovid, the *Disticha*, Senecan texts, Boethius, and so on.[7] (Material from both collections will appear throughout this book.) Maxims and exempla from these collections that promote self-interested silence as the best policy reach late medieval English poets and dramatists primarily through two textual channels, in both of which they are joined by Stoic sayings attributed to Cicero and Seneca the Younger that advocated control of the emotions, pursuit of virtue, and living according to a rational assessment of the natural order. In both sets of texts, this classical material is framed, as in the commentary on the *Disticha*, by Jewish wisdom literature and Christian scripture, biblical and patristic. In both, therefore, moral thought is conveyed primarily by *sententiae*, short authoritative sayings that are complete in grammar and thought, that seem self-evident, and that are easy to notice, memorize, absorb, and put to use in specific situations. The first set of texts, three treatises of advice that the mid-thirteenth-century Northern Italian lawyer-notary and judge Albertano da Brescia wrote for his sons, link the calculated use of speech to the equally calculated practice of refraining from speaking. As a *causidicus* (pleader of cases, lawyer) and judge in the strife-torn cities of Northern Italy with their entrenched codes of honor, Albertano promoted the prudent practice of silence as a means of preventing civil conflict and advancing communal welfare, as well as a means of advancing and protecting oneself in an uncertain public world. In the second stream of instructional moral writing, the very same textual amalgam enables clerical writers from the late twelfth century on to develop *taciturnitas*, the inclination to stay silent amid speakers, as a useful, but demanding, discipline that protects oneself and others from hasty, unrestrained, and destructive speech. Guided by prudence, the taciturn, biding their time and assessing situations, are able to restrain a natural loquacity that might reveal too much of their thoughts and emotions, overcommit themselves, or forestall gathering wise counsel in social and political life.

Albertano da Brescia presents his *De arte loquendi et tacendi* (1245), widely disseminated in England throughout the fourteenth and fifteenth centuries, as a treatise that empowers a professional elite, in James Powell's words, "to examine critically the role of language in the preservation or destruction of order within the commune." For Albertano, because language inevitably expresses relations within the political community, any utterance has the power to affect human welfare and so has an ethical, as well as political, dimension. Within a communal web of speakers, to keep silent is to exercise "moral control over the power of language" to do good or evil.[8] In the first sentence of his brief preface, Albertano justifies writing an instructive treatise on speech and silence by insisting that no one can master the tongue, authorizing his stark, universalizing claim with James 3:7–8, a passage central to Christian medieval moral writing about speech: "Natura bestiarum et serpentum, volucrum et ceterorum domatur a natura humana; sed linguam nemo domare potest" (For the nature of beasts and of serpents, of birds, and of the rest, is tamed by the nature of humans, but the tongue no one can tame).[9] To account for the tongue's wild nature and this failure to govern it, he turns to Cicero's Stoic distrust of violent emotions as transmitted largely through Martin of Braga's sixth-century *Formula honestae vitae* (Rules for an honorable life). Nothing can be done steadily or properly, Cicero insists, by someone whose mind is blinded by strong and confusing emotions, like anger, laziness, and lust.[10] To prevent hasty and vehement speech, destructive as it usually is, Albertano advocates a pragmatic regimen very much in line with Cicero's promotion of *cautio* (wariness) as a good emotion. Before breath brings words to the mouth, he says to his son Stephanus (who was preparing for a career in law), potential speakers should examine in silence the circumstances in which they find themselves, measuring them with six points he has devised from his own knowledge (*scientia*) as a notary and lawyer engaged in public life: Who (are you)? What? To Whom? Why?

How? When? (Quis? Quid? Cui? Cur? Quomodo? Quando?).[11] Each of the six sections of *De arte* is devoted to explaining what points should be considered when potential speakers ask one of these questions. For example, under "Cui?" they should ask themselves if the person present is a friend or an enemy, foolish or wise, loquacious, ill-willed, and likely to be drunk. To weigh speaking situations by these circumstances should enable them to gauge the likely effects of speaking or not speaking on both themselves and others present. This circumspect analysis forms a key element of a transformative *forma vitae* (rule of life), a term that signifies a disciplined way of life under religious rules, usually in a monastic community. However, as Powell observes, Albertano, under Seneca's influence (and that of Martin of Braga's Senecan *Formula vitae honestae*), extends his rule of life to the whole community.[12]

As he works out practices of silence, Albertano founds them on *utilitas*, both usefulness and personal advantage. To be guided by personal interest in Albertano, even to pursue material profit, does not equal self-serving pragmatism. Rather, he follows Cicero, as the greatest of Roman forensic orators and civil officials, in identifying the expedient (*utile*) with the morally right (*honestum*), as Patricia Demarco explains in a fine essay on Chaucer's Dame Prudence in the *Melibee*, the source of which (via a French intermediary) is Albertano's third and last treatise, the *Liber consolationi et consilii* (The book of consolation and counsel; 1246). As long as an agent does not harm others and so impair bonds within the community, his true interest, as he (of course, the male in Alberto's perception of Italian communes) practices his profession skillfully, contributes to the social good. In this, he must be guided by the virtue of prudence, defined by Cicero as the practical knowledge of things to be sought or avoided.[13]

Taciturnity is the necessary first step in Albertano's process of prudent speech. To drive home the need for such initial silence, he turns, in his first two sections about the speaker's self ("Quis?"), to Jewish wisdom literature, as well as to maxims from late antique collections. Like Roman maxims, the wisdom books develop an ethic that advises gauging the likely outcomes of different courses of action. Yet they see this ethic as part of a quest for wisdom, which is gained by reflecting on the order created by God/Wisdom with its regularity and set modes of causality. The seekers' wisdom grows as they examine the consequences of human acts within this divine economy, and they develop prudent practices for making their lives more productive and for insulating themselves from loss and disaster.[14] Within this cautionary ethic, verbal restraint becomes the means of averting the destructive consequences of some acts of speech. Those whose passions drive them to speak without considering the situation, Albertano writes, are like Solomon's unwalled city, open to its enemies (Prov 20:28). Unless speakers weigh their words first in silence, as if in a balance, bridling their tongues as a spirited horse is bridled, they may let words slip that vigilant enemies might seize on and use to inflict evils on them (Sirach 28:29–30). Then he concludes this section by recalling that schoolboys' dictum that any lawyer of his time was likely to have memorized, the distich with which this chapter began: "Virtutem primam esse puta compescere linguam: / Proximus ille Deo, qui scit ratione tacere."[15] To hold the tongue is the first resource, in time as well as importance, any reasonable and virtuous person would fall back on when encountering a conversation.

In Albertano's three treatises, this initial act of restraining speech may lead to sustained silence when that might benefit the speaker or others. For the final point that prudent speakers should consider about themselves, Albertano insists that they must always look to the effect of what they could say. What will it accomplish? What might it endanger or destroy? In words Albertano attributes to Pamphilus, the lover in a twelfth-century comedy,

> Principium finemque simul prudentia spectat.
> Rerum finis habet crimen et omne decus.
> Verbi principium, finem quoque conspice verbi,
> Ut possis melius praemeditata loqui.

> Prudence considers at once the beginning and the end.
> The end of affairs is a misdeed or every honorable deed.
> Look to the end of an utterance as well as the beginning,
> So that you may be able to speak better what is premeditated.

If you have any doubt about the effect being beneficial in the long run, Albertano advises Stephanus, you should remain silent rather than speak. The wise know it is more expedient to maintain silence, as Cato declares, for then their speech will not work against them: "Nil tacuisse nocet, nocet esse saepe locutum."[16] As a prudent person, you should especially be wary of voicing precipitously any doubtful counsels, any courses of action you or your allies are considering but have not settled on, writes Albertano to his son Iohannes in the *Liber consolationis et consilii*, which deals more extensively than the earlier treatises with how to gather and act on advice wisely in unstable social and political situations.[17] Behind all these warnings in Albertano's treatises lies a deep suspicion of superfluous speech of any kind: it is always foolish because it is always either dangerous or off-putting.[18]

Other silences that Albertano advocates are designed directly to avoid contentious speech that might escalate into violence. Do not involve yourself in the affairs of others if they do not concern you, he writes to Stephanus, lest rash speech mix you up in others' quarrels and wreck your relations with others beyond them. If you are injured by something others have said, he writes in setting forth what should be spoken or omitted ("Quid?"), you should respond with silence because injurious and insulting speech inevitably incites anger that hardens into enmity. Moreover, both Cicero and Jesus Sirach insist that injuries and insults do not just harm individuals; they unsettle cities and kingdoms, often leading to unrest and violent changes in rule. Albertano concludes these urgent entreaties to his son by quoting what he believes to be a *sententia* of St. Augustine: "Gloriosius est tacendo injurias fugere, quam respondendo superare" (To flee injuries by keeping silent is acting more honorably than to overcome by responding).[19] With this *sententia*, he turns upside down the feudally derived sense of honor. A good name and social respect come from silence in the face of insults, not from vengeful speech and actions. For, by restraining inflammatory counterinsults, the silent exhibit admirable self-control and a commitment to preserving civic peace and amicable relations with fellow citizens.

In Albertano's three treatises, especially *De arte*, the practice of silence protects and advances civic welfare, just as it protects and advances the speaker and their friends. All depends on that initial act of verbal restraint that opens up the opportunity to measure, in silence, the speaking situation by the six circumstances. Only then can a person determine the right time and place to speak and, if that does not emerge, remain silent. Indeed, the title *De arte loquendi et tacendi* recalls the *sententia* of Solomon that is Albertano's mantra: "tempus tacendi et tempus loquendi" (There is a time for keeping silent and a time for speaking; Eccl 3:7b). But it does so with a difference. Whereas Jewish wisdom offers only general moral statement and exhortation, Albertano understands silent circumspection and deliberated speech as a craft within a prudent way of life that demands, he writes in the penultimate sentence of *De arte*, disciplined practice.[20]

Perhaps under Albertano's influence, late medieval English courtesy books for boys and men take up circumspect silence (albeit briefly) as a practical strategy for protecting and advancing the self in social life. (Courtesy books for women, like *The Book of the Knight of La Tour-Landry*, do not imagine them in public life, their prescriptions for practicing silence addressing only life in domestic spaces and, occasionally, in the streets.) In the eighth chapter of Caxton's *Book of Good Manners*, Cato's distich "Nam nulli" is translated to warn men not to engage in combative exchanges, which might escalate and harm them, whereas "scylence causeth to haue peas."[21] In what may be a debt, direct or indirect, to Albertano's circumstances of speech in his widely circulated *De arte*, Caxton's *The Book of Curtesye* urges young men serving their masters to observe seven conditions before they speak, if they must speak at all:

> And yet in auenture / yf the caas require
> Ye most speke / but ye muste thenne percaas
> Seuen condicions obserue / as ye may now hyre
> Auyse you wel / what ye saye / & in what place
> Of whom / & to whom, in your mynde compace
> Howe y shall speke / & whan tak good hede
> This councelith the wise man withoute drede.[22]

Yet this concession to speech (if it is carefully calculated) comes after advice to stay silent in congested social situations, above all refusing to pass on any talk about one's master. These admonitions to be silent and to speak only circumspectly lie side by side with other advice on how to observe social hierarchy and order, like greeting people properly in the street or not picking one's nose at the table. In their general precepts on silence, derived from the "wise," they resemble earlier collections of proverbs and the fifteenth-century *Dicts and Sayings of the Philosophers*, in which advice is often akin to Albertano's: do not reveal your secrets, even to friends (who may turn on you); do not speak evil of others and so gain or preserve friendships; do not blurt out anything in conversation but spy out the speaker's thoughts instead.[23] Sententious lyrics and longer admonitory poems convey similar advice from the wise, sometimes offering the circumstances of speech as a way to keep secrets or win good repute for refusing to pass on damaging gossip. "Consail and Teiching at the Vys Man Gaif His Sone," for example, invokes them so the son can fulfill the wise father's imperative "hald the styll": "And be weil war quhome of þu spek, / Quhen and quhar to quhome & quhy."[24] In these various forms of monitory literature, all is designed to promote valuable friendships, prevent social gaffs, protect oneself from enemies, and calculate how to advance oneself socially. The political strategies of silence, so central in Albertano's treatises, are wholly absent in these courtesy books and sentential lyrics. Hence, the following chapters on silences at the royal court and during inquisition will set them aside.

The discipline that makes silence possible is presented as even more arduous, but equally or more beneficial, in clerical moral texts because of monastic traditions stretching back to the solitaries of the Egyptian desert. Abbot Agathon, according to at least half a dozen moral works circulating in late medieval England, judged silence to be so useful (*utile*, as in Albertano's treatises) that he held a stone in his mouth for three years so that he would learn taciturnity.[25] While some of this material on silence is embedded in texts written for religious communities, like the chapter on claustral silence at the end of the Dominican Guillaume Peyraut's massive *Summa de vitiis* (late 1230s), even it was used as general Christian teaching in sermons, catechesis, the confessional dialogue, and personal admonition. Other instructional texts, like the Middle English *Alphabet of Tales* (a fifteenth-century translation of Arnold de Liège's *Alphabetum narrationum* of 1308) or the catechetical *exempla* of the *Speculum laicorum* (A mirror for laypeople; thirteenth century), were designed from the outset to reach the laity, less often directly, of course, than through clerical mediation. Some were framed for clerics and/or laics in specific estates, like the *Compendium morale de virtutibus* (A moral encyclopedia of the virtues) by the ecclesiastical and royal administrator Roger of Waltham (d. 1341), a treatise on virtues in public life, in which material on taciturnity appears most extensively in chapters on how those who preside over others may attain greatness of character (*magnificencia*), on how ecclesiastical and civil administrators may shun the vices arising from their positions, and on how priests should deal with the administrators they serve. Because of its fix on administrators (it was dedicated to Edward II), it looms large below. Just as Albertano directs his treatises to his sons in their professions and to his fellow lawyers, even though they prescribe practices for all citizens, so these texts invariably consider carefully the specific duties of priests, as well as the general obligations of all Christians. Necessarily, then, New Testament, patristic, and, in some contexts, canon law texts become important resources. Nevertheless, the fundamental ethical traditions that inform clerical moral writing on silence remain, as in Albertano's treatises, those of Roman popular morality, Stoicism, and Jewish wisdom literature. Clerical writers often attribute both Roman and Jewish *sententiae* to "sapiens" (a wise man), indicating their sense that these are related ethical traditions on silence.

Like the English commentary on the *Disticha Catonis* with which this chapter began, Christian moral texts understand prudence as the virtue that should govern choosing and maintaining silence, just as it does in choosing when and how to speak (or act) effectively. Ciceronian prudence is appropriated more explicitly and fully by clerical writers than by Albertano in *De arte*, yet it is also more thoroughly Christianized. Guillaume Peyraut draws on *De officiis* (On duties) for Cicero's basic conception of prudence as the practical knowledge of what to seek and what to flee. Yet he begins his treatment of prudence by quoting Augustine, who insists that its driving force when it makes choices is love, that the goods it chooses aid humans in moving toward God, and that the evils it avoids impede humans from that movement.[26] Similarly, the fourteenth-century Dominican Robert Holcot, in his influential commentary on the book of Wisdom, expounds and then Christianizes the Ciceronian doctrine that prudence has three parts: the memory by which the *animus* repeats what has happened, the intellect that considers it, and the foresight (*providentia*) by which the past is used to grasp what is to come. He insists that God, of His grace, rushes in to teach humans what is expedient to remember, what they should meditate on to deal well with the present, and what they should expect so they make good plans for the future.[27] All of prudence's workings, concludes Roger of Waltham, following "Seneca" (Martin of Braga, actually), should be directed to ensuring that nothing that happens will be sudden or unexpected, that the prudent will never be deceived. Above all (he returns to Cicero here), prudence prevents people from committing to a course of action that they will later regret because it did not turn out well or even endangered them:

> Et Tullius. "Illud quidem ingenii est ante constituere qu[i]d accidere possit in utramque partem et quid agendum sit cum quid evenerit,

nec committere ut aliquando dicat 'Non putabam sic accidisse.' In illum enim defectum periculose et imprudenter accidit."[28]

And Cicero: "Indeed, it is for the intelligence to establish beforehand what could happen both for good and for ill and what should be done when any given thing might happen, and not to begin unreflectively so that one would have to say "I was not thinking that it would have come to pass in this way." For in the absence of that, things fall out dangerously and unwisely.

This understood, it is not surprising that, according to Peyraut, to be prudent is to love taciturnity ("Prudentis est taciturnitatem amare").[29] (Taciturnity, the inclination to remain silent, a noun never used in Albertano's treatises, is often preferred over "silentium" in clerical moral texts.) To be inclined to silence in a situation gives time to reflect on alternative courses in light of past experience, personal and that provided by authoritative texts, and then time to choose what is likely to be the most useful or beneficial one.

What constitutes utility and benefit for clerics understanding prudence in this way and writing for their own class, in part? According to the English compiler of the widespread comprehensive treatise on speech *De lingua* (late thirteenth century), the prudent and taciturn person, like a flower that opens in the presence of the sun but closes in its absence, knows the most suitable time to speak for God's honor or others' welfare ("ad honorem Dei uel utilitatem proximi") but also keeps their mouth closed humbly when they perceive that speech will not be useful.[30] Insisting, too, that *utilitas* should dictate when to speak or keep silent, the extract "Tacere" from the *Pera peregrini* (The pilgrim's scrip) advises the wise to regard the tongue as a liminal space between the interior self and the world of speech and, before using it, to recall four circumstances of speech ("quid," "cui," "quando," "quo loco" [in what place]) in order to weigh whether to speak or remain silent.[31] For the clerical class after the initiatives of the Fourth Lateran Council (1215), the forms of speech most central to others' welfare were, of course, preaching and correcting sins, especially the sins of those who were in their pastoral care. The great reformist writer and teacher of leading English clerics Pierre le Chantre even adds two more circumstances of speech to Albertano's six, "qualia" (of what kind) and "ubi" (where), so that a priest may gauge how to speak most effectively for the benefit of others. Sometimes, he writes, a circumspect priest will judge that, under the circumstances, he should not preach or correct at all but should remain silent because his potential audience would not benefit: if it does not have the capacity to absorb what he could utter, if it is made up of despisers of the truth and so incorrigible, or if he does not have the eloquence needed for a specific occasion.[32] When the fourteenth-century Dominican John Bromyard wishes to illustrate the value for all people of such silent, discreet observation and the beneficial speech (*utilis* again) it enables, he turns to the fairy-tale exemplum of the aged nobleman and his three sons. In order for the father to judge to which son he should bequeath all he possesses, he asks each in turn what bird's nature and character (*conditio*) he would choose to have. "The eagle," replies the eldest, "because it flies the highest and dominates other birds." "The falcon," replies the middle son, "because it eats delicacies." "The swan," replies the youngest, because he wishes to have a long neck (that liminal space) "so that he could weigh well every word before it passed through the long neck from the heart to the mouth, determining if it should be spoken or not" (ut de omni verbo deliberare posset, antequam ad os de corde per longum collum transiret, si dicendum esset uel non). The wisdom of the youngest, in true fairy-tale fashion, ensures that he will inherit everything.[33] In an interesting variation, the *Speculum laicorum* has the father award the two elder sons his lands and the youngest only part of his goods because the last's prizing of circumspect speech indicates that he will acquire all he needs through it. Indeed, he becomes a high-ranking court official.[34] Although the son's desire to consider speech carefully in silence works to his own advantage in both versions, the *Speculum* presents the exemplum to illustrate how speech, lay as well as clerical, should be judiciously targeted, rather than used idly, so that it can soften the angry, quell the envious, rouse the lazy, coax the bitter, console the desperate, and in general become a source of good. Bromyard presents it alongside the speech of another exemplary figure, the Virgin Mary, who speaks only for the benefit of others, as when she procures wine for the wedding guests. In both, a contemporary tale that promotes self-advancement is recast by commentary and context to stress that all people ought to be concerned for how their speech may benefit others the most.

To the benefits that taciturnity may create for others by providing space to shape effective speech, clerical writers join the benefits for potential speakers themselves, self-protection chief among them. Clerical discourse on speech, I argued several decades ago, is built on Augustinian semiotics:

speech is a gift from God, unique to humans, to enable them to transmit their inner thoughts to others. Exercising that function carelessly can carry a destructive kick. Even more than Albertano, clerical writers see the tongue as a violent, driving, almost independent member of the body, often figured as a horse without reins or a fire, a heedless agent of destructive verbal transgressions and excesses, a provoker of violence and criminal or sinful acts of all kinds.[35] One peril that thoughtless and excessive speech brings, states *The Book of Vices and Virtues*, is imprudent disclosure of the inner self, especially thoughts, apprehensions, emotions, and projects that others might regard as foolish. With a simile from animal husbandry, it reminds its readers that "bi þe wordes mowe [may] men knowe þe wittes and þe folies of a man, as men knowen a swyn bi þe tonge, wheþer he is hole or mesel [diseased]." This homely figure locates danger in the tongue itself as the organ of speech and suggests that self-revelation can alter one's life, even impair it and put it under threat. Only discreet "mesure in wordes," as Solomon insists, can stem the turbulent flow of "folie wordes and outrageous [out of bounds; excessive]," for heedless speakers are compared by the *Book* to a mill without a sluice that runs wildly when the water does, an image that reminds this translator of the *Somme le Roi* (Book of the king) of the untamable tongue of the Epistle to James. Only holding back words at the sluice of discretion or weighing them in a balance (the wisdom metaphor again) can make one confident that "þat þer be no þing to vndertake [chide] ne [nor] to reproue hem wiþ."[36] Likewise, the *Speculum laicorum* warns its readers that because words are the mirror of the heart ("speculum quidem cordis verba sunt"), they should be wary of speaking loosely and disclosing foolishly too much of their inner selves.[37]

In a political context, excessive, self-revelatory speech not only can hand enemies and rivals material for attacks or, at least, subversive criticism but can incur blame for revealing what ought to be kept hidden. "Exigua est virtus prestare silencia rebus, / At contra gravis est culpa tacenda loqui" (Modest is the virtue of keeping silent about things; / On the other hand, weighty is the guilt for speaking what ought to be kept silent). Thus, Roger of Waltham turns to Ovid's *Ars amatoria* to drive home to those who hold public offices the danger of revealing what should be kept secret. The very sweetness inherent in words, he writes, can insinuate its way into ears and delude people into divulging secrets, just as drunkenness and love do. Eventually such disclosures reach the whole populace, for the garrulous are never content to tell what they know to one pair of ears.³⁸ Roger's contemporary the Dominican Simon of Boraston underscores the assertion (Quintilian's, he believes) that nothing is more difficult than keeping silent by retailing a Roman anecdote about the boy Papirius and his garrulous mother. Although a boy not yet of age, Papirius, as the son of a Roman senator, was permitted to accompany his father to deliberations in the Senate chamber. One day, when the grave issue debated could not be brought to a conclusion, the Senate adjourned until the next day with the stipulation that no one divulge the curial subject. On Papirius's return home, his curious mother berated him violently for keeping the matter secret. He found refuge in a lie. The Senate, he said, was considering the question of whether it was better for a man to have two wives or for a woman to have two husbands. Unable to restrain her tongue, his mother told all the women of Rome, who, rushing into the Senate chamber the next day, lobbied for two husbands. Amid total confusion, Papirius explained his ruse. The Senate then commended him for his prudence in keeping the matter secret.³⁹

Clerical warnings against revealing secrets in public life also find their way into mirrors for princes written by prominent clerics interested in administration. Walter Millemete's mirror for the newly enthroned Edward III, *On the Nobility, Wisdom, and Prudence of Kings* (1327), devotes a whole chapter to how Edward should never divulge his counsel, his secret plans, except to his most trusted advisers, and then only when he must. Otherwise, his stratagems might be betrayed and brought to nothing.⁴⁰ Behind this caution lies a basic political assumption, stated by Egidio Colonna (Giles of Rome), the Augustinian friar and theologian who tutored the future French king Phillip IV: "what is iseid [said] in counsaille scholde be prevey [secret]. For manye nedes ben ilett by wriyng [necessary things are prevented or hindered by going amiss] and tellyng out of counsaille." This forms the fourth point about counsel in his *De regimine principum*, widely read in fourteenth- and fifteenth-century England and translated by John Trevisa for Lord Berkeley (*The Governance of Kings and Princes*), most likely between 1399 and 1402. (*De regimine* became a major source for Hoccleve's *Regiment of Princes*, as we shall see.) Setting aside the traditional etymology of *consilium*, *The Governance*, hewing closely to Colonna's Latin, claims that the term "is componed [composed] of con þat is to menyng togederes, and of silio, siles, þat is to meynynge be stille in scilence. So þat consilium þat is counsaille scholde be what manye men knowen and ben stille and spekeþ not þerof." Colonna ties this essential quality of counsel to the public good. Outside of public counsel, people may choose to make public whatever contributes to their profit, but, if they are part of public deliberation, they must keep its secrets because the common profit demands that common needs not be hindered by someone divulging public secrets.[41]

As well as transmitting secrets, according to moral texts, excessive speech inevitably is damaging to anyone, especially in public life, while remaining silent has several social and political advantages. Speaking too much in itself makes anyone hated, according to Guillaume Peyraut, who, like the compiler of *De lingua*, cites Sirach 9:25: "Terribilis est in civitate sua homo linguosus, et temerarius in verbo suo odibilis erit" (A loquacious person is dreadful in his city, and the rash in speech will be hateful).[42] Talkative people, writes Roger of Waltham, fatigue an audience, driving its members to hate them.[43] In place of such repellent verbosity, clerical writers, including Peyraut in his treatise on the formation of rulers (*De eruditione principum*), recommend speaking rarely and briefly after preserving an initial silence to formulate something pithy.[44] Indeed, Peyraut and John of Mirfield both claim that few words make a person worthy of love, a claim anchored in the saying of a Roman wise man. When asked by someone how he could please people, the wise man replied, "If you will have done very good things and spoken few words" (Si gesseris optima et locutus fueris pauca).[45]

Beyond the value of silence in heading off excessive speech, it has the power in clerical texts, as it does in Albertano, to prevent strife from erupting. "Seþþe [Because] amonge alle þyngus þes to haue is nedful, nedful þenne to hem is silence, wherof þes cometh, for myche strif and ire is fordone [prevented] and leued [left behind] þorw [through] kepynge of silence." Thus, *The Book for a Simple and Devout Woman* (first half of the fifteenth century) recommends silence amid fraught situations, as do many clerical moral texts, on the authority of Jewish wisdom literature: keeping still quiets the anger of a foolish person, according to King Solomon (Prov 16:10).[46] The most effective remedy that Roger of Waltham prescribes for one's own anger, as well as another's, is to abstain from, or at least delay, words (and, of course, actions). Thus, silence prevents quarrels, litigation, and ultimately violence by quieting down both parties.[47] When he advises public figures on attaining greatness of character, Roger takes up the case of those rulers who suffer insults and shaming words. He takes as his authority Cicero, who recommends suffering them in silence, one mode of patience, to be explored much more fully in the chapter 4. Like other clerics writing on silence, he makes the exemplar King David. Semei, a kinsman of Saul, began cursing David when he was cast down by his son Absalom's rebellion, calling him a usurper and crying out, "Egredere, egredere, vir sanguini et vir Belial" (Go away, go away, man of blood and man of Belial), while casting stones at him. Although one of David's attendants offers to cut off Semei's head, the king forbids violence, refuses to speak back to Semei, and commands his attendants to let Semei continue insulting and cursing him. For Roger, exhibiting silence in the face of shaming words, rather than replying with vituperation or even violence, is a key way of behaving with *magnificencia* (greatness, nobleness), an essential virtue for people in public life.[48] As in Albertano's treatises, ensuring the good name necessary for social stature and public trust entails meeting insults with silence.

All clerical moral texts that have sections devoted to "Taciturnitas" or "Silencium" consider loquacity its worthless opposite. By dispersing the force of speech, verbal excess vitiates the extraordinary political and social value that clerical writers see in this unique gift from God: it enables humans to transmit their thoughts to each other and so order their common life. For clerics, loquacity stems from a failure to measure speech, to use a *modus* (measure, method) or *moderamen* (means of controlling) to distribute speech and silence according to the circumstances of specific political and social interactions.[49] Given the complexity of social and political life, all that clerical moral texts can offer speakers for this task, apart from the circumstances of speech, is norms, authoritative sayings, and exempla—largely from the past—to assist them in the present as they attempt to discern likely outcomes. In doing so, they share Albertano's confidence that humans are capable of disciplined self-governance, especially control of vehement emotions and appetites, the forces behind verbal excess. Such carefully moderated speech opens the way to secure prudently what humans seek for themselves and for others to whom they are bound in political, social, and religious communities.

CHAPTER 2

THE ART OF POLITICAL SILENCE
The Prudent King of Hoccleve's *Regiment of Princes*

Although chapter 1, on prescriptive moral writing, largely in Latin, provides groundwork for all five chapters on Middle English literature, its focus on prudent silences in institutional life particularly informs this chapter. Its norms, even its *sententiae*, shape the strategies of royal silences that Thomas Hoccleve advocates in the troubled reign of Henry IV (1399–1413). A longtime clerk in the Office of the Privy Seal, Hoccleve wrote, late in the reign, *The Regiment of Princes*, a mirror for princes advising Prince Henry, soon to be king, on how to perform kingship in ways that would make him the authoritative moral center of a well-governed England. In the code of conduct necessary for Henry to fulfill the public duties of his position, Hoccleve gives a prominent place to cautious silences grounded in Roman maxims and exempla, Jewish and Christian scripture, and Aristotelian ethics—a place far greater and more sharply marked than in his sources and other mirrors for princes. When scholars have taken up silence in the *Regiment*, they have tended to concentrate on Hoccleve's oppressed silence in the opening dialogue, on the societal constraints on speech that hem him in as a royal bureaucrat, and on the ways the poet manages to break his silence to offer the prince counsel without offending him.[1] I focus on the prudential silences the poet advises the prince to practice from the time of his coronation, silences that Hoccleve advocates throughout the mirror in conjunction with virtues and royal duties. The habit of taciturnity and the sustained silences it sometimes generates, he argues, should shape Henry's thinking, speech, conduct, and even authority. They should become tools for keeping oaths and promises to his subjects, for avoiding dangerous self-revelation, for gathering a wide range of counsel, for displaying exemplary self-restraint, and for manipulating advisers, enemies, and the English people as a whole. By conforming his already prudent self to Hoccleve's advice about practicing a prudent taciturnity, the Lancastrian prince would be able, as king, to avoid political misfortune and at the same time benefit his people.

When Hoccleve wrote *The Regiment of Princes* (from late 1410 or early 1411 to no later than spring 1413), Henry IV had ruled England for over a decade. It was to be widely transmitted, especially among the aristocracy, down through the politically unstable century.[2] Outright rebellion against the new dynasty, vacillating attempts to control magnates by royal largesse and by threats or punishments, recalcitrant parliaments, wars on multiple fronts, and popular discontent over taxes and over a costly royal household form the context in which Hoccleve wrote. More than a decade after the deposition of Richard II, Henry IV was still struggling to rule in ways that would consolidate his kingship.[3] The *Regiment* begins by recalling this political instability and misfortune, as the melancholy Hoccleve, the poet's narrative self, muses about "The welthe unseur of every creature, / How lightly that Fortune it can dissolve" (lines 16–17), a universal uncertainty that directs him to think of the recent fall of Richard II for misrule and the fall of many other lords (lines 22–25).[4] Hoccleve immediately links the political to the personal. Although he has held a position as clerk in the Office of the Privy Seal for over thirty years, he has also experienced the vagaries of Fortune. He has not been able, he tells an impoverished old man, to meet the expenses of his household because his annuity has not been paid every year in full and in a timely way by the king, whose recurrent financial woes due to war, civil unrest, and overindulgence affect the whole royal bureaucracy. Thus, his own experience also witnesses to how political instability can trigger the misfortunes of subjects. The old man proposes that Hoccleve address his and the kingdom's insecurity (although a royal clerk cannot be overly explicit about the latter) by composing a poem for Prince Henry, who has already shown political promise by astutely controlling the Council and winning confidence from Parliament during his father's illness. Henry's "hi [high, great] prudence" would direct him to embrace the sound advice on kingship Hoccleve's poem would bring, and he would reward the impecunious poet in exchange (lines 1898–953).

As the title indicates, *The Regiment of Princes* will prescribe for Prince Henry a regimen, a way of life in which admired virtues, acculturated habits that maintain consistent action for the benefit of all, generate principles of practical politics (*MED*, s.v. "regiment" [n.], 2 and 1). The plural "princes" suggests that those principles and virtues have been derived from observing rulers over time so that they are applicable to all effective governance. Indeed, Hoccleve presents himself as a compiler of instructional materials from the past, as Nicholas Perkins's fine study of the poem explains, a scribe who, far from assuming "unwarranted authority" in advising the king-to-be, assembles materials from authoritative texts with him in mind.[5] In his marginal glosses throughout the poem, Hoccleve quotes and even cites some of the biblical, patristic, and classical texts from which he takes wise sayings and exempla, making it clear that the *Regiment* draws from the textual nexus from which other writers on public life, like Albertano and the clerics of chapter 1, compiled their instructional works.[6] In the proem that introduces the direct advice to princes, Hoccleve acknowledges at length his three main sources: the immensely popular pseudo-Aristotelian *Secreta secretorum* (The secret of secrets), in which wise old Aristotle instructs the young Alexander in how he should manage his body and adhere to virtues (his regimens) so that he will make political and military decisions advantageous to himself and those whom he rules; *De regimine principum*, strongly influenced by Aristotle's *Nicomachean Ethics* and *Politics*; and the *Libellus de moribus hominum et de officiis nobilium super ludo scaccorum* (Book about the conduct of humans and the duties of nobles with regard to the game of chess) of the Dominican Jacopo da Cessole, a collection of exempla about the various orders of society (lines 2038–135).[7] Like the first two, mirrors for princes or handbooks for effective rule, Hoccleve will develop the essential virtues for a ruler to possess: justice, pity, mercy, chastity, patience, magnanimity, largesse, and prudence. Indeed, the *Regiment* is largely organized by virtues: they inform most of the carefully demarcated sections of the poem (headed, for example, "De misericordia" or "De regis magnanimitate"). In these ways, Hoccleve prepares the prince, as a reader, for what the poem will furnish him with: accepted principles of rule stemming from personal virtues. Although a fairly lowly royal clerk, financially dependent on the king and those who commission his scribal labor, Hoccleve has the authority of a literate man who has absorbed and can employ Latin writings from antiquity to the present, supplemented, of course, by his own observations from the Exchequer ("I sumwhat knowe a kynges draght" [move in chess], line 2120). Indeed, he often marks the marginal Latin glosses with "scriptum est" (it is written), a visual attestation, as Jane Griffiths observes, to this authority and the trustworthiness of the written tradition itself.[8]

Such a text of orthodox political/ethical principles, as Hoccleve studies since Paul Strohm have stressed, assures the prince, who, like his father, was "aware of the textual basis of power and authority itself," that it will confer some legitimacy on the contested and turbulent Lancastrian rule.[9] Yet the *Regiment*'s proem promises much more: a design for a virtuous way of life that fosters stability and welfare for both king and subject. The old man urges Hoccleve toward the end of their dialogue to translate a treatise "Growndid on his [the prince's] estates holsumnesse" (line 1950). "Holsumnesse" conveys a state of well-being, a virtuous state free from any kind of corruption, decay, or loss. Like the legendary tutor Aristotle drawing up the *Secreta* as a letter to instruct his former pupil Alexander, Hoccleve claims to write the *Regiment* out of "Myn inward wil that thristith [thirsts for] the welfare / Of your persone" (lines 2027–28), welfare that is resistant to the threats to rule, reversals of political fortunes, and disastrous outcomes that Richard II and, to some extent, Henry IV had experienced. (Hoccleve also, of course, writes for more than the prince; many of his passages indirectly criticize the failures of Henry IV, as Judith Ferster has shown.)[10] In the conclusion of the proem, he prays that God will grant Prince Henry, when he accedes to the throne,

> Swich governance men may feele and see
> In yow as may been unto His [God's] plesance,
> Profyt to us and your good loos [fame, reputation] avance.
> (lines 2161–63)

As in Albertano's *De arte*, good conduct in a person of influence at once promotes his own interests and those of his society, especially at a time of disorder and uncertainty. Like God, whom the new king will represent, even image, Henry will be an exemplar because he rules, forming a pattern for his subjects' conduct. His good governance will profit others, as himself, not only by his astute decisions but also by the virtues that shape them and that they manifest. The *Regiment*, as Larry Scanlon puts it neatly, treats the king "as society's moral center."[11]

Prime—that is, both first and of greatest importance—among the regnal virtues is prudence, the virtue that enables and directs the work of all others. The *Liber regalis* (The book of the king), the late medieval coronation service recorded under Richard II, regarded prudence as the central virtue ensuring good governance. As the king-to-be prepares during the night to be crowned, he must pray for "prudenciam circa regni gubernacionem" (prudence regarding the government of the kingdom), along with devotion to God and justice to the people. He is to have been instructed in these three virtues by the Dean of Westminster.[12] In the *Regiment*'s section "De regis prudencia" (On the prudence of a king), Hoccleve presents the virtue as Cicero and medieval moral writers had: a virtue of the practical intellect that works in three ways to ensure good outcomes.

> Prudence is vertu of entendement [understanding];
> Shee makith man by reson him governe,
> Whoso þat list [desires to] be wys and prudent
> And the light folwe wole [is willing to follow] of hir lanterne,
> He muste caste his look in every herne [nook]
> Of thynges past and been [are] and that schul be:
> The ende seeth and eek [also] mesurith she.
> (lines 4761–67)

As a faculty of understanding ("entendement") searching the past and examining the present in order to assess the likely outcomes of potential actions, prudence enables people to act with calculation, imposing control on their conduct and the world around them. Although Hoccleve treats regnal prudence in and of itself in only one section (lines 4747–858), as he does the other virtues, he presents it as necessary for all the other virtues to operate, directing them (he is referring to the three other cardinal virtues of "attemperance, strengthe, and right") as to how to work "Aftir hir reed [advice], withouten whom no man / Wel unto God ne the world lyve can" (lines 4754–60).[13] Although Hoccleve has the old man characterize Prince Henry as a prudent person already, shaped by rigorous reading and the examples of his Lancastrian forebearers, the *Regiment*'s account of prudence and the other virtues is designed to assist Henry in maintaining, in all the pressing business of kingship, the consistency and stability of character central to Stoic, Aristotelian, Jewish, and Christian ethics.[14] Only then will he be able to withstand the vagaries of Fortune and make decisions under pressure that benefit both himself and his people. For Henry's prudence, Hoccleve concludes in the vein of clerical moralists like Robert Holcot, must be directed by love, love of his people rooted in a love of God and then in a sense that his future will be determined by how well he guides and governs his people (lines 4803–58). For if he governs with his eye on prudence, like an archer on the mark, "his peple hath sikirnesse [security] / Of reste and pees, welthe, joie, and gladnesse" (lines 4851–52), securing, in turn, their love.

In the *Regiment*, a king depends on continued good repute ("loos") in order to rule effectively and to have a significant influence on his subjects. Hoccleve's great predecessor Aristotle, the poet claims, devoted his whole epistle to instructing Alexander "how to susteene his honour" as he ruled (line 2044). Essential to preserving that good name in the *Regiment* is prudential taciturnity and, in some cases, a considered refusal to speak at all. For among the grave threats to any king's governance of himself and his kingdom could be his own tongue.

The untamable tongue of the Epistle to James, the impetus for Albertano's prudential circumstances in *De arte* and for clerical norms for speech, comes to the fore as a threat near the end of the second section of the *Regiment*'s mirror. After the brief first section on a king's dignity, Hoccleve examines how essential it is for effective rule that a king keep his oaths and promises, especially his coronation oaths (lines 2192–464):

> Alle natures of beestes and brides [birds]
> And of serpentes been ymakid tame [may be tamed],
> But tonge of man, as it wel knowe and kid [shown] is,
> Nat may be tamed. O fy, man, for shame!
> Silence of tonge is wardeyn of good fame,
> And aftir repreef, fisshith clap [fishes for chatter] and foulith.
> The tonge of man al the body deffoulith.
> (lines 2437–43)

In the margin beside this stanza, Hoccleve gives the Latin he has Englished, James 3:7 followed by 3:6, firmly authorizing his universalizing claim, just as his appeal to common knowledge does ("as it wel knowe and kid is").

Between the two Englished verses in the stanza, he bluntly states how the uncontrolled tongue damages all people: it disgraces them in their own eyes and those of others, a loss both internal and social/political. The power of the tongue to damage speakers seems unlimited. Even after speakers are disgraced and censured, their tongues continue to wag ("fisshith clap"), degrading them yet further. Here, as in clerical moral writings, the tongue seems its own agent, independent of the rest of the human body and relentless in its continual movement. The couplet's near repetition, "foulith" / "deffoulith," stresses that the tongue, although just one organ, oppresses and pollutes the whole body. Unlike Albertano's treatises, where the untamable tongue risks primarily involving speakers in conflicts and damaging their prospects, and unlike clerical writing, where it subverts institutions and dismembers others' social selves, the *Regiment*, as a mirror for princes, locates the tongue's damage in the speakers' own ill repute, the loss of the "good fame" necessary to preserve their social standing and the relations with subjects necessary for them to do the work of their "estate."[15] For a king, this loss would be the greatest if he were to violate an oath.

Hoccleve sees the future king's coronation oaths (Hoccleve uses the plural) as performative, as Larry Scanlon has observed: in the ceremony, they enact practical constraints on royal prerogative and power.[16] Just as Hoccleve stresses that destructive speech is produced by the tongue as a bodily organ, so he presents oath taking as a physical act performed by the tongue: "Tho [Those] oothes that at your creacioun / Shul thurgh [through] your tonge passe, hem wel observe" (lines 2192–93). By pledging himself in this public, physical performance at the beginning of a reign, a king establishes a contractual relation that can be broken if he fails to adhere to what his words avow, in those oaths or in any others he utters. Such a failure would bring his trustworthiness into question. Because it is only trust that makes a nation possible, gathering individuals into a shared polity ("By feith is maad the congregacioun [gathering, community] / Of peple" [lines 2206–7]), it is only because of subjects' trust in a king's fidelity to his word that he exercises "dominacioun" and they obey him (lines 2208 and 2212). So, throughout his reign, a king should swear only oaths and make only promises he is certain, after careful consideration and with prudential foresight, that he can observe: "Or [before] a kyng swere, it is ful necessarie / Avyse him [to deliberate, take thought] wel" (lines 2332–33). Forswearing, lack of "trouthe," leads to "wikkid ende and cursid aventure [fortune, chance]" (line 2204), what Hoccleve proclaims that he can assist Prince Henry in avoiding once he becomes king in uncertain times. As in Roman popular morality, opposite courses lead to radically different outcomes. Hoccleve also makes an ontological argument for adhering to oaths. A key source of royal legitimacy for him, as we have seen, is a king's likeness to God, and since God is "trouthe itself," the ground of all reality as well as faithfulness,

> than may the vice
> Of untrouthe [faithlessness, oath breaking] nat in a kyng appeere,
> If his office shal to god referee.
> (lines 2410–13)

Reminding the king-to-be of James 3:2 (given as a marginal gloss: "Si quis verbo non offendit perfectus est, et cetera"), Hoccleve concludes that, in order not to vow anything that he does not wish to, or cannot, perform, a king must be "parfyt" in speech. He must be "He that by word nat giltith [does not offend]" (line 2415). He must be habituated by prudence—that is, by memory, by analysis, by foresight of consequences—never to utter a transgressive word.[17] Otherwise, he forfeits his moral—and his ontological—kinship with God, and so his honor, his exalted stature among his people, to whom he is tied by speech that depends on trust.

Given a king's need for absolute integrity in speech to prevent loss of good repute and trust, what can keep a king from uttering words that might damage him, perhaps irreparably, when the tongue is an untamable force? "Silence of tonge is wardeyn of good fame" (line 2441), declares Hoccleve, using an image from the Jewish wisdom books (Pss 38:2 and 140:3), where the Psalmist pleads for a "custodia" (guard) on his mouth. As in Albertano's treatises and clerical writings, in the *Regiment*, taciturnity must be the default position in any public situation, the initial guard or protector that prevents unwary utterances. Only when the tongue is kept in abeyance can prudence perform its complex work of memory, analysis, and foresight ("Prudence wakith whan the tonge sleepith, / And slepith ofte whan the tonge wakith" [lines 2434–35]). Then it can determine when and how to speak profitably and safely. Along with this advice comes, of course, more fundamental advice from the wisdom books, given in Latin in the margin with its source (Sirach 9:5) carefully noted: avoid loquacity and escape the ill will it generates ("Whoso that hatith mochil clap or speeche / Qwenchith malice" [lines 2430–31]). Excessive speech will sully a king's reputation, make his stature fade away in the eyes of his subjects, and obscure the special character of his rank: "For mochil clap wole his estat desteyne" (line 2419; *MED*, s.v. "desteinen" [v.], 3 and 2). A gloss attributed to Aristotle in the opening section on speech marks another adverse consequence of loquacity.[18] The people "thriste [thirst] and yerne" to hear the words of their king, but, if he speaks excessively,

> mennes eres dulle of his mateere;
> For dullyng hem, dulleth the herte in feere [together]
> Of hem that geuen to him audience.
> In mochil speeche wantith nat [does not lack] offense.
> (lines 2423–29)

When this warning about the soporific effect of verbal excess on hearers appears in clerical texts, it is usually taken from Roman forensic oratory, though often capped by Proverbs 10:19, as in the *Regiment*: "In multiloquio non deerit peccatum" (In a multitude of words, offense will not be lacking). Albertano devotes a whole section ("Cui?") to how to assess audiences, especially their receptivity, and another ("Quomodo?") includes a subsection against prolixity, a tissue of sayings from Seneca and Jewish wisdom books introduced by Proverbs 10:19. As we have seen, clerical moral texts advocate that priests develop a keen awareness of audience so that they can assess how their speech might affect those whom they are obliged to inform, reprove, and move to salvific penitence. More generally, they caution all Christians against the vitiating effects of superfluous speech. The wisdom imagery of physical restraint runs throughout these stanzas of the *Regiment*: the king must preserve his honor by governing his tongue with "mesures reyne," the control over words asserted when initial silence allows him to determine what and how much to say (line 2420). Nicholas Perkins understands that a king who guards his tongue and measures his words shows "his special nature, his distance," because he can constrain "a potentially destructive part of his physical body."[19] Perkins reads the *Regiment* searchingly and fruitfully in terms of the constraints on speech constructed by late medieval English politics and by a "proverbial tradition designed to regulate and restrict the circulation of speech," a tradition that features Cato prominently and includes Albertano's treatises (although Perkins does not analyze them).[20] Yet in these stanzas on restraint of the tongue, Hoccleve's images and *sententiae* are drawn from the wisdom books and the Epistle to James, emphatically marked by five extended marginal quotations. In truth, non-biblical and nonpatristic sayings appear only twice in this entire section on oaths and speech (272 lines). What is Hoccleve offering his king-to-be in this early and expansive consideration of royal taciturnity and royal speech following the section on making and fulfilling oaths, shaped by and ostentatiously authorized by Jewish and Christian scripture as it is? More broadly, what does his mirror as a whole offer Prince Henry?[21]

As scribe and poet, Hoccleve offers Henry divinely given prescriptions and proscriptions that will, by their very scriptural origin, be efficacious, effective for all humans, of course, but particularly for the one who bears the image of God as oath maker and ordainer of the hierarchical political world as it is, the God that Hoccleve, Henry, and his soon-to-be subjects acknowledge. (Much is made throughout the *Regiment* of Henry's piety and his orthodoxy, just as much is made of God as the locus and fountain of the virtues necessary for an earthly ruler, like justice, mercy, and largesse.) Only by consistently applying these *modi* or *moderamina*, which we find both in Albertano's treatises and in clerical writers, these means of governing the tongue intently and consistently in the often-murky give-and-take of early fifteenth-century English political life, will Henry manage to employ silence and, therefore, speech in strategic ways that preserve, even enhance, his honor—indeed, his kingship itself. Why should a king-to-be, acculturated to be prudent, be reminded of these norms for refraining from speech? In the press of life at court, surrounded by the contending voices and pressed by the urgent decision-making that Hoccleve envisions, Henry will need to check constantly his feelings, his emotions, his first thoughts, and therefore his speech, lest he speak precipitously from a sense of royal prerogative, not from an awareness of the all-too-real constraints on his powers. Indeed, as Larry Scanlon has argued, the *Regiment* as a whole centers on a king's constant need to restrain his powers.[22]

In certain types of interchanges with Henry's subjects-to-be, the *Regiment* cautions him to remain silent altogether for much the same reasons that Albertano and clerical writers give their readers. Silence becomes key to effectively gathering and implementing sound counsel, a fundamental concern of mirrors for princes. As Henry listens to multifarious and often divergent advice from his councilors and other stakeholders in the realm, he should keep silent about what actions he is considering: "What that yee thynke do, lat it be deed; / As for the tyme, let no word appeere" (lines 4868–69). Several advantages arise from this royal silence. As king, Henry must at least appear to be seriously seeking out counsel from those whose office or interests incline them to advance certain reasons for policies and actions. Moreover, if he is to act wisely, Henry will need to recognize that, even though divinely appointed, he is a "man soul," a single person whose apprehension, thought processes, and judgment may err. "Good conseil," as an exchange of information and ideas, may prompt him to avoid mistakes (lines 4859–65). If he does not divulge his own thinking, then he can listen carefully to the speech of all those who are entitled to advise him, determining what is wise counsel but not disclosing the course of action on which he is settling (lines 4870–73). By not closing down advisers and by not announcing a course in the midst of the communal process, he allows all those who speak to believe that their thinking is weighed and enables himself to get as much apt advice as he can, make a full assessment of it, and learn much about advisers' reliability. Prince Henry, Derek Pearsall notes, was always active in seeking out advice when he presided over the royal council in his father's illness, even if he did not act on what was advocated by advisers.[23] Another, perhaps even more important, benefit of royal silence about counsel emerges in the *Regiment*. If Henry were to divulge "your conseil which that yee han take," a clause that suggests both the deliberations and his decision, it could reach his enemies and force him not to execute what he judged the wisest course (lines 4922–48). As Egidio Colonna and his translator John Trevisa insist by their etymology for *consilium*, to have a role in formulating counsel entails silence about decisions in order to ensure the common profit. For Henry when king, both the common profit and his own will depend on his silences.

A second kind of profitable royal silence, one counter to the feudal culture of honor, emerges in the *Regiment*'s section on patience as a royal virtue: silence that preserves peaceful relations between people, a central *topos*, as we have seen, in Albertano's treatises and in clerical texts on taciturnity. Hoccleve invokes both Gregory the Great and the "Socrates" of cautionary adages when he claims that one type of patience is not to speak in anger so one does not arouse anger in another. In urging Henry to remain silent when he is provoked by a subject, Hoccleve retells many classical and biblical exempla of nobles and kings. Foremost comes the great clerical exemplum of King David remaining silent when insulted by Semei, with the biblical passage given in a couplet as well as quoted in the Latin marginal notes. Although Semei was speaking ill of the king, even cursing him, not only does the king refuse his attendant's offer to slay him, but he suffers the insults and curses in silence, not rebuking Semei or restraining him (lines 3480–93). When Hoccleve narrates at length the traditional exemplum of Duke Pisistarus and his friend Aristuppus, he stresses the shame Aristuppus brought on the duke by rebuking him and spitting on him in front of the ducal retinue. Incited by the violent emotions so distrusted by writers on silence from the Stoics on, anger and sorrow, Aristuppus speaks hastily, without any consideration of his words or their likely consequences. The public shame brought on by this degrading speech and act ("vilenye") is so great that the duke's sons, like King David's attendant, offer to slay the offender. Such a breach of another's honor, of course, led to many killings and protracted feuds in both Albertano's Italian communes and English society (as Chaucer's Dame Prudence, the descendant of Albertano's Prudentia in his third treatise, reminds us). The duke's response ("And he therto no word spak in that place" [line 3549]), his renunciation of retaliatory insults, both heads off violence and opens the way for reconciliation when Aristuppus, struck again by violent emotion, repents of his speech the next day (lines 3543–70). With patient control of speech, which Hoccleve sets in contrast with Aristuppus's "wordes felle [wicked, cruel, violent]" (line 3545), the duke "broghte al to reste and pees" (line 3563). By restraining violent speech in response to insults and by restraining his own impulse to strike out, Prince Henry will realize, as a Christian king, the patience of silent Jesus in His passion (lines 3613–26). (This pre-eminent exemplum of patient silence and some of the imaginative literature it generates are explored in chapter 4.) Thus, Hoccleve conveys to the prince that he himself may become an exemplar of kingly restraint of speech acts and bodily acts, joining the line of Jewish, Greek and Roman, and Christian heroes of patient silence. As such an exemplar, he could move his own people to restrain violent speech and retaliation, helping to maintain peace in a new reign that follows a time of conflict.

For a king to practice these two forms of protective silence, Hoccleve observes, he must avoid overindulgence in food and drink. If anyone drinks delicate and strong sweet wines "outrageously" (beyond bounds), he warns.

They birien [bury] wit and forbeeden silence
Of conseil; they outrayen [annihilate] pacience;

They kyndlen ire.
(lines 3830–35)

As in the stanzas on excessive speech, Hoccleve's remedy is to avoid superfluity by imposing a *modum* on the appetites, measuring out food and drink, like other pleasures, so that superfluity never leads to heedless speech that might disclose counsel or inflame anger.

Hoccleve's extended and comprehensive treatment of strategic silences in public life contrasts sharply with the very limited ones in his sources and in the only other mirror for a young Lancastrian prince, the *Active Policy of a Prince*, compiled, probably in the chaotic late 1460s, by George Ashby, a clerk of the signet to Queen Margaret.[24] One of Hoccleve's sources, Jacopo da Cessole's *Libellus* (to judge from William Caxton's close translation *The Game and Pleye of the Chesse*) never even mentions silence, even when telling the exemplum of Pisistarus's patient response to the abuse from his friend Aristuppus. The *Secreta secretorum*, much like the *Regiment*, advises kings to avoid loquacity and keep silent about their own plans when hearing advice but does so very briefly. However, these are the only sections where it treats silence in spite of listing restraint of the tongue as a royal virtue.[25] Egidio Colonna is so reliant on Aristotle's *Ethics* and *Politics* that his *De regimine principum* only brings up silence when treating effective gathering of counsel, as Aristotle does.[26] Altogether, Hoccleve's sources never envision silence as a political strategy in any situation except those that demand listening to others. Ashby's *Policy*, written for Edward, the last Lancastrian Prince of Wales, probably during his exile in France, would seem to promise a more extended consideration of taciturnity because prudent circumspection dominates the poem's first section, 126 rhyme royal stanzas organized around past, present, and future. However, keeping one's "entent" to oneself, as in the *Secreta* and *De regimine*, is the only type of silence recommended for Edward when he becomes king, although Ashby extends silent listening from gathering counsel (lines 359–65) to pondering secretly how much truth there may be in "tales" told by others (lines 625–31).[27] To the *Policy*, Ashby appended his incomplete *Dicta et opiniones diversorum philosophorum* (Sayings and thoughts of sundry wise men), 181 excerpts, mainly from the thirteenth-century *Liber philosophorum moralium antiquorum* (The book of ancient moral philosophers), each followed by an English rhyme royal stanza on its subject.[28] To brief general exhortations to practice verbal restraint, including Cato's "first virtue" distich (line 960), Ashby adds only one stanza claiming that taciturnity brings security to a ruler by protecting him from the consequences of rash speech and by rendering his thoughts opaque to those surrounding him (lines 1219–25). Ashby's limited and entirely self-protective advice to avoid speaking hastily and voluminously throws into sharp relief the many situations in which Hoccleve insists that a king's silences may protect his people, as well as him.

Throughout the *Regiment*, from the unruly tongue uttering unfulfillable promises to avarice propelling foreign wars, Hoccleve presents urgent appetites and vehement emotions as a major threat to successful rule. Hoccleve's king must cultivate virtues, like patience and mercy, that can not only check volatile emotions but also help to create the consistency and stability in speech and action that people expect from their rulers. Central to virtuous restraint in all situations is prudence, with its power to direct a ruler to bring apt past situations to bear on the analysis of present ones and then weigh likely outcomes. In this political code of restraint, stability, and prudent choices, the resource of taciturnity enables a king to escape the dangers of committing himself hastily, enables him to assess situations and people and to deliberate amid the noisy hive of a court, the unpredictability of political actors, and the press for decisive action. Taciturnity could help Prince Henry, once king, to retain his honor as a "true king," one on whose oaths and promises his subjects may rely. Because of cautionary initial silence, he could also decide rightly when to keep certain policies and necessary actions secret until they are shaped by the counsel that promises the most beneficial consequences for him and for his subjects and, then, until they are enacted. Such habitual verbal restraint also would enable him to practice that most difficult of all silences for feudal lords: the patient silence when slighted or insulted that will maintain peace with those with whom he must deal. Authorized, even enjoined, by texts from classical, Jewish, and Christian antiquity and advocated by the clergy in catechesis and sermon, both taciturnity and the sustained silence it sometimes devises would make a new King Henry an exemplar for his nobles—indeed, for all his subjects. In all these ways, taciturnity and shrewd silence together constitute in the *Regiment* what the historian of women's rhetorics Cheryl Glenn calls "a strategic position of strength," a crucial one in a time of political, even dynastic, uncertainty.[29] Even then, however, another type of circumspect silence, the *mala taciturnitas* (evil taciturnity) of comprehensive clerical writing on silence, would threaten Henry's reign-to-be, just as it has his father's. Silence by royal advisers could dangerously limit gathering counsel, threaten communal welfare, exacerbate violent quarrels, and damage the king in his subjects' eyes, all political hazards that strategic silence aims to avert. To this evil twin of useful taciturnity in the *Regiment* and its nearly contemporary poem *Mum and the Sothsegger*, chapter 3 turns.

CHAPTER 3

CORRUPT POLITICAL SILENCES
Mum and the Sothsegger

The textual web of Jewish and Christian scriptures and of classical maxims and anecdotes that undergirds the advocacy of public silences in Albertano da Brescia's treatises, late medieval clerical works, and Hoccleve's mirror for Prince Henry is torn apart in the anonymous alliterative satire *Mum and the Sothsegger*, written in 1409, just before the *Regiment*. Like Hoccleve, its author comes across as a royalist familiar with Lancastrian legal and parliamentary affairs. Unlike the *Regiment*'s traditional model of advice about rule from an informed (if somewhat marginal) royal servant, the "uplandish," often colloquial, style of *Mum* places it "outside the discourses of dominant institutions," as Helen Barr and Kate Ward-Perkins observe.[1] Although Hoccleve denounces the destructive silences of flattering advisers as part of his comprehensive treatment of political silences, in *Mum*, silence, embodied in the shape-shifting courtier-bishop Mum, emerges only as a self-interested practice that subverts just and wise rule. Although Mum speaks readily enough when he wishes to persuade, to threaten, and to distract, he chooses not to report social injustices to the royal court or check the ill-conceived designs of the people in power: mayors, lawyers, nobles, and clerics, as well as King Henry IV. In all arenas of public life, Mum's opposite, the public-spirited truth-teller ("Sothsegger"), is despised, cast out, and threatened with torture and death.

Mum's rejection of truth-telling and embrace of self-serving silence, the poem's narrator realizes, may be justified by the *Disticha Catonis*, with its ethic of avoiding harm and maximizing personal benefit. However, behind the *Mum*-poet's satiric vision of corrupt political silences lies John Wyclif's martyrological rhetoric dramatizing the dangers of telling the truth in a church dominated by powerful clerics who betray their own offices with their wicked silences.² And behind his polemics lies a clerical tradition of unmasking a vicious type of taciturnity, *mala* (evil) or *nimia* (excessive) or *indiscreta* (ill-advised) *taciturnitas*: the failure to offer needed advice, the shirking of corrective speech that might antagonize the powerful and wealthy, and negligence in positions that demand giving instruction. In sections on evil taciturnity, included in almost all treatments of silence, clerical writers leave behind Roman popular morality, with its concern for benefiting the actor, and even Stoicism, deriving their moral norms entirely from Christian scripture and canon law. This material opens a way for the *Mum*-poet to subvert the self-serving prudential reasoning of Mum and his many adherents, providing texts that counter what the poet sees as the corrupt, but dominant, way of life in every level of English institutions. These biblical and legal texts also validate the truth-teller's dissenting way of life, in which everything, including life itself, is risked in order to disclose to officials and the king himself injustices, corrupt practices, and destructive policies. Yet, as a royalist like Wyclif, the poet envisions reform as operating only within received political structures, just as clerical moral writers did within the practices of the institutional church. Over a decade ago, I wrote about how the *Mum*-poet authorizes his satire and promotes political reforms by appealing to fraternal correction as a practice mandated by canon law and pastoral teaching.³ Now I turn to the other side of the poem's fundamental and often quasi-academic debate: Mum's defense of his strategic silences as the good life of a "wise man," a defense rarely considered by scholars, who tend to focus on the poet's satire of bureaucratic and legal culture.⁴

Because of the renewed commitment to preaching, correcting, and admonishing that emerges in the late twelfth-century circle of Pierre le Chantre, clerical moral writers, unlike Albertano da Brescia, explore this dark side of taciturnity, which occurs, in the words of *De lingua*, "cum tacetur veritas dicenda uel ad honorem Dei uel ad salutem sui uel ad utilitatem proximi" (when the truth is kept silent which ought to be spoken either for God's honor or the speaker's own salvation or another's benefit).[5] So important did this evil taciturnity become in the economy of salvation that the Franciscan *Summa fratris Alexandri* of the mid-thirteenth century reasons that taciturnity may be a greater sin than any sin of the tongue because the value—*utilitas*, again—of speech is greater than that of silence and so the damage created by withholding speech when needed is greater than that created by breaking silence.[6] While this culpable silence could be committed by any Christian who failed to speak words of edifying counsel to people in need of it, clerics devote most of their exposition to their own class.[7] A priest betrays the truth not only by openly speaking a lie instead of the truth but also by not proclaiming and defending it. So declares the ecclesiastical and political administrator Roger of Waltham, in the words of a decretal ascribed to Gratian:

> Non ille enim solum proditor est veritatis qui transgrediens veritatem pro veritate palam loquitur mendacium. Sed etiam ille qui non libere pronunciat veritatem quam libere pronunciare oportet aut qui non libere veritatem defendit quam libere defendere convenit, proditor est veritatis.[8]

> Indeed, a betrayer of truth is not only one who, deserting the truth, openly speaks a lie instead of the truth, but even he is a betrayer of the truth who does not openly proclaim truth that is fitting to proclaim openly or he who does not boldly defend truth that is fitting to defend.

Roger takes up the sin of taciturnity in the tenth part of his compendium, dealing with the virtue of humility in rulers and the courage or boldness (*animositas*) needed by priests in order to resist rulers' vicious designs. The priestly office demands that its holders put in a clear light and reprehend sins that are committed by anyone whomsoever ("officium arguendi").

To explain why some priests fail to carry out their responsibilities of advising and correcting, Roger turns to that Roman civil and ecclesiastical administrator Pope Gregory the Great: they fear losing the favor of the powerful. This fear can be so overmastering, Gregory explains, that, when asked by a powerful person, they do not hesitate to deny the truth in a legal case (or possibly the more general sense of "causa": affair), even if that disadvantages someone else.[9] Clerics' fear of the powerful is always accompanied, observes Pierre le Chantre, by greed, as they fear to lose gifts from the wealthy.[10] Stoic, patristic, and medieval moral writers agreed that fear, as aversion to and flight from an imagined destructive event, was a powerful emotion that could precipitate rash actions, and, as Barbara Rosenwein has shown, some Christian writers, like Augustine and Jean Gerson, understood avarice, as a passion for accumulating wealth, to be an emotion, too.[11] In conjunction, these powerful emotions could outweigh, even efface, any consideration of clerical loyalties and responsibilities. The French Franciscan Nicolas de Byard, writing outside of Roger's administrative world, finds reasons in addition to fear for this culpable silence: priests' cowardice in reproving the powerful (such priests are like birds of prey that only attack chickens), laziness (like that of the man in Matthew's gospel who hides his talent in the ground), foolish worldly anxieties (like those of the overly solicitous hen that hides an egg among its already-hatched chicks), and consciousness of their own sins.[12] By choosing not to speak when the circumstances obligate them to do so, these clerics deny Christ the truth and abandon their flocks to the wolf, acting as dumb dogs not having the power to speak, in the common metaphor derived from Isaiah 56:10. Such dumb dogs are the most imprudent of dogs ("canes imprudentissimi") in John of Mirfield's *Florarium*, failing to use foresight and circumspection to carry out their fundamental duties.[13] They even fail to obey the evangelical imperative of fraternal correction, by which all Christians are bound to reprove sins they witness. Roger develops the communal consequences of such a failure: by not confronting sins openly, priests seduce the ignorant and foolish into sinning, and all of them—priest, initial sinner, and those seduced—may be damned, their blood on the hands of the silent priest. In the blunt English of the *Book for a Simple and Devout Woman*, "So if eny of þe peple for þe prelate holdeþ hym stille deye, as gulti is he of his deþe as he hym hadde slayne."[14] To drive home silent priests' responsibility, clerical writers again and again work the common metaphor of sin as a wound. By seeing evils and not correcting them, silent priests withdraw the medicine or salve that would draw out the poisonous fluids from the wound and so prevent death.[15] Against these silent priests who incur destructive consequences for themselves as well as for others (and God insofar as they fail to carry out His desire that humans be clawed back from sin), Roger and other writers set the example of John the Baptist, who, even in prison, inveighed against the adultery and incest of Herod and Herodias so that people in the future would not be tempted by their example.[16]

Evil taciturnity is akin to its polar opposite, loquacity, in its effects and so in its gravity, Carla Casagrande and Silvana Vecchio argue, largely from twelfth- and early thirteenth-century texts written in France. Evil taciturnity denies the value of language as a fundamental pedagogic resource, while, as chapter 1 explains, *multiloquium* disperses its force. Moreover, since both vicious extremes stem from a failure to measure speech, clerics offer means for judging when to stay silent and when to speak according to kinds of social interactions.[17] These norms are, of course, inculcated so that individuals in specific situations can assess the circumstances but, perhaps even more importantly, so that they can restrain vehement emotions like fear and greed, the forces behind the vicious extreme of evil taciturnity that denies others vital teaching ("vitalis edificacio"). Where evil taciturnity differs markedly from useful taciturnity is its context: most of the time clerics fail to rebuke and teach when power relations are asymmetrical (priest and noble) or at least contestable (archbishop and king), when they are responsible for advising the wealthy and people in institutional positions of power.

John Wyclif does not treat evil taciturnity comprehensively in a *distinctio* or chapter on silence, as earlier clerical writers had done, but sporadically in his increasingly polemical theological treatises of the late 1370s, so often assaults on the hierarchy of the institutional church. Wyclif's culpable taciturnity follows the broad outlines of clerical moral writing since Pierre le Chantre: clerics remain silent out of laziness and, especially, greed, including fear of losing temporal goods and positions; they resist God's intended end for the tongue; they slay both the souls of those whom they are bound to care for and their own.[18] In *Tractatus de mandatis divinis* (Treatise on the divine commandments), for example, Wyclif reasons that such silence directly stands in the way of God's intended end for the tongue ("directe obviat fini lingue"), citing the conventional *sententia* that the mouth should be open for life-giving teaching just as it should be closed against destructive speech. Therefore, he rechristens *mala* or *nimia taciturnitas* as *proditoria taciturnitas* (traitorous taciturnity). For him, clerical failures to correct sinners amount to treachery against God, a violation of a divinely given office: "Cum enim sacerdotes et prophete pastorum et speculatorum ex mandato Domini gerant officium, patet quod eorum taciturnitas foret Dei prodicio"

(Because, indeed, priests and prophets among pastors and watchmen hold an office by the commandment of God, it is clear that their taciturnity would be a betrayal of God).[19]

What is new in Wyclif's treatises, especially in *De veritate Sacrae Scripturae* (On the truth of holy scripture), written during 1377 and 1378 while bishops were initiating legal hearings about his potentially unorthodox positions, is the dramatic scenario of division within the institutional church, where those who proclaim the truth of the gospel are hounded by those who consent to lies out of servile fear ("timor servilis"). Instead of earlier clerics' concern with correcting the sins of people in their pastoral care, especially the wealthy and the powerful, Wyclif sees his duty and the duty of all true Christians (his followers would christen themselves "true men") as preaching against enemies within the institutional church, especially in its hierarchy. The culpable silences of *prelates* (a term that may refer to all priests or to members of the hierarchy), Wyclif claims, are responsible for every human evil and the ruin of all the people ("taciturnitas culpabilis prelatorum est causa tocius ruine populi").[20] New, therefore, too, is his dismissal of what he understands as a temporizing argument: that he and other true believers should hold back because denouncing institutional evils would cause scandal to the faithful, a debilitating awareness of the church's corruption and failures that might lead people to lose faith in it. Both Bede and St. Bernard drew the conclusion, Wyclif himself concludes, that it is better that scandal should arise than that the truth should be abandoned ("quod 'melius est quod scandalum oriatur, quam ut veritas relinquatur'"). Otherwise, lies will become stronger than the truth.[21] So, Christians must defend the truth to the death. In *De veritate*, sinners' panicked moves to keep the truth about themselves hidden mean that faithful preachers must be willing to face martyrdom. Wyclif develops those traditional biblical exemplars of faithful preachers from earlier discourse on *mala taciturnitas*, Jesus and John the Baptist, so that what causes their deaths is the institutional sins that Wyclif denounces in the contemporary church: the greed of the clerical class (scribes and pharisees, labels he often tars his contemporaries with) and the attempts by culpably silent officials to suppress faithful preaching.[22]

Given Thomas Hoccleve's recurrent self-image in his poetry as a fierce opponent of Wycliffites and given the prominence that traitorous taciturnity had assumed in John Wyclif's later works three decades earlier, it may seem surprising that evil taciturnity becomes a recurrent topic in *The Regiment of Princes*.[23] Although strategic silences are essential instruments for an effective king's thinking, speaking, and acting in the *Regiment*, self-interested silence from those who surround the king, in Hoccleve's view, threatens English governance, indeed, the Lancastrians' hold on power. In contrast, two of his main sources, the *Libellus* and the *Secretum*, never mention the silence of flatterers, and John of Trevisa's translation of *De regimine* does so only in one sentence about deceived nobles.[24] Hoccleve treats this evil taciturnity most extensively as a failure of "pitee"/"pietas," wholehearted devotion to, and aid for, people suffering calamities (lines 2997–3000). Flatterers, imagined by Hoccleve as cruel for their indifference to the fate of their king and their kingdom, first of all use speech to promote what the king already thinks and desires (lines 3039–87). Hoccleve had inveighed against flatterers who cloak how lords' "gouernance is despysid / Among the peple" in his earlier *La male regle* (The ill-governed life), where he warns against the misfortune and ruin that follow from such deception. However, there he limits flattery to seductive, deceptive speech because his invective is prompted by a confession that he overpaid flattering boatmen when they addressed him as a person of stature and consequence.[25] Here, in the *Regiment*'s account of flattery at court, Hoccleve turns to another mode of flattery, deceiving silence:

> A gloser [sycophant, deceiver] also keepith his silence
> Often where he his lord seeth him mistake.
> Lest that his answer mighte doon offense
> Unto his lord and him displesid make,
> He halt his pees—nat o word dar he crake [utter];
> And for he naght ne seeth [says], he his assent
> Geveth therto by mannes jugement.
>
> Whoso that woot [is aware of] the purpos of a wight [man]
> That is ygrowndid upon wikkednesse
> And nat ne lettith [does not at all prevent] it unto his might,
> Favourith it, as the book can expresse. (lines 3088–98)

To mark out evil taciturnity as an essential part of a treatise on effective rule, Hoccleve paraphrases, in the first two lines, a Latin definition of flattery and places the original in the margin, attributing it to the twelfth-century theologian and biblical exegete Hugues de Saint-Victor: "Adulator est ille qui tacet et dat consensum ne offendat quem hortat habere propitium" (at line 3088; A flatterer is one who stays silent and gives consent lest he offend the person whom he pleads to be favorably disposed toward him).[26] By terming the silent flatterer a "gloser," Hoccleve indicates that silence, like speech, may be used to obscure the truth of a matter, just as a glossator of a passage might interpret it in a way that masks its sense and import (*MED*, s.v. "glosen" [v.], 1 and 2). Driving home with repetition the decision to stay silent, Hoccleve weighs carefully what kind of moral culpability an adviser's willed silence about a ruler's errors carries. First, using "lord" instead of "king" here allows Hoccleve to stress the feudal allegiance and devotion that the adviser owes to the ruler, increasing his obligation to him. Then, to authorize his claim that the silent assent to, even favor, the wicked deeds they observe in the making, he appeals to canon law ("the book"), that essential source for clerical norms on evil taciturnity, and in the margin he notes "Qui tacet, et etcetera." "Qui tacet consentire videtur" (He who keeps silent seems to consent), a maxim added to the *Decretals* in the late thirteenth century, brings the authority of canon law to Hoccleve's ethical analysis, an authority he refers to elsewhere when instructing Prince Henry on crucial royal duties (like what is necessary to swear an oath validly at line 2353).[27] Such tacit approval of a king's destructive actions, like false praise, stems primarily, as clerical writing down to Wyclif insists, from avarice, which Hoccleve later characterizes as the pursuit of "profyt singuler" instead of "profyt commun," a pursuit that causes war and internal disturbances by depriving a king of checks on his initial impulses (lines 5244–71). Throughout the *Regiment*, as we have seen, Hoccleve asserts a king's need to check strong emotions and hastily conceived actions by taciturnity as an initial silence that fosters cautious discernment and the gathering of counsel from all sides. The culpably silent adviser withholds counsel because he fears offending his lord and so forfeiting "thi lucre and thi cofres warmnesse [material value, prosperity]," his only reason for playing his part in the court's game of dissimulation. He does so even when he realizes that the consequences of his silence will be his lord's loss of good repute, so central to effective rule in the *Regiment* (lines 3039–59).

The destructive consequences of such tacit approval for the kingdom as a whole are developed in the final section of the *Regiment*, where Hoccleve presents flattery as a breaker of the peace and a furtherer of war. Because kings have become accustomed to tacit approval, the very people who could advise them knowledgeably about military strategy and the on-the-ground costs of war—the knights, squires, and yeomen who have spent their blood in the king's wars—cannot do so (lines 5279–85). If they are to be heard at court, they must adopt curial silence about uncomfortable truths; if they are forthright, they will be sent packing. Either way, the king and kingdom are more likely to suffer needlessly destructive and draining military adventures. The destructive effects of counsel skewed by silence are developed more fully in the section on royal largesse and prodigality. There Hoccleve describes how injudicious and excessive royal spending impoverishes heavily taxed marginal laborers, a significant complaint during the reigns of Richard II and Henry IV. Yet a king may never grasp that his prodigality is inciting popular discontent that will eventually harm him. Although "scriptures," authoritative writings, amply tell of these consequences for any people and any ruler, "Fauel [flattery] nat reportith tho [those] scriptures." Instead, because the flatterer fears royal displeasure, he hides the truth that relevant texts contain (for example, clerical moral writing often treats the consequences of prodigality),[28] even though they are "His lordes soules salve" (lines 4439–42). Such destructive silencing of crucial Jewish and Christian scripture and other moral writing brings down God's wrath on the flatterer, the consequence of evil taciturnity in clerical writing:

> Who that for drede of any lord or sire
> Hydeth the trouthe and nat wole it out seye,
> He upon him provokith Goddes ire
> For that more than God of man hath ye [has an eye to]. (lines 4453–56)

Here Hoccleve paraphrases a key sentence on evil taciturnity from canon law, which he gives in the margin: "Quisquis metu alicuius potestatis veritatem occultat iram dei super se provocat quia magis timet hominem quam deum" (Whoever, because of fear of another's power, hides the truth calls God's wrath down upon himself because he fears a human more than God).[29] Through their silences about their master's ill-conceived designs, about the deleterious effects of them on the commons, and about relevant literature of advice, royal advisers, whether clerics or laics, sunder the conjunction of personal and common profit that Albertano and clerical writers claim that prudent silences in public affairs will generate. Silent flatterers calculate that their status and wealth depend on cloaking troubling matters that they know will subvert the welfare of both king and subject. They see the king not as the nation's ruler but only as the powerful dispenser of favor, position, and wealth within the court, able to cut off their curial benefits if they displease him.

In the anonymous *Mum and the Sothsegger*, deeply influenced by John Wyclif and his followers, not only do public figures abandon communal profit for personal profit, but the poem questions whether they can be fused at all, as Albertano's treatises, non-Wycliffite moral writing, and most of the *Regiment* claim. The royal adviser Mum, a man of many identities, justifies his opportunistic silences by appealing to popular prudential reasoning about consequences, a position that the *Disticha Catonis*, that main vehicle of Roman popular morality, seems to validate. In a sustained contrast to Mum, who thrives at the center of secular power, the Sothsegger, an impoverished and despised truth-teller, leads a seemingly futile life out of the court. Yet this way of life rests, the narrator discovers, on Jewish and Christian scripture and canon law, the main resources for clerical writing (including Wyclif's) on *mala taciturnitas*. The *Mum*-poet marks his work as political and social satire with an urgent public voice by writing in alliterative verse, the medium of *Piers Plowman* and other satires of political and ecclesiastical abuses, like *Richard the Redeless* (after 1400) and *Pierce the Plowman's Crede* (late 1390s). While the *Regiment* confines itself to a generic portrayal of culpably silent advisers at court, *Mum*'s reformist zeal is explicitly turned against the clergy, as well: priests, friars, and, especially, bishops who functioned as royal advisers during the reign of Henry IV, as during the reigns of his predecessors. As reformist satire, it aims to unmask the aims, methods, and shaky self-justifications of those who serve only themselves in public life, secular and ecclesiastical, moving readers who might have tolerated the abuses of the silent and their consequences to reject Mum's way of life. Like Hoccleve's exposure of silent advisers in the *Regiment*'s section on *pietas*, *Mum* also discloses, albeit slowly and progressively as satire does, the ethical norms that the silent violate, not least of all because of their institutional responsibilities.

The sole manuscript of the *Mum* opens (the beginning is lost) amid an account of the failures of court officials to address the causes of continuing popular unrest a decade into Henry IV's rule. Although Henry is praised early in *Mum* as a skilled warrior and gracious ruler (lines 206–26), the poem retails the growing popular resentment over heavy taxation and the commoners' complaints that wrongs have not been amended and that their lawsuits have been scuttled.[30] The royalist author presents Henry as unaware of the commoners' complaints because no one who flourishes at court will tell him the truth. Bent on their own profit, flattering should-be advisers hide popular grievances, while frank truth-tellers not only are never heard, as in the *Regiment*, but are cast out, hunted down, imprisoned, tortured, and even killed (lines 31–232). As Jenni Nuttall states, "by 1409 the professed Lancastrian commitment to truth-telling and reform was considered to be a temporary and pragmatic measure rather than a genuine gesture," and the royal household largely became inaccessible to truth-tellers.[31] Given Wyclif's and his followers' binary view of the church, it is hardly surprising that the *Mum*-poet, as a Wycliffite sympathizer, casts his discursive satire as a conflict between a pious out-of-power truth-teller and a greedy, violent practitioner of cautionary silence who is depicted with a miter at a crucial juncture. By doing so, he aligns the political crisis in the realm with the crisis within the English church as painted by Wyclif's unsparing polemics. Just as he appropriates the Christian practice of fraternal correction of sin, taught and enjoined by the clergy as a means to reform individuals, to legitimate truth-telling to the king and his advisers, so he appropriates clerical writing on taciturnity down through Wyclif to delegitimatize the silences of royal advisers and clerics. In this process, he opens up fissures in the classically and scripturally shaped tradition of discreet silences in public life: fissures between the practical intellect operative in prudence and the loving will informed by Christian imperatives, between silent circumspection and fidelity to the truth, between personal profit and public welfare, between Roman popular consequentialist ethics and Jewish wisdom. By repudiating the syncretic tradition stretching from Albertano and Pierre le Chantre to the *Mum*-poet's near contemporary John of Mirfield, he creates a new ethic of silence and speech in public life, understanding differently the circumstances of speaking situations and weighing differently the consequences of refraining from speech.

Much as a commanding figure from *Piers Plowman* might do, Mum breaks off abruptly the narrator's initial musings over truth-telling about unrest, and, like some of the figures in that progenitor of *Mum*, he personifies a way of life that is thrust upon the somewhat baffled narrator. Mum's opponent, the truth-teller, never speaks in the poem. Mum himself initiates a disputation by attacking the narrator for being so foolish as to even consider the value of truthful counsel. Then, accentuating the difference in power between them, he introduces himself as a master of court life and as the narrator's own master, the figure who both rules and tutors him, as if he were unable to govern and instruct himself:

> "I am Mum thy maister," cothe [said] he, "in alle maniere places,
> That sittith with souuerayns and seruyd with greete.
> Thaire wille ne thaire wordes I withseye neuer.
> But folowe thaym in thaire folie and fare muche the bettre,
> Easily for oyle [oil], sire, and elles were I nyce [foolish].
> Thus leede I my life in luste of my herte,
> And for my wisedame and witte wone [dwell] I with the beste . . ."
>
> (lines 243–49)

With this entry, Mum himself unwittingly sets up an ironic contrast between his name (for "mom" means an inarticulate sound) and his brash, imperious, and voluble speech. Against the ostracized truth-teller he sets his social success at court: a pleasure-filled life at the tables of kings and magnates, dispensers of favor, status, and gifts. To justify initially his tacit approval of rulers' foolish actions, which he frankly declares flattery (oil is a metaphor for flattering words), Mum simply credits his wisdom and "witte," the clever use of his practical intellect that he has just mocked the narrator for lacking (line 238). Mum sees no need to cite written authority as justification. For him, naked self-interest and its reward, elevated social standing, work as wholly persuasive appeals. So does the naked claim that wisdom and "witte" dictate never speaking against the will of the powerful, even when those prudential qualities, critical for a responsible adviser, enable him to detect what is willed as foolish. While he claims to be the narrator's master, he is acutely conscious of the king's power to confer and to include or exclude.

To counter Mum's claims, the narrator resorts mainly to two traditional tools of discourse on *mala taciturnitas*, working in concert: written authority and the consequences for the person who could speak out and, especially, for others. First, he turns to canon law, a crucial authority on evil taciturnity, as we have seen in clerical writing:

> And yit thou suffris [allow, countenance] thy souurayn to shame hym-self
> There thou mightes amende hym many tyme and ofte.
> *Facientis culpam habet, qui quod potest corrigere negligit emendare in secretis etc.* [Anyone who neglects to amend what he could correct secretly bears the fault of the doer] (lines 273–74a)

The Latin *sententia* is written by the poem's scribe in the margin of its only manuscript, as are all the Latin sentences or fragments incorporated into the poem's lines by its only editors since the original edition of 1936: Helen Barr (1993, the edition I use) and James Dean (2000). All of these Latin lines, Barr argues, authorize the English passages to which they are attached, sometimes supporting speakers' positions. In some passages, the Latin is Englished in the poem itself. In addition, she perceives that this practice of including authoritative Latin *sententiae* mimics the practice of *Mum*'s progenitor *Piers Plowman*, in which Latin (and French) lines are included in the text of the poem itself in most manuscripts. For these reasons, she, like Dean, includes the Latin within the lines of the poem itself in her edition, and, in my reading, I also regard them as integral to the poem.[32] This Latin *sententia* (without "in secretis") about the guilt of those who fail to correct evils, which begins a *causa* from the *Decretals* ascribed to Gratian, was often cited in England throughout the fourteenth century and before.[33] Appearing in the *Decretals* amid *causae* reproving clerics at several levels (bishops first) who fail to fulfill the office of teaching and correcting sins, it was used by ecclesiastics to justify remonstrating against the actions of the politically powerful, as Thomas Beckett did, quoting it when he wrote to King Henry II from exile to protest against the irreverent treatment of the church and its dignitaries by the secular power.[34] Yet the language of the *causa* is so general that it could be quoted in catechetical material on correcting evils and that it could be used, as William of Ockham does in his *Dialogus*, to argue for the culpability of anyone who fails to correct the errant.[35] Therefore, when the *Mum*-poet appropriated this *sententia* from canon law to subvert the triumphalist claims of a member of Henry IV's court, he was not writing in an unprecedented way. By adding "in secretis" to the legal statement (or keeping it from a source), he stresses the great consequences of evil taciturnity: the king's loss of reputation, which, for a royalist like him (and Hoccleve), precipitates loss of the people's trust and thus subverts rule.³⁶ The faithful adviser works in secret to prevent misconceived actions, cloaking his criticism of the king. Yet "in secretis" does more than that. It restricts telling uncomfortable truths to the king to people with access to him by reason of their office, status, or royal favor. Only they could do so privately. So, the *Mum*-poet's Wycliffite commitment to truth-telling is circumscribed by his royalist sense that it should be done only within received political culture, a limit stated more openly later in the poem. He may draw on Wyclif's condemnation of *mala taciturnitas*, but he does not share Wyclif's passionate promotion of denunciatory speech even when it inflicts damage on institutions and their officials. This obligation to inform and correct the king in private and its restriction to people at court both subvert Mum's practice of withholding the truth. As a silent man at court witnessing his own lord about to embark on shameful actions, he allows the king to proceed and damage his *fama* ("thou suffris thy souuaryn to shame hymself"). Thus, the narrator exposes Mum as a mere profiteer whose adoption of unwavering cautious silence as the only successful way of life at court sacrifices, for his own profit, public welfare, loyalty to his lord, and obedience to fundamental Christian law.

The narrator of *Mum*, like his ancestor Will of *Piers Plowman*, is a creature of second thoughts—and more. Once Mum departs, he recalls with wonder how Mum proved his opinions "by profitable poyntz y-nowe [enough]" (line 281). As he mulls over the competing claims of truth-telling and remaining mum, he realizes that Mum's portrayal of the sorrowful, rejected truth-teller is validated by the schoolboy dictum from the *Disticha Catonis* that is cited as authoritative, as we have seen, by Albertano da Brescia and by clerical writers on taciturnity:

> And cleerly Caton construeth the same,
> And seyth soethly, I saw hit in youthe,
> Nam nulli tacuisse nocet, nocet esse locutum.
> That of "bable" cometh blame [rebuke, ill repute, shame] and of
>   "be stille" neuer,
> And a wise worldly worde, as me thenketh. (lines 289–92)

This dictum begins a conflict between different ethical traditions on the uses of silence that runs throughout the narrator's journeys. In the narrator's search for confirmatory texts, he realizes that Mum lives by a Roman consequentialist morality that values a cautious appraisal of likely consequences. As a result, he never says anything that might harm himself in any way. To speak unreservedly about what one observes in the realm ("bable") would incur censure and rejection by others jockeying for position and power in the competitive world of the Lancastrian court. Since speech always carries risk and can work against the speaker, as Albertano and clerical writers assert, sometimes using this very Catonic dictum, silence is the best policy for a politic man at court.[37] However, Mum's silence is not only Albertano's, clerics', and Hoccleve's silence as a necessary first step in assessing the circumstances in any situation and deciding when and what to speak, if at all. It is silence, no matter what the consequences for others, whenever a royal adviser senses that his lord desires a course of action. It is silence born of greed and fear of loss that is condemned in the *Regiment*. In step with Cato's "wise worldly worde," Mum has reduced to personal profit the wide-ranging purposes of silence as a resource in public life according to Albertano's treatises, clerical moral writings, and the *Regiment*: to foster a multivoiced process of advice giving, to avoid rash oaths and promises, to cloak planned actions from enemies, to avoid verbal and then physical strife in honor cultures, to prevent disclosing foolish thoughts and feelings that others might exploit. He has sundered personal profit from profit for other individuals and for the whole body politic, in contrast to Albertano, Hoccleve, and most clerics, who weld together the three arenas of profit.

Given Mum's self-exposure and the narrator's marshaling of canon law and consequences against him (even if a dictum from the *Disticha Catonis* seems to unsettle the latter's position), where can the poet take the "matiere" or "case" of Mum and the Sothsegger, to use the legal terms he so often draws on to characterize the conflict between ways of life that the narrator must judge? First, his narrator turns to reading books of wisdom, then, in a journey of years, to observing how Mum operates in and affects different domains of communal life. In both ways, the poet moves from disclosing the consequences of self-serving silence for the king to those for his subjects, from the great magnates to humble rural folk in their parish churches.

Rather than recalling more of the *Disticha Catonis*, the narrator reads in wisdom literature, "Sidrac and Salomon-is termes, / And Seneca the sage" (lines 304–5): a widespread encyclopedic French text of the thirteenth century attributed to the ancient sage Sidrach, Jewish wisdom books, and texts attributed to Seneca as a Stoic philosopher.[38] These ethical strains provide no support whatsoever for Mum's way of life, which the narrator considers fashionable foolishness ("nycete of the newe iette" [line 312]), as does a Doctor of Theology he consults, who adds the adjective "noyous" (line 375) to stress that harm it brings. By contrast, the narrator's reading delivers the customary principle "How that good gouuernance gracieusely endith," which the Doctor of Theology later proclaims the only text relevant to adjudicating the conflicting ways of life (lines 313, 377). Yet the bemused narrator fails to figure out how to apply the wise saying, given its generality, to either way of life, and neither the Doctor nor others versed in learned texts offer him any help. Nonetheless, this principle pits Jewish wisdom and Stoic ethics against Mum's naked self-advancing consequentialism, at best somewhat in tune with Roman popular morality as encapsulated in that distich of "Cato." Just as the latter ethic cloaks with silence the political, economic, legal, and social abuses of which King Henry is unaware, the former provides a sure, albeit general, foundation for public life: governance is to be judged by whether or not it produces results that enable people to prosper and win their good will.

The abuses of office and power throughout the realm emerge during the narrator's journey in search of compelling answers to his question "Whether Mvm is more better or Melle-sum-tyme [Speak Sometimes] / Forto amende that were amysse into more ease" (lines 526–27). In all domains of institutional life, he observes how "worldly wise" silence overmasters and corrupts every estate and almost every person. As the sphere of Mum (and *Mum*) moves beyond the court and the harm Mum inflicts on King Henry and the kingdom in general, the poet makes specific and immediate the multifarious consequences for governance when officeholders, even institutions, adopt Mum's way of life. Thus, he reveals the codes of silence which people with even a little power use to prey on those whose well-being, spiritual and material, is entrusted to them.

First the narrator surveys religious institutions, where conventional Wycliffite satire of clerical abuses should not obscure for readers how silence maintains those abuses. The parade begins with the friars, who have resorted to "kepte cunseil and cloos [secret and private plotting]" to devise, and then to cloak, means to accumulate wealth and power. Under the guise of offering expert spiritual guidance, they have shouldered their way into hearing confessions and so controlling penitents. During the sacrament, they ferret out the sinful desires, aims, and schemes ("intentz") of lords and ladies. Then they leverage that knowledge to enrich themselves and feed their endless acquisitiveness. Even the poor cannot escape their devious stratagems, dependent, as they were, on confession to be granted remission of their sins (lines 457–65). Then the narrator overhears a parish priest giving a sermon itemizing the tithes he desires, a catalogue ranging from wool and cheese to chives and garlic, its breadth and detail conveying the grasping reach of clerics over all that human labor produces from the earth. Meanwhile, Mum, who serves as the priest's "meen" (intermediary), standing between the priest and the people in his pastoral care, keeps him from preaching about how tithes should be dispersed and how he should labor along with his parishioners. So, he buries in silence how much he sets aside for himself, rather than sharing it with the poor as he is obligated to do by his office according to canon law, a source arcane enough that only he in the parish would be likely to know it (lines 592–628).[39] Thus, even the humblest rural priest can use the very medium designed to declare basic religious obligations, preaching, in order to cloak his exploitation of those whom he should be teaching. Throughout the church, the narrator concludes, the "worldly wise and wynners [profiteers]," love their "mates" "Mvm and the monaye," the alliteration tying circumspect silence to its object: financial gain (lines 670–73). They remain silent about both their obligations and their own profiteering practices, with the result that corruption becomes normalized and people do not think to ask for the truth. To silence the narrator and cut short his exposure of clerical corruption and the clerical conspiracy of silence, Mum, now wearing a miter as a representative of the hierarchy, advises him to submit to his rule of silence and to look out only for himself. Then, like a bishop characterized by Wyclif, he threatens him with madness and death (lines 578–81, 675–79), the extremes to which the hierarchy goes in order to protect clerics' crass exploitation of laypeople through the very pastoral practices designed to instruct, guide, and save those in their pastoral care.

The stratagems that guarantee Mum's mastery of civil, as well as well as of religious, institutions, and the consequences for the less powerful, emerge more fully as the narrator's years-long search throughout the realm draws to a close. As Albertano da Brescia recommends, Mum discreetly observes others conversing (with a lock on his lips), but only to detect the will of the wealthy so that he can enter the conversation in a way that wins their thanks and gifts (lines 681–97). In every town the narrator enters, the mayor, as a magistrate charged with ensuring fair trade, prizes Mum as a companion.

Mum sits apart from the court's proceedings, observing silently how he can manipulate the legal processes so that the rich gain at the expense of the poor. Biding his time, he sees how to omit procedural stages that might disadvantage a rich man who is being sued by a poor one; by his carefully calculated lies, jokes, and fawning speech, he distracts plaintiffs from anything in the proceedings that they could protest; throughout a case, he refuses to speak for one party when the mayor favors another (lines 801–17).[40] In these ways, the prudential verbal restraint that Albertano and clerical writers recommend for leaders in public life works to exclude the poor, and others without powerful patrons, from due process. The mayor, in turn, rewards Mum with gifts and a high place at mayoral feasts. In this situation, Mum does not just keep silent to avoid antagonizing the person of power, as he does at the royal court, but he uses his silence as a strategy to further the mayor's designs and those of the rich in general. The narrator's experience of Mum's "worldly wise" moves and the consequences of them only lead him to end his search where he began: by realizing anew that Mum is a "maister among men of good [goods collectively, prosperity]" and that, as a result, he lives a merrier life than a truth-teller does (lines 844, 849).

Despite this pervasive culture of silence that he has built, the ever-garrulous Mum reveals, in a passage that startles modern readers early in the narrator's journey, that he and his "mummers" are well aware both of the costs of their silences and of their own culpability for them. Indeed, Mum's spats with the narrator close with Mum acknowledging that clerics, especially bishops (like him), are obligated to advise, correct, and reform magnates to prevent them from slaughtering each other (as they had done throughout the reign of Richard II and the first decade of Henry's reign). In support, he quotes and Englishes expansively the ecclesiastical legal maxim on consent that Hoccleve inserts a year or two later into the *Regiment*'s section on silent advisers:

> And also in cuntrey hit is a comune speche [saying]
> And is y-write in Latyne, lerne hit who-so wil:
> The reason [principle] is 'qui tacet consentire videtur.'
> And who-so hath in-sight [knowledge] of silde-couthe [outrageous, immoral] thingz,
> Of synne or of shame or of shonde [disgrace] outher,

And luste [desires] not to lette [prevent] hit, but leteth [allows]
   hit forth passe,
As clercz doon construe that knowen alle bokes,
He shal be demyd doer of the same deede. (lines 743–50)

The *Mum*-poet gives the maxim prominence, even for a text that resorts frequently to legal terms and principles: it is the only Latin phrase worked into his verse.[41] He also gives it great authority: it is quoted all over the realm, yet it is also approved by the most learned of scholars. He even develops the dictum in two sharply different ways. He prefaces it with the homely metaphor about warning comrades of a coming shower so they can take shelter (lines 737–42), and he follows it up with a related civil law stipulating that, if someone who is interrogated about a felony stands "still as a stone," that person will be convicted for the crime (lines 751–57). Finally, Mum applies the principle once again to prelates: not to counsel magnates for rancor toward their fellows is to be culpable for the murders and unrest throughout society that the vacuum fails to prevent (lines 759–66). In this astonishing and unexpected move, the poet has Mum develop a canon law text about the culpability of silent advisers more extensively and acutely than the narrator did earlier in condemning Mum's silences at court (with "Facientis culpam"). Yet, for all of Mum's awareness of the maxim's authority and centrality in forestalling crimes, dishonor, and social disorder, Mum finishes his exchanges with the narrator by declaring that, out of fear of coming into conflict with others, he will follow "no waie but wit [practical cleverness that secures advantage] go bifore" and that he will learn from no one but himself, "My maister and maker, Mvm that I serue" (lines 776–79). Once again, he is acutely aware of the powers of the people above him in the political hierarchy, here the magnates' clout and capacity for violence. Whereas the poem's editors have attributed this startling self-reference to inconsistency in character or a memory lapse by the poet, surely it is perfectly in character. The Mum who declares from the first that he is teacher and controller of all, including the narrator, sees himself as self-created and self-controlling.[42] Whatever ecclesiastical law may enjoin and however much it is in keeping with daily experience and civil law, it has no more claim on him than any other clerically authoritative writing on silence does and no more role in shaping his life at court and in the church. Crafty use of silence to secure wealth and status, in large part by not challenging people with greater political powers, is all that matters.

When the poem comes to settle the debate between Mum's way of life and the Sothsegger's, it does so on the grounds of consequences, to which Mum appeals regularly for support, and of written authority, which Mum has ignored or deliberately set aside throughout his exchanges with the narrator. In a new revelatory dream, the exhausted narrator is counseled by a wise old gardener and beekeeper, who tends a well-ordered paradise, rooting out the weeds and killing off the drones before they devour all the honey of the worker bees and their king (yes, king; lines 869–1285). This authority on good governance rejects Mum because of the consequences of his silences seen throughout the poem—mercenary tricks, oppression, treachery, felonies, plundering, riots, unjust judgments against the poor, bribery—festering problems that silent advisers, including prelates, keep from king and council (lines 1115–55). Mum is "especially active in parliament," where, Wendy Scase has registered in her study of legal and literary complaint, formal complaints about wrongs should be made so that parliament and king may provide remedies. Instead, lords and knights of the shire fail to lodge complaints because of fear (lines 1117–40).[43] Mum, of course, has acknowledged the injustices that he enables the rich and clerics to perpetrate and the violence that he has decided not to check, setting them aside as collateral damage in his pursuit of status, money, and goods. In this dream, the beekeeper counters this position by proclaiming that such silences violate injunctions to correct evils in Jewish wisdom books and Stoic texts. An uncompromising *sententia*, said to be from the ancient sage Sidrach, undermines the silent observers of political evils: "Qui potest contradicere peccato et non contradicit actor est peccati. Sidrac" (The person who can speak out against sin and does not is a doer of the sin; line 1140b). (Words very close to these are spoken by the dying reformist bishop Robert Grosseteste in Matthew of Paris's *Historia Anglorum*. Grosseteste is lamenting the failure of clerics, including those of his own Franciscan order, to reprove sins.)[44] These sinful followers of Mum's way of life, the beekeeper asserts, need to hear a truth-teller proclaim the reformist texts that the narrator assiduously studied after his first encounter with Mum: "Salomon and Seneca and Sidrac the noble" (lines 1209–12). The beekeeper weighs Jewish wisdom literature and Stoic texts as more significant authorities on silence and speech than self-authored and "Cato's" "worldly wise" wisdom, just as the narrator embraces Daniel's authority on the value of dreams, rejecting a distich of "Cato" that dismisses them as mere illusion (lines 873–75)—a clash of fundamentally different ethics that recalls the poem's progenitor, *Piers Plowman*.[45] As a student and agent of good governance, the beekeeper thus affirms the value of authoritative texts, Jewish and Stoic. They become in *Mum* the means of reforming those who are involved in advising and governing and so the means of checking exploitation and violence throughout the realm.

Traditional wisdom literature, however, cannot be used to reform public life unless it shapes the lives, the fundamental values and choices, of those who proclaim it. The narrator's other name for the Sothsegger, "Melle-sumtyme," recalls the basic Solomonic *sententia* that is used by clerical writers to define proper taciturnity: "tempus tacendi et tempus loquendi" (There is a time for keeping silent and a time for speaking; Eccl 3:7b). The truth-teller of *Mum*, like the narrator himself, is not the babbler, the forever imprudent speaker, that Mum brands him. He, like Mum, chooses to use silence, as well as speech, strategically, looking carefully for the most effective circumstances in which to speak the truth.[46] Yet speaking the truth even in this well-judged, circumspect way costs the truth-teller, as the narrator's recollection of "Cato's" distich initially indicated. Throughout the narrator's journey, even before Mum makes his claims, as we have seen, the truth-teller is seen living at the margins of life, rejected in favor of Mum's way of life, despised, and persecuted. At the journey's end, after the mayor's feast, the narrator finds the truth-teller nursing his wounds in an out-of-the-way shop. Despite recognizing this ostracism, the poet vindicates the truth-teller's mode of living with an ultimate textual authority, Jesus's Beatitude "Beati qui persecucionem paciuntur propter iusticiam. evangelium" ("Blessed are those who suffer persecution on account of justice. The gospel" [line 847b, from Matt 5:10]). This Wycliffian practice of contrasting social ostracism and danger with scriptural affirmation for proclaiming truth comes into the poem in interstices like this and like the praise, amid extended scenes of clerical corruption, for the martyrs who suffered death because of their love of the Creator (lines 630–51). In these ways, the truth-teller's way of life is aligned with, and vindicated by, textual authority, in contrast to Mum, who sets aside texts just as the silent flatterers of the *Regiment* do when they refuse to utter "scriptures" that the king needs to hear. Proclaiming Jewish and Stoic texts to the powerful and informing the king and council of abuses and unrest, the truth-teller chooses to play his part in the salving of the nation's wounds and the curing of its diseases (to use the poet's frequent metaphors), working to redress the abuses that Mum cloaks or perpetrates. As the *Mum*-poet adapts to political life Wyclif's thinking on *taciturnitas proditoria*, textual authority propels the Sothsegger, the beekeeper, and, finally, the narrator to decide which consequences matter most: good governance and public benefit, the consequences of bold reformist speech, instead of material gain, status, and even life itself.

Clerical moral discourse on *mala taciturnitas* constitutes the textual matrix out of which John Wyclif and the *Mum*-poet develop the evils of political silences, Wyclif in polemical theology, the satiric poet in the anything-but-mum Mum as he reveals all about revealing nothing. Mum embodies in both the English church and state the dumb-dog *praelatus* characterized by Pierre le Chantre and many after him: whether priest or bishop, he keeps silent about error and destructive acts out of a fear that he might lose both his temporal goods and his position. Thus, he, and Mum later, fail to provide the corrective advice that their privileged positions and their access to the powerful obligate them to offer. The *Mum*-poet also inherits from clerical moral discourse his (and Wyclif's) passionate concern that the truth should not be suppressed, although in traditional clerical writing, that truth is the whole of Christian moral teaching, while in *Mum*, it is more often the truth about legal, economic, ecclesiastical, and political abuses. However, when clerical writers consider vicious silences, they do so in the larger context of the multiple benefits of prudent silence, almost always given first place and more space: calculating the most persuasive way to utter salvific words, screening out speech that might put off hearers, protecting personal and communal secrets, shunning verbal contention and violence (as in Albertano da Brescia's treatises). Yet it is Mum, far more than the truth-teller, who, as clerical writing advocates (as does Albertano), practices this cautious taciturnity in specific public situations, surveying in silence the circumstances and the drift of conversations, then using foresight to grasp the likely consequences of speaking or remaining silent. For the *Mum*-poet, prudential silences open the way for royal advisers to avoid giving truthful reports about the state of the realm and checking the will and devices of the powerful whose parasitical boon companions they triumphantly remain. In contrast, despite all that Hoccleve shares with the *Mum*-poet—Lancastrian royalism, concern with the King Henry's reputation, the greed of those silent advisers who fear the displeasure of the powerful king, and the remedy of truth-telling advisers who operate in the traditional political roles of advisers—he embraces taciturnity as essential to effective governance, seeing in its practice the benefits that clerical writers before Wyclif attributed to it. Yet there is another major reason for this crucial difference besides the *Mum*-poet's Wycliffism.

The poems' dissimilar genres, with their conventions, imagined readers, kinds of narrator, and attitudes toward traditional moral texts, also dictate, I think, these different stances toward silence. In writing a mirror for princes for Prince Henry, Hoccleve, like the authors he absorbs and imitates, focuses on the education of the prince, instruction by a learned man in the many dimensions of successful governance. As a late medieval mirror, the *Regiment* is profoundly shaped by Aristotelianism in its structure (by virtues), its insistence that royal rule rests on royal ethics, and its confidence that Prince Henry is well on his way to becoming the stable moral exemplar to the nobles and commons that an effective ruler must be. Among the virtues, Hoccleve prizes, as essential to good governance, a prudence that recollects past examples, uses them to analyze present situations, and forecasts future outcomes. Taciturnity, then, becomes necessary for the work of prudence itself, forestalling precipitous speech and hasty decisions. By contrast, *Mum and the Sothsegger* focuses not on the king but on the moral, religious, and political failings of officeholders and advisers throughout ecclesiastical and, especially, secular government, from humble parish priests to bishops and from mayors to royal advisers. In the *Mum*-poet's bleak, almost apocalyptic, dream vision of Henrician England, aimed at anyone interested in reform, sustained strategic taciturnity has no legitimate place. It is simply a tool for the corrupt at every level to further the designs of the rich and powerful and to profit themselves. Moreover, as a dream vision, *Mum* radically alters how instructional moral materials are appropriated and, even, understood. Hoccleve presents large swathes of advice undergirded by classical sayings, biblical verses, canon law, and exempla, gleaned from his deep and wide reading in all the learned Latin ethical traditions available to a scribe in his middle age and to a well-tutored prince. That is, he offers the prince, and, beyond him, Lancastrian nobles and other advisers, a comprehensive body of learning designed to direct and exhort them as they seek to rule in strategic ways that establish, maintain, and even repair their relations with the commons and with each other. Because these instructional materials stretch back to Jewish and classical texts and up to the fourteenth century (through canon law and Hoccleve's three main late medieval sources), they are understood as comprehensive, unitary, and monovocal. They promise to continue the process of constructing and confirming the virtues of effective rule as habits that must be inculcated. Hoccleve is their assured mediator as a scribe-poet. In dream vision, by contrast, instructional materials are embedded in a spinning kaleidoscope of contemporary English political, ecclesiastical, social, and economic life as witnessed by a troubled, far-from-certain, and far-from-assured dreamer. Rather than offering instruction to a political elite, he narrates dreams in which various figures that appear and disappear at random, like Mum and the beekeeper, attempt to persuade him. In dream visions, individual Latin sayings work as local tools in argument and urgent reflection, initiating, reinforcing, focusing, and capping arguments in the changing dialectic.[47] These arguments force responses from the narrator: sometimes counterarguments, sometimes assent, sometimes reflection. Whoever the speaker may be, these Latin dicta appear not as part of a firm body of learning but as part of the narrator's experience, heard, absorbed, and applied by him to support how he and others might operate in the business of church and state. In weaving Latin sayings into the web of the narrator's experience and that of his interlocutors, the *Mum*-poet presents moral material, like arguments, as part of the clothing its figures don and as weapons they take up in the fierce contentions between different ways of acting in public life. Necessarily, then, this moral material is fragmented and multivocal, its different strands, like the Roman consequentialism that initially seems to justify Mum's way of life and the Jewish wisdom and Christian scripture that rejects it, often at odds with each other—or seemingly so. By setting these texts against each other and self-interest against the common good, *Mum and the Sothsegger* exposes fissures in seemingly monovocal clerical moral writing on silence and in genres, like the mirror for princes, that adopt its range of material. For clerical manuals, as Alcuin Blamires has divined, often contain unresolved problems and unacknowledged tensions, largely due to the embrace of multiple ethical traditions.[48]

CHAPTER 4

PATIENT SILENCES UNDER INTERROGATION
Jesus in the York Cycle and William Thorpe

In *Mum and the Sothsegger*, as in the *Regiment*, asymmetrical power relations lie in the background, save for those between Lancastrian king and adviser. The soldier reduced to beggary or the poor man whose case is overthrown in a mayoral court by Mum is never characterized, his circumstances never developed, his oppression never voiced by himself. The strategies of silence and circumspect speech within the established arenas of power are all that matters. Now this book turns to the silences (and carefully chosen speech) of those who were subjected to inquisition by religious and civil rulers: Jesus and his avowed fifteenth-century followers, who were also considered religious dissidents and outsiders. Patience, rather than prudence, undergirds their silences, which serve to preserve their integrity under verbal assaults by people with the power to suppress and isolate, to order corporal punishment, and to impose death. To understand how patient silence was understood to work for those who were subjected to coercive power, no Middle English texts offer us more than the trial pageants within the mystery cycles, especially that of York, in which the silent Jesus is interrogated vigorously by the hostile high priests, Pilate, Herod, and Pilate once again and is abused verbally and physically throughout by their brutish soldiers. Amid all their threats, boasts, insults, mocking games, and juridical ploys, Jesus's silence is a potent sign, just as his physical stillness is. But, given the ambiguity inherent in silence as a sign, how and what does it signify to his powerful inquisitors and to late medieval English audiences? With the valuable silences of instrumental moral writing and of Hoccleve's *Regiment* behind us, we might also ask, "How then does his silence benefit himself and others, those present as speakers around him and the audience of York citizens?" After exploring the pageants in these terms, we can turn to those followers of Jesus who were, like Jesus, subjected to violent and abusive language, especially by institutional interrogators during Lancastrian rule. First we turn to a narrative introduction to patient silence, a type of silence so radically different, in many ways, from the prudential silence of king, adviser, lawyer, and influential cleric in chapters 1, 2, and 3.

When the pilgrim sets out for the heavenly city in *The Pilgrimage of the Lyfe of the Manhode* (ca. 1450), the anonymous translation of Guillaume de Deguileville's first recension of his *Pélerinage de la vie humaine* (1333), Grace Dieu begins arming him by giving him a surcoat with an anvil on the back. This startling image, so at odds with what the senses can perceive and what the culture allowed, comes with an equally astonishing claim: "whoso hadde neiþer handes ne feet, and were tached to a pile [stake], but þat he hadde þat upon him withoute more he shulde neuere be venquished, but he shulde with gret wurship [reputation, high status] be victour of all hise enemys."[1] How can a simple cloth garment, let alone one with a weighty anvil on the back, prevent anyone from being defeated in combat, especially when the person is tied to a stake and without hands and feet? In this way, Deguileville introduces the paradoxes of patience. Grace Dieu then explains that the garment itself torments its wearer and that the tormenting itself protects the wearer: it is made up of sharp points that pierce the flesh and "of prikkinges he bicometh armed." How can needling, incessant pain defend someone under assault? Moreover, everyone clothed in this surcoat will see clouds make their grain grow, pestilences fill their cellars, sicknesses make them strong, torments delight them, and poverty become recreative. As the shift from the physical to the affective suggests, this surcoat represents something that reverses common and supposedly natural experience and so the value a warrior culture assigns to it. Finally, Grace Dieu names the garment Patience, "madd to suffre peynes and to susteyne grete prikkinges, for to be as an anvelte þat stireth not for þe strok of a feþer, for to resseyue and endure al with good wille, withoute murmurynge."[2] Murmur, the sin of the tongue in which believers complain about hardships, is in the Jewish scriptures and in medieval clerical writing the besetting sin of those who had entrusted themselves to a hidden God but then became fearful and angry at the suffering that came to entail. In the Gawain-poet's biblical narrative *Patience*, the prophet Jonah falls back on murmur when he resists God's command to preach repentance to the alien and violent Ninevites.[3] While the Gawain-poet begins with a prologue on patience as a wise resource in dealing with events beyond one's control, Deguileville and his translator delay moral language in order to convey the way patience, as a virtue (a source of strength and power), defies and reverses claims that the comfort, strength, and defense of the body are all that matter, or at least matter most. But Grace Dieu issues two conditions for suffering to have value and become a source of strength: it must be accepted readily and with a willing disposition, and it must never be complained about or protested ("withoute murmurynge"). These stipulations make patience all the more radical in its reversal of ordinary human conduct. Not surprisingly, the woeful and naïve pilgrim doffs the surcoat with the rest of his uncomfortable armor before he even begins his journey, just as Jonah flees in the direction opposite to Nineveh. If even they, prophet and avowed pilgrim, reject patience, how can it ever become a human resource?

One of Grace Dieu's allusive images already suggests the answer: the man bound to a stake and defended by the surcoat is the Jesus of Passion iconography bound to the cross. Directly after naming the surcoat, Grace Dieu makes this explicit: "This doublet wered on Ihesus whan in þe crosse for þee he was hanged: vpon him it was rihted [fitted] and prikked [sewn] and mesured aright at his rihts [properly]. Al he suffrede and al endurede, and no woord seyde ne sownede."[4] What confirms that Jesus's suffering is endured with patience is his silence, stressed by the alliterated verbs. This silent Jesus Grace Dieu presents as an exemplar for the pilgrim, whose injuries will take the form not so much of physical torments as of verbal abuse and acts that shame him: "If þer be any þat missey [speak evilly of] þee, or þat dooth þe vileynye [ill, especially ill that shames], turne þe bac towardes him: lawhe [laugh] in þin herte, and sey no woord. It shulde nothing recche [trouble] þee to haue þe berkynge of howndes."[5] To be patient, the pilgrim, when spoken of evilly, must not speak at all in response, even though he knows his silence would allow his abusers to continue to try to torment him with repetitive and animalistic speech. In Grace Dieu's exhortation to the pilgrim to make Jesus's example the source of his own patience, she presents the redemption of humankind as the cause for which Jesus willingly suffered. The pilgrim's twin reasons for enduring suffering silently should become attaining "divine" patience in itself and thus claiming heaven as a reward because the abusers' verbal assaults will forge his crown of martyrdom. This the pilgrim never attains. Undefended by his surcoat and anvil, he blunders through an idle life, succumbing to the Seven Deadly Sins, spouting insults even when he speaks first, caught in tumultuous sea of the world. When Tribulation appears with a hammer, she cannot forge a crown because there is no anvil and surcoat of Patience like those Job had.

How does patient silence defend those who, unlike the pilgrim, practice it in often-fractious encounters with others? How can their silences "do" anything at all when their thoughts, emotions, and intentions are not conveyed by speech to the people around them, especially to those who are inflicting the injuries? Given these questions inevitably raised by those who are counseled to practice patience, before turning to the York pageants themselves, we should grasp what fundamental ideas about patience as a virtue, especially patience when suffering verbal abuse, were inculcated, directly or indirectly, by instructional moral materials during the two centuries in which these pageants were constructed and altered by clerics and laymen.

No writer of antiquity had more influence on late medieval moral materials about patience than that sixth-century Roman patrician Pope Gregory the Great through his homilies on the gospels and his commentary on the book of Job. For example, nineteen of the forty-nine *sententiae* under the rubric "Paciencia" in the widely circulated *Manipulus florum* (A handbook of the finest parts) of Thomas of Ireland are drawn from Gregory's writing.[6] Preaching on the lection ending "In patientia vestra possedebitis animas vestras" (In your patience you will possess your souls; Luke 21:19), Gregory delivers what became the most influential pithy formulation of patience: "Patientia vero est aliena mala aequanimiter perpeti, contra eum quoque qui mala irrogat nullo dolore morderi" (Truly patience is to endure evils from others with equanimity, not to be stung by any resentment against the one who imposes the evils).[7] These evils, he explains, often come from the people around us in the form of persecutions, losses (*damna*), and insults (*contumeliae*).[8] Another *sententia* common in the late Middle Ages also specifies insults as a major type of assault on the self that the patient bear: "Paciencia est virtus contumeliarum et omnis adversitatis impetus aequanimiter portans" (Patience is the virtue that bears with equanimity the onslaughts of insults and all adversity).⁹ Gregory's Christianized equanimity involves choosing not to be moved to hatred against perpetrators but to love them as brothers. What makes possible this tall order, so contrary to the customs of a patrician Roman culture yet central among gospel injunctions, is the end that Gregory's auditors should have in mind (the end for Deguileville's pilgrim): the glory of eternal reward (*retributio*), which eclipses temporal injuries.¹⁰ The cause or end (*causa*) for which one suffers determines if one is truly patient in late medieval treatments of the virtue, as Ralph Hanna has explained. Another definition of patience (this by Cicero) often cited in medieval moral texts, and connected to Gregory's, stressed enduring willingly what is difficult and dreadful for the sake of living a virtuous life or gaining benefits: "Patientia est honestatis vel utilitatis causa rerum arduarum et terribilium voluntaria et diuturna perpessio."¹¹ With the compelling end of heavenly reward in the eyes of their minds, all people, Gregory insists, may vigilantly respond to loss and insult by refusing to repay act with act and word with word.

Gregory's preoccupation with the inner life of the patient also emerges in his commentary on the book of Job, although in a slightly different way, one also adopted by late medieval moral writers. In the *Moralia*, he considers the integrity of the patient, their constancy. The just mind of Job, he writes, was not broken by the loss of externals, however great. The patient person may be worn by adversity but not bent from the straight line of his hope.¹² Beyond remaining intact, the patient realize a fullness of life that the impatient reject. Just as grain is pressed out when the husk is cast off in threshing and as redolent roses arise amid thorns, the patient, those with the fortitude of Job, are nourished and refreshed by the experience of enduring with equanimity evils inflicted on them by their neighbors.¹³ Picking up this theme, Guillaume Peyraut draws on the Stoic Seneca to applaud the magnanimity, the greatness of soul, of patient people. As chapter 1 explains, high and late medieval clerics found their writing on speech and silence on distrust of vehement emotions and the rash reactions they incite. Because the settled moral disposition of the patient prevents them from being overwhelmed by, and acting on, violent emotions, their constancy or integrity marks them out as superior to others, especially their tormentors, who act out of rage, hatred, envy, and other turbulent emotions. In this way, Peyraut writes, as did Gregory, the patient conquer: they resist the power of their own strong emotions, overcoming themselves in a greater act than conquering a city (an image taken from Proverbs 16:32).[14] (Gregory frequently associates this self-conquering patience with *mansuetudo*, mildness, as well as with humility, both suggesting that the patient will to ignore the claims of worldly status when attacked by others.)[15] In this way, Peyraut concludes, the patient possess their souls, as Jesus enjoins, their dominion consisting of an interior self free from the appetite for vengeance, an external self (the tongue and hand) free from insults and violence.[16] So, for Gregory and clerics influenced by him, patience defends people by disposing them to react to suffering imposed on them by controlling their emotions and by remaining constant, characteristics prized in several strands of late medieval culture, as J. D. Burnley has observed in his contrast of the raging tyrant and the philosopher.[17]

This willed and sustained endurance of evils imposed unjustly by others extends the effect of patience beyond the self. Patient people's very self-containment, their refusal to speak or act out of anger, overcomes their persecutors without striking a blow or even picking up a weapon, writes Peyraut. By showing their adversaries that they have more inner strength, more resources, than their adversaries do, the patient overcome malice, concludes the author of *distinctiones* in Bodleian Library (MS. Bodl. 4), and in this way they fulfill the popular adage that "paciencia vincit."[18] As a result, those who have inflicted the evil can be thrown into perplexity and confusion, which is exacerbated when they perceive that they have failed to achieve what they sought. The vernacular catechetical compendium *Disce mori* (mid-fifteenth century) justifies, in part, its exhortation to "be pacient and dispise þe despites of contumelie (abusive language) doon vnto þee" by how patient silence affects the angry perpetrator:

> God yaue to þe mouthe ii dores, þe teeth and þe lippes, not with oute cause lest þe tonge shuld lighly [easily, hastily] hurte þe soule, as hit doth ofte, not restreyned with inne his closures, namely whan wrath setteth þe herte afyre. For and [if] þou wolt stryue in wordes ayenst an irous [irate] man, þou shalt not þerrine ouercome, but rather prouoque hym, for and þin aduersarie see þee angrie, he hath founde in þee alle þat he sought, and if he fele þat þou passe ouere in cilence, he is discomfited or elles by þin example he is amended.[19]

Disce mori thus offers its readers the silence of the patient as a remedy against wrath. When the silent refuse to be goaded into a wrathful response, then agency and, with it, moral choice, falls to the abusers, who may choose to end the abuse, even change their way of life, instead of just feeling defeated and confused.

This concern with how patient silence affects others makes exemplarity central in clerical writing about taciturnity, as well as about patience. Occasionally exempla were drawn from pre-Christian antiquity, like those of patient Socrates and his chiding wife and of Caesar's forbearance with public insults, but usually they were taken from Jewish and Christian sources, often both in that order.[20] The messengers of King Hezekiah stand silent as the Assyrian king threatens their people (2 Sam 18); King David (as in Hoccleve's *Regiment*) refuses to retaliate when insulted by Semei; Mary Magdalen remains silently washing Jesus's feet as his host reproaches her (Mark 14:3–9 and the other three gospels); the woman taken in adultery does not speak back to her harsh accusers (John 8:1–11).[21] As in the *Regiment*, too, the main exemplar of patient silence was Jesus, practicing verbal restraint throughout his ministry but especially during the interrogations following his arrest and during the beatings and mockery by soldiers. Jesus's refusal to respond in "stryfe of words" is the first of "foure maneres of patiences" that he taught, according to the *Memoriale credencium* (An outline for believers), a manual of theology for laypeople (first half of the fifteenth century). A list of genres of abusive speech follows, along with some illustrations, and then the compiler concludes, "In alle þes reprefyngus of wordus he opened not onus [once] his mouthe fort [to] excuse him ne for to defende him ne forto vndernymme [rebuke] hym [them], but mekeliche suffred for to teche vs vertu of pacience. Ne whenne he was falsliche accusid in his passion, set ward [guard] vppon his mouth and answered not."[22] Instead of protesting or attempting to set his abusers straight, Jesus abides by Jewish scriptures. The "ward vppon his mouth" comes from Ps 38:2 ("posui ori meo custodiam") and Ps 140:3 ("Pone, Domine, custodiam ori meo"), passages cited again and again in clerical moral texts on taciturnity and patience.[23] While repetition and parallel syntax convey Jesus's constancy, the writer also states three times the intention behind it: to teach others the virtue of patience. Patience is something to be acquired by observing the remarkable—indeed, the unparalleled—integrity of Jesus's restraint. In *De lingua*'s chapter on taciturnity, it, like the *Memoriale*, presents a catalogue of abusive speech, but it does so from the ordinary experience of all people, establishing their kinship with the Jesus of the interrogations and Passion:

> Et de salvatore nostro legitur Marci [14:61] quod "tacebat et nichil respondit" ad ea que obiciebant ei. Is. 41 [42:14]: "Tacui, semper silui, paciens fui." Isidorus *De institutione bone vite*: "Quamuis quisque rideat, quamuis exasperet, quamuis insultet, quamuis iniuriam faciat, quamuis conviciet at litem provocet, quamuis afficiat contumeliis, tu tace, tu dissimula, tu non loquaris, tu exerce silencium; iniurie non respondeas, conuicia non retorqueas. Disce a Christo modestiam, disce toleranciam. Iniuriam passus pro nobis, relinquit nobis exemplum, nam palmis percussus, flagellis cesus, sputis derisus, clavis confixus, spinis coronatus, cruce damnatus, semper tacuit."[24]

> And we read about our Savior in Mark 14:61 that "he was silent and did not respond" to those things with which they were reproaching him. Isa 42:14: "I stayed silent; I was quiet; I was patient." Isidore's *On Instruction for a Good Life*: "Although someone may ridicule, although he may exasperate, although he may scoff, although he may cause an injury, although he may revile and provoke a quarrel, although he may inflict insults, remain silent, hide your feelings, do not speak, practice silence, do not respond to the injury, do not throw reproaches back. Learn from Christ restraint; learn endurance. Suffering injury on our behalf, he gave us an example, for struck with palms, beaten with scourges, mocked by spitting, transfixed by nails, crowned with thorns, condemned to the cross, he was always silent."

Although the compiler begins with the gospel account of the high priest's questioning and a Psalm believed to prophesy Jesus's conduct, Isidore's passage conveys the various ways that all people experience humiliating and threatening speech from people attempting to make them suffer, feel injured, and react with retaliatory words, especially insults. Then the exhortation presents Jesus's steady silent endurance in a situation so brutal and relentless that its very extremity, its very unlikeness to believers' experience, suggests that surely they can endure by similarly refusing to speak.

The patient and silent Jesus of medieval moral writers stands at the center of the York cycle, as he is brought by taunting soldiers into three courts, interrogated four times by powerful and antagonistic inquisitors, then goaded by soldiers—a spectacle on pageant wagons witnessed up close by an audience assumed to be Christian. Of the forty-seven "textual imitations of past theatrical performances" for the craft guilds, stretching from the fall of the angels to doomsday, a dozen dramatize the events recorded in the gospels that begin with Jesus's entry into Jerusalem and end with his death.[25] Four present interrogations: *Christ Before Annas and Caiaphas* (29), *Christ Before Pilate I: The Dream of Pilate's Wife* (30), *Christ Before Herod* (31), *Christ Before Pilate II: The Judgement* (33).[26] (The titles are modern.) The York interrogations by the priests are developed far more fully than those in the single Chester cycle trial pageant, in the N-Town collection (an episode of less than sixty lines), and in the Towneley collection plays (with their focus on the accusers and the soldiers). Moreover, the Chester, Towneley, and N-Town trial plays only treat Herod in a brief episode. For these reasons, I choose to consider the four York pageants extensively, with only glancing references to the Chester and Towneley plays. Although scholars hesitate to accept J. W. Robinson's proposal that these four York pageants, plus two others, were given their extant form largely by one dramatist ("The York Realist"), the plays share characteristics that Robinson identified: alliterative verse, the use of "close detail" to develop character and atmosphere, an emphasis on the mental processes that lead to decision, and an interest in argument.[27] With these techniques, the records of the pageants, even by themselves, present a sharp, sustained contrast between the bullying monologues, verbal strife, and legal wrangling of the powerful, obsessed with speech as a tool to gain and maintain control over others, and the almost always silent, unmoving Jesus, a contrast designed to engage, move, and stimulate reflection in an urban audience attuned both to the liturgy and religious instruction and to political and legal struggle.[28] That audience, as Richard Beadle has argued, was "audiate," if not literate. Its members possessed the competence both to register detail and to pick up overall patterns, competence acquired by frequent and sustained listening to texts, especially verse, being read aloud.[29]

The playwright(s) of the York trial pageants chose to magnify this contrast, as did those of the Chester cycle and the Towneley compilation, by including very few of Jesus's utterances in the three synoptic gospels. The four plays present him speaking only three times, once to the high priests (in four brief segments) and twice to Pilate. As Rosemary Woolf has pointed out, they could have chosen a very different way of presenting Jesus: they could have created a major speaking role for him by using a gospel harmony to include many of his words from all four gospels and even by pulling in teaching from elsewhere in the gospels, as did the playwright(s) of the N-Town Passion plays.[30] Given Jesus's silence, the York playwright(s), like those of Chester and Towneley plays, chose to convey Christ's nature, as Larry Clopper has argued, by contrast with the antagonists who surround him in a series of confrontations.[31] Each play begins with an expansive public harangue, moves to political jockeying between Jesus's antagonists, develops the interrogation of Jesus, and ends with the soldiers threatening and taunting him. The genres of speech that the antagonists employ, I argue first, disclose what they believe the sources of their power to be, how they attempt to control others, and what they are seeking to accomplish. Jesus's refusal to engage in each genre conveys something of his otherness: his different sources of power, his different intentions, and the different effects he desires to have on others. His silence, however, is a riddle to his inquisitors and their henchmen. They are provoked to puzzle out what it conveys of his emotions, thoughts, and purposes. In the process, their obvious misconstruals, like those of the speaker in this book's opening anecdote from John of Mirfield, reveal their own obsessions with authority and aristocratic status, developing the contrast with Jesus even more sharply. The silences also pose, of course, hermeneutic challenges for the York audiences, engaging them more intently in the counterpoint of silence and seemingly endless verbiage and moving them to grasp what causes Jesus's refusals to speak. In the end, I conclude, Jesus's silence may move spectators not only to consider the value of patient silence but also to question, even come to detest, the kinds of speech his antagonists employ, the obsessive speech of domination and self-protection practiced by oppressive religious and political leaders and by their violent henchmen, speech that brings into question the worth, even the legitimacy, of the very institutions they head.

Each pageant begins with a monologue by a powerful man, designed to silence spectators, that links the people in the streets of York to the bystanders and crowds of Jerusalem.[32] (Their compelled silence will be contrasted by Jesus's voluntary silences when the same figures demand not that he become silent but that he speak.) Threats, the most violent in the York cycle since Pharaoh and the first Herod (pageants 11 and 19), are the interrogators' currency in these versions of the conventional opening claims on attention made by the pageants' first speakers. Herod, waving his sword, out-Herods even Pilate in his threats:

> Pes, ye brothellis [wretches] and browlys [brats] in þis broydnesse [wide area] inbrased,
> And freykis [people] þat are frendely your freykenesse [boldness] to frayne [ask about],
> Youre tounges fro [from] tretyng of triffillis be trased [reined in],
> Or þis brande [sword] þat is bright schall breste in youre brayne.
>   (31, 1–4)[33]

Driven to clear space for his own speech, Herod is aware of the appeals of everyday talk, its recurrent interweaving of speakers, its social bonding, and its shared light "chatt" (Pilate's term at 33, 3). Against those appeals, he sets threats of extreme violence to those who are present, threats given vehemence by alliteration, vividness, and detail (he will beat every limb and hack all their bones to pieces). As Claire Wright has worked out in elegant detail, the irregularity of the alliterative lines here and their violent consonance assault the audience with sounds conveying Herod's volatility and, therefore, how unpredictable his strikes would be.[34] Inevitably his threats morph into extravagant boasts of power. His violent suppression of opponents moves to the natural world itself when he brags that "Dragons þat are dredfull schall derke [shrink back] in þer dennes" and that he can join weapons with wild giants. These romance-hero boasts are so out of whack with the city setting (Jerusalem in York) and Herod's sumptuous clothing that they expose him to ridicule, especially when undercut by the bathetic last one: he can slaughter swimming swans (31, 12–15). The genres of absolute power, threat and boast, teeter over easily into the comical and the foolish, revealing the chasm between fantasies of absolute power and banal reality, although bathos does not make Herod's love of violence any less dangerous. By contrast, the silent Jesus of this and the surrounding pageants refuses to utter threats and boasts, to use speech of any kind that aims to create fear and thus coerce and oppress others. Beyond that lies his rejection of what Herod's speech threatens so vividly: the use of weapons—indeed, violence of any kind—to force others to submit to one's will. His silence following and amid the threats and boasts of political and religious leaders, directed against him during interrogation and torture as they are against the citizens of York at the outset, becomes even more striking as courtiers, messengers, and soldiers recount his miracles. These reports culminate in Jesus's act of bringing Lazarus back to life just before he enters Jerusalem, the action the York audience has recently witnessed in pageant 24. In these miracles, as in restoring Malchus's ear in pageant 28, Jesus displays an astonishing power over human bodies and natural forces that contrasts with Herod's vaunting: he acts with power rather than boasting about it, and he acts to heal and revivify bodies rather than threatening to maim and destroy them. In all these ways, the nature of Jesus's powers and his uses of them begin to emerge as utterly other than those of the coercive rulers in whose power he rests.

Although Pilate, like Herod, begins both of "his" pageants with threats of violence designed to control the audience, even its disorderly movements, he turns quickly to the sources of his power and position in *Pilate 1*, as does Caiaphas in the first pageant of the four. Pilate boasts of high lineage, the ground of his political authority: he is a son of the emperor, a status his wife then proclaims as unequaled. This exalted state ("Loo, Pilate I am, proued [acknowledged] a prince of grete pride" [30, 19]) led the Romans to appoint him governor of recalcitrant Pontus, where, he boasts, he repressed the people ruthlessly (30, 9–24).[35] Percula adopts the language of boasting as her due as his wife, praising herself for her mental acuity, her "comly and clere" countenance, her "ful clere" body, and her sumptuous clothing, all sources of her status (30, 37–45). Pilate's and Percula's need to engross their standing elicits flattery, just as Herod's does from his courtiers. Even the Bedellus (messenger), who firmly marshals both of them so that the initial legal practices of Jesus's coming interrogation are properly observed, addresses Pilate as "schynyng schawe [spectacle]," exactly the image the couple strives to create, and then proclaims him a "liberall lorde" and "gentill juger" (gracious judge; 30, 55–58), qualities sharply at variance with the arrogance, threats, and ruthlessness displayed by his monologue.

In the preceding pageant, Caiaphas also begins by proclaiming his status as a lord who rightly demands silence from bystanders, forging, even more than Pilate and Herod, an elaborate claim to speak at length and be heard with attention: "And sese [cease] sone of youre sawes [words], and se [pay attention to] what I saye" (29, 2). The dominance that Caiaphas asserts rests on his learning and expertise in religious law:

By connyng [expertise, learning] of clergy and casting [use] of witte
Full wisely my wordis I welde [wield] at my will,
So semely in seete [a judge's chair] me semys for to sitte,
And þe lawe for to lerne [teach] you, and lede it by skill,
Right sone. (29, 5–9)

All of Jesus's interrogators speak of themselves "in relation to the law" and use law to maintain power, not execute justice, as Sarah Beckwith argues.[36] And that legal language can become an instrument of oppression because it is rooted in the person of the ruler, who seeks his personal interest, not in the community, as Emma Lipton observes about two of Pilate's speeches.[37] Yet Caiaphas alone founds his authority and power solely in law. Eschewing the threats of secular lords, he boasts instead of how his legal training within a learned caste (the clergy as a professional body) and his native quickness of mind enable him to speak so wisely that he has gained the status of high priest. This status, in turn, justifies his control of how Jewish law, as both rules for conduct and the Jewish religious system, is taught and how cases are decided (29, 10–14). Against him in court, he boasts, no "lord ne lady lerned in þe lawe," no experienced bishop or priest, no erudite clerk may defend themselves. On these grounds, he asserts, "I haue þe renke [sovereignty] and þe rewle of all þe ryalté [kingdom]" (29, 14–18). Legal learning, legal expertise, and legal position determine the right to rule a nation founded on religious law and custom. "Wherfore," he concludes, "takes tente [pay attention] to my tales [acts of speaking], and lowte [pay homage to] me" (29, 22). By this right, quite unlike Pilate's lineage, he assumes control of speaking situations, expects attentive listening, and exacts absolute obedience. Through contemporary legal language and through dress, the pageants portray the Jewish priests as medieval English bishops, as Richard Beadle, Sarah Beckwith, and other scholars have noted. To their courts, infamous for their bureaucracy and inquisitional practices, the audience of the York pageants was subject, just as it was to secular rulers intent on confirming and entrenching their power through the fifteenth century.[38] Like those bishops and like Herod and Pilate, Caiaphas and Anna enjoy a late medieval aristocratic way of life that enacts their exalted status: they dress extravagantly in ways that mark them off from others; they tightly control access to their households and courts (no one who does not dwell in the priests' court may speak in the "case" of Jesus); they demand obeisance from courtiers and from Jesus in the forms of bowing and kneeling; they all engage in courtly wine ceremonies. Through their boasts, as through their threats (for all later threaten Jesus, as do their soldiers), they display a constant need to reassert and aggrandize their status and power and, beneath that, a fear that both might not be acknowledged, perhaps even be contested.

Christ Before Annas and Caiaphas begins to dramatize, early in the sequence of interrogations, other reasons why Jesus might be silent amid the boasting of secular and religious authorities. As we would expect from medieval moral texts, Jesus's silence is rooted in patience. Indeed, as the soldiers insult Jesus as "ladde" and threaten to teach him to make obeisance to Caiaphas and Anna as "lords" (29, 239–41), they lead him into the priests by a rope. This stage prop, as scholars have noted, was meant to recall the messianic prophecy central in moral discourse on patience and silence: "As a shepe lad to sleing [slaughter] and as a lombe tofore þe clipper [shearer], so he openiþ not his mouþe" (Isa 53:7).[39] As the expected response to insistent claims of power, Jesus's patient silence conveys a humility and mildness (qualities linked to patience by Gregory) quite at odds with the arrogance displayed by Caiaphas, as it is later by Pilate and Herod. In his patience and humility, he rejects not only their ends of asserting, maintaining, and aggrandizing their power over others by threats and boasts but also the institutions that give them such power and cultivate such pride: established law-bound religion and secular imperium. Such a rejection rests on a refusal to acknowledge the very grounds of the rulers' authority: lineage and legal acumen. The allusion to the lamb, however, suggests more, indeed what is almost a contradiction: submission to their control—but only physical control—over him. Because this submission does not extend to acknowledging their authority or even answering most of their questions, its roots lie within him, inaccessible to his antagonists. On the other hand, the York audience, saturated with images of the Lamb of God, must have seen Jesus's unprotesting patience as an acceptance of the powers, however corrupt, and the conditions, however degrading, under which the will of God can be achieved.[40] That is, they would have grasped the cause for which he suffers in silence (so crucial from Gregory on), seeing Jesus as a willing sacrifice, like the Isaac of pageant 10. So, Jesus's imperviousness to, and outright defiance of, the claims and speech of institutionalized power grows out of confidence in God's disposition for himself and humankind. In this way, he shares silence with a hidden God who meets human evil with forbearance and endurance, like the God of Reason, as we shall see, in the third dream of *Piers Plowman*.

Abuse and insults, other genres of speech also used by the interrogators of Jesus and their courtiers and henchmen, also serve to establish, they think, their political and social superiority. When the Bedellus insists that Percula leave because Jewish law excludes women from legal proceedings, she calls him, despite his unvarying courtesy to her, a "horosonne boy" and a "cursid carle" (30, 59–63). Both of her nouns indicate a servile position and low, perhaps illegitimate, birth, as well as social ineptitude. With these insults, she continues to establish her status based on lineage and courtly conduct, belittling a man who is countering her will. "Boy" becomes the stock insult directed at Jesus by his lordly interrogators, marginalizing him, placing him outside of their spheres of judicial, religious, and political life, just as do their slighting remarks on his provincial and artisan-class birth (a carpenter's son from Galilee).[41] Caiaphas concludes his opening monologue by commanding his soldiers to bring the "boy into bayle [custody]," and they promptly echo him, as does his fellow priest Anna (29, 26–31). In their use, "boy" also brands Jesus as a miscreant and ruffian, a wretched disturber of Jewish life and a violator of law and custom who refuses to obey authority (*MED*, s.v. "boie" [n.], 1, 2a, 3). Far from being the casual insult of the soldiers wrangling with each other for "worship," "boy" is carefully targeted to delegitimatize Jesus, marking him as someone who lacks any social, religious, or legal standing, let alone the exalted one that Caiaphas's speech claims for himself.

Jesus's silence in the face of insults also marks a refusal to retaliate verbally, as we would expect from *The Pilgrimage of the Lyfe of the Manhode* and clerical moral materials on patient silence.[42] When Jesus does not answer the high priest's question about his parentage and upbringing, Caiaphas, enraged, calls him "boy" and repeats his question. But Jesus responds by addressing him as "Sir" and simply replies, "sothly I saye / Þat I schall go to my fadir þat I come froo [from,] / And dwelle with hym wynly [worthily] in welthe allway" (29, 293–95). Jesus's simple expression of trust in the transcendent changes the arena of speech from secular to divine relationship, suggesting an equanimity founded on otherness, just as his silence does. This inherent composure itself obviates angry speech. Jesus does not struggle for self-control as Gregory's and Peyraut's patient Christians must do before they can master their tongues. Herod's anger in the third interrogation greatly exceeds that of Caiaphas throughout the four plays, as Jesus refuses to play the game that the king and his household have contrived: banter with Jesus as if he were a professional fool come to entertain them but also, as Sandra Billington observes, as if a King of Fools, the unlikely ruler of popular king games.[43]

> Saie, can 3e not knele?
> We shalle haue gaudis [jests] full goode and games or [before] we goo.
> Howe likis þa [thou]? Wele, lorde? Saie. What, deyull, neuere a dele?
> I faute in my reuerant [I am being dishonored] in otill moy,
> I am of fauour, loo, fairer be ferre [far].
> Kyte! Oute! Yugilment! Vta! Oy! Oy!
> Be any witte þat Y watte [know] it will waxe were [danger, suspicious conduct].
>
> *Saeuitia perimet* [Fierce violence may destroy],
> Such losellis [miscreants] and lurdaynes [rascals, wretches] as þou, loo,
> *Respicias timet* [Be wary. Let him fear.].
> What þe deuyll and his dame schall Y now doo? (31, 236–46)

By calling Jesus "lorde" after demanding that he kneel to him and after addressing him with the familiar "thou" instead of the formal "3e," Herod seeks to mock Jesus as a witless and uncouth alien to courtly life, a butt of aristocratic games. Jesus's refusal to speak under these terms enrages Herod so far that he veers into French, Latin, and even nonsense words, as well as demeaning Jesus with insults and threats, as we would expect from his opening harangue. His French and Latin, of course, convey his exalted political position, plus his sense of aristocratic status, but the nonsense words interlarding them indicate that Herod's fury begins to make his speech unintelligible. This code-switching and gibberish, fueled by frustration at failing to realize his terms for the encounter with Jesus, accentuates the emotional control of the silent Jesus. Not only does he reject angry speech, but he also refuses to join in the quarrels that arise constantly between the priests and the secular rulers and between Pilate and Herod, all affronted if their claims for jurisdiction are slighted or contested. (It is, of course, this very struggle for both that prompts the high priests to send soldiers to apprehend Jesus and bring him into court and, in the fourth pageant, to tip Pilate, afraid that Jesus's kingship threatens his imperial position, into condemning him to a traitor's death.) Unlike the conquering patient Christians of Gregory and Peyraut, however, the almost always silent Jesus seems to have no chance of converting those who assault him verbally. Indeed, Herod just continues to spout multilingual insults and threats, plus yet more impatient questions. Jesus's inquisitors are as impervious to the value of patience—and to Jesus's constancy, humility, and equanimity—as Jesus is to the claims of coercive power, exalted status, and angry retaliatory insults.

Herod's extravagant macaronic language and his attempt to create a comic playlet point to another use of speech that Jesus is rejecting throughout all four pageants: speech as a tool to amuse oneself at the expense of others. The encounter with Jesus is to provide jests ("gaudis") and games, entertaining a bored aristocrat by tricking the supposed charlatan Jesus into humiliating himself and providing an occasion for Herod to display linguistic variety and mastery. Even the more dangerous interrogations are regarded by Caiaphas, Anna, Pilate, and their soldiers and courtiers as "good sport." Even as Caiaphas turns again to worming out a statement of divine sonship that they have planned to use to indict Jesus, he assures Anna, "We schall haue game or [before] we goo" (29, 288). Jesus's silence then indicates that he is as immune to idle talk and to verbal gamesmanship as he is later to the soldier's horrifying blend of childish games and brutal torture. He refuses to speak to Herod because he only seeks to have Jesus, whom he believes to be an "incantator" (sorcerer) perform miracles just for him to satisfy his vanity, as a macaronic Good Friday sermon from the era of the York plays declares. What religious profit for others could there be in such a situation if he spoke or used spells (as Herod expects)?[44] Ironically, as V. A. Kolve recognized some time ago, it is Jesus's very refusal to speak that Herod takes initially as a sign that he is playing games, interpreting Jesus in terms of himself and so never seeing him as he is.[45]

The absurd verbal displays of Herod and his emotional volatility bring to the fore all of the antagonists' varied, voluminous, and highly charged uses of speech to cow others and enforce their wills on them, even to reduce them to silence so that they can dominate the situation with threats, boasts, insults, quarrelsome assertions, and jests. Of the four pageants centered on interrogation, *Christ Before Herod* dramatizes Jesus's refusal to speak in these ways to the nth degree. He never speaks in the course of his long encounter with Herod, his sons, his courtiers, and his soldiers. In the next pageant, *Christ Before Pilate II: The Judgement*, his only speech finally manifests to the antagonists and the audience the basis of his patient silence and rare, brief speech in all the preceding interrogations and tormenting games by soldiers:

> Euery man has a mouthe þat made is on molde [earth],
> In wele and in woo to welde [wield] at his will;
> If he gouerne it gudly like as God wolde [would desire],
> For his spirituale speche hym thar not to spill [he ought not to waste].
> And what gome [person] so gouerne it ill,
> Ful vnhendly [evilly] and ill sall he happe [fare];
> Of ilk tale [each word] þou talkis vs vntill [you speak to us]
> Þou accounte sall, þou can not escappe. (33, 300–307)

This startling statement about the uses of speech comes in response to Pilate's urging that Jesus excuse himself if he is able to, that he answer his accusers. Other vernacular accounts of Pilate's urgent request, like that in the *Cursor mundi* or the *Northern Passion*, do not record any such response; indeed, the *Cursor*'s Pilate stresses Jesus's refusal to speak by first questioning Jesus about his silence twice, then pleading with him twice to speak. Not present in any of the gospel accounts of his Passion, this speech summarizes Jesus's teaching throughout his ministry that speech is a voluntary act that God will judge (especially Matt 12:54–57 and Luke 6:45).[46] Jesus begins, as clerical moral writers do, with the physiological organ of speech: the tongue. As created by God, it is an instrument of speakers' wills so that what distinguishes speech acts, and what speech acts manifest to others, is what speakers feel, desire, think, and intend. Their speech is inherently "spirituale" in two ways: divinely given and originating from their souls (*MED*, s.v. "spiritual" [adj.], 2a and 4a). Jesus's verbs, "gouerne" and "welde," used so often in clerical moral literature on speech and taciturnity, come from Jewish wisdom texts, where they convey speakers' moral responsibility to use the divine gift of speech in ways that lead to beneficial consequences for themselves, for others, and for God. Jesus offers no norms for how to govern the tongue; rather, what matters is that speakers subject their wills to God's. Therefore, his steady silence stems from the speakers around him choosing to speak what God does not intend, what, instead, is determined by the errant wills of those who are enmeshed in, and profiting from, corrupt institutions. Jesus's speech throughout his ministry has consisted of what he claims God desires him to utter, religious teaching and consolation, genres that have no place in these courts, even in the mouths of religious leaders for whom legal knowledge is used for judicial jockeying, not instruction. Yet Jesus's instructional speech does more than voice his own understanding of how speech should be used—and does so plainly and directly, in contrast to his antagonists' elaborate game-playing, at times insulting and at times deadly. In this, his last and longest utterance in the four pageants, he prompts his antagonists to reflect on how they have chosen to speak, especially during their interrogations. Are their wills as speakers in harmony with the divine will?

Although the inquisitors are not moved to reflection and, possibly, some amendment of life by Jesus's speech, they are provoked throughout by his silence into frustrated, angry, adversarial, and face-saving attempts to construe his silence in ways that justify their tightly defended ways of life. His silence is a riddle that they are driven to solve. It discomfits them, throwing awry the plans they have so carefully contrived before he is led in by the soldiers, plans designed to achieve their legal, social, and political ends. It confuses them because Jesus does not fulfill their expectations that he will defend himself against accusations or protest his torture. It angers them because they take Jesus's refusal to answer their questions as an affront to their dignity, authority, and power as priests and rulers. The terms in which the confused and angry inquisitors frame Jesus's silences arise from their own thoughts and emotions, confirming what their genres of speech convey or even disclosing further their own sense of themselves and of the political, social, and religious standing to which they are entitled. The gap between their misconstruals and Jesus's identity becomes obvious to a York audience informed by the earlier pageants about Jesus's ministry, affected emotionally by the oppressors' violent language early in each pageant, and conditioned, as Pamela King has developed, by iconography, by worship, and by Christian catechesis, even at its most minimal.[47]

Those who are within the enclosed court of the high priest attribute Jesus's silence to cunning in service of deception. Before Jesus is hauled into court, Caiaphas and Anna choose to see Jesus's "wondirfull werkis" (Caiaphas's term), his healings of the sick and lame, as witchcraft, given his humble parentage (29, 34–53). When, in the last of the four interrogation pageants, Pilate's banners bow to Jesus despite the efforts of the strongest soldiers, they accuse him of the related crime of sorcery.[48] Any power beyond their comprehension or their own reach as priests with institutionalized religious power must be due to a diabolical agent. Therefore, when Jesus responds with silence to Caiaphas's question about his parents and upbringing, Caiaphas assumes that he is cunningly cloaking the truth ("lyste him be nyse [he wants to be cunning]" (29, 284). He and Anna see Jesus in terms of themselves as someone who uses trickery to acquire authority and power over others, whereas the York ministry plays have dramatized Jesus primarily as a teacher who speaks the truth directly and plainly to all, while his antagonists, even in the early *Christ and the Doctors*, constantly seek to entrap him with verbal nets they have woven, a dynamic contrast that Alexandra Johnston has explored.[49] In this, the York pageants are akin to the early fifteenth-century *Metrical Life of Christ*, perhaps a source for trial ones, which represents Jesus as escaping with silence the dilemma contrived by the accusers of the woman taken in adultery in order to trap him into culpable speech. Instead of either breaking the law's punishment or refusing to show mercy to her, the *Life* states emphatically, "He spake no worde in þat stounde [dangerous occasion]," instead writing their sins in the sand. Then, when they have left in shame, he refuses to judge the woman and encourages her to save herself.[50] In the York cycle, Jesus's silence under inquisition adheres to his strategy throughout his ministry for evading verbal traps and speaking only to edify those who are receptive.

Although Caiaphas harps on Jesus's cunning wiles and sorcerer's tricks throughout the four pageants, it is he who introduces a quite different, even contradictory, explanation for Jesus's silence in a phrase that Herod later uses, too: "his langage is lorne" (29, 278; and 31, 19). Their identical exclamations erase Jesus as an agent: he is powerless to speak; he has been dispossessed of speech. For Caiaphas, seeing himself throughout as "prince of all priests" and Jesus as a "chorle" (churl), his exalted status has made the bumpkin tongue-tied, as has the aristocratic manners and dress of the court: "Boy, be not agaste if we seme gaye [sumptuously dressed, noble, merry]" (29, 289). Driven to save face because of Jesus's sustained silence, Herod and his courtiers all assume that he is a simpleton or a madman. Later, a courtier moves to cloak lèse-majesté by inventing yet another flattering explanation: Jesus is overawed by Herod's magniloquence and loud voice. Assured of his royal stature, Herod gives voice once again to a loud outburst, chock full of Latin, and when Jesus remains a "stoke or a stone," the king makes an even more absurd effort to save face: "þe rebalde [wretch] seis vs so richely arayed, / He wenys [thinks] we be aungelis euere-ilkone [each and every one]" (31, 281–82), a line quickly echoed by a flatterer and embroidered by the eldest son. To paper over the court's confusion, that son and Herod devise a playlet. To humiliate and mock Jesus, the soldiers dress him in white and address him as a natural fool (as opposed to a professional fool earlier), actions that dramatize all of their explanations for his silence: that he is deprived of his wits and his tongue by rusticity, ignorance, awe, fear, or simple-mindedness. In the closed-off courts of ritual, flattery, displays of power, and games, the antagonists who surround Jesus assume he refuses to play a part because he is incapacitated in some way, despite members of their courts giving reports of his miracles.

In contrast to the antagonists' misconstruals, the York audience has witnessed a far different reason for Jesus's patient silence: the divinely given cause for which he endures in silence relentless verbal abuse, threats, inquisition, and torture. Before Caiaphas and Anna arrive in Pilate's court to accuse Jesus falsely, the devil disturbs Percula's sleep. Unlike the priests and rulers who denigrate Jesus throughout the four pageants, the devil recognizes Jesus's exalted birth (a "gentilman") and his true nature:

Be [By] any syngne [sign] þat I see þis same is Goddis sonne;
And [If] he be slone [slain], oure solace will sese,
He will saue man saule fro [from] oure sonde [custody]
And refe vs [deprive us of] þe remys [realms] þat are rounde. (30, 161–64)

The miracles that prompt the priests to entrap Jesus and to amuse themselves at Jesus the charlatan manifest to the devil not only his divinity but also his purpose in the world: to endure death so that humankind will be delivered from diabolical control. So, in an irony running through all four pageants, Jesus is silently suffering the accusation that he is being aided by diabolical agents so that he may free humans from the devil's power. Yet for him to reveal why he endures the accusation in silence would be to fail in his purpose, the cause for which he is suffering patiently: to be the willing sacrificial lamb of Isaiah's prophecy. This reason for Jesus's silence is given often in biblical commentaries, Middle English biblical narratives, clerical writing on taciturnity, and allegorical poems (remembering the cause that Deguileville's Grace Dieu gives for Jesus's silence). *The Metrical Life of Jesus* uses repetition to stress how astonishing Jesus's silence is to Herod, who has offered to save his life if he would perform marvels for Herod:

> And while þe Kyng saide his wille,
> Oure Lord stode þere ful stille,
> Als stille as any stone,
> Worde wolde he speke none.
> Saynt Austyn saiþ witterly [plainly]
> Þat was for þe skil [reason] why,
> Hade he spoken anyþinge,
> And done miracles bifore þe Kyng,
> Þe Kyng wolde his lif haue saued,
> And his deþ þere delayed.
> And Crist wist [knew] wele his þoght,
> And to be saued willed noght,
> For he wolde in alle wise
> For mannes sake dye & ryse,
> And altogeder done be
> Vppon þe Iewes owne degre [In the Jews' own way].
> Forþi oure Lord as any mayde
> Stode stille, and noght saide.[51]

Jesus's very silence veils the cause for which he suffers patiently, and by submitting in silence to the authorities, by not contesting unjust accusations, and by letting the juridical procedures, corrupt as they are, take their course, he accomplishes his purpose, God's purpose. In the process, the patient Jesus vanquishes his antagonists, human and diabolical. Agency has passed to Jesus from his antagonists, as clerical moral writing declared it does when the patient resist with equanimity the designs of their abusers and accomplish their own purposes. Steadfast silent resistance to coercive speech, undergirded by a God-given cause, emerges in the York trial pageants as real power.[52]

Yet there is a final step in the four York pageants, a step beyond the interrogations: Jesus's silence as he is brutally struck and flogged by Pilate's soldiers, actions recalled, we have seen, by Isidore and the author of *De lingua* as they present Jesus as an exemplar of patience.

> IV MILES   Nowe flynge to [flail at] þis flaterer [deceiver] with
>   flappes [blows].
> I MILES   I sall hertely hitte on his hippes
>   And haunch.
> II MILES   Fra oure skelpes [blows] not scatheles [without injury]
>   he skyppes.
> III MILES   3itt hym list [he chooses to] not lyft vp his lippis,
>   And pray vs to haue pety on his paunch.
> IV MILES   To haue petie of his paunche he propheres no prayere.
> I MILES   Lorde, how likes you þis lake [game] and þis lare þat
>   we lere [teach] 3ou. (33, 366–74)

Regarding torture as a game, the soldiers mock the seemingly powerless Jesus by addressing him as "Lorde," a title both political and religious, by switching between the respectful "thou" and the familiar "you," and by casting their violent acts as teachers' lessons. These parodies of kingship and discipleship take full form in response to Jesus's silence. The soldiers are nonplussed by his refusal to plead that his body be spared as they continue to flog him, stopping only when they worry about killing him and so depriving Pilate of the public spectacle of crucifixion. For the last time in the trial pageants, Jesus's sustained silence is stressed by his antagonists, accentuating the visual image of a still Jesus amid the swirl of violent talk and action. In this last stage of interrogations and torments, the silent Jesus stands even more as a figure who is beyond what others can expect—no, beyond what they can imagine of a human being. His constant silence, as Rosemary Woolf incisively says, becomes more than "a manifestation of his unquestioned submission to human suffering"; it becomes "a sublime expression of his divinity."[53] As Greg Walker characterizes the effects of early English drama, it has a "capacity to suggest rather than to state, to hint at depths, complexities."[54] Jesus's identity and his patient silence are unfathomable to his powerful antagonists not only because he does not live by their laws and customs (an alien in their midst) but because he has wholly submitted himself to God's will, because he is one with God.

If one effect of Jesus's extraordinary patient silence on the York audience would have been to shadow forth his far-from-ordinary nature, one manifested in the earlier pageants of his birth, baptism, and transfiguration, how far could he serve as an example for his fifteenth-century English followers, ordinary human beings? Let us focus on late Middle English texts in which women and men who are engaged in seeking a holy life, are, like the Jesus they seek to imitate, interrogated by religious authorities who use judicial systems to condemn those who engage in disruptive religious practices, question their authority, and reject their materialistic ("worldly," believers would have said) way of life. Like the York cycle's high priests, Herod, and Pilate, these late medieval inquisitors spew threats, insults, and mockery to cow, denigrate, and marginalize those over whom they wield power by their institutional offices. Like Jesus, Margery Kempe (whom we will consider briefly) and the Wycliffite William Thorpe refuse to reply in kind. Unlike Jesus, who breaks silence only rarely and briefly to confess faith in God and his purposes, they speak at length, believing that they are bound to testify to what they believe. So, what purposes does silence serve in the texts witnessing to their exemplary lives, *The Book of Margery Kempe* and *The Testimony of William Thorpe*?

Margery Kempe, of course, is far from silent when interrogated by Henry Bowet, Archbishop of York, and the learned men, many of them lawyers, who surround him. Not only does she readily rehearse the Articles of Faith, but she attacks clerical sins at length, taking refuge, as I have argued elsewhere, in the clerically constructed practice of fraternal correction that empowers subjects to rebuke *prelati*, clerics who have power over them through institutional roles.[55] In this, she follows the example of the disputative early Christian female saints (St. Catherine of Alexandria, for example) she admired, who vigorously resisted imperial interrogators. Yet *The Book of Margery Kempe*, offering her as a holy woman to be imitated, also presents a Margery Kempe who falls silent at times when attacked and threatened. A few days before she is interrogated by Archbishop Bowet, a priest at York Minster seizes the collar of her white clothing (he objects to her wearing a virgin's color), saying "'Þu wolf, what is þis cloth þat þu hast on?'" In response, she "not wolde answeryn in hir owyn cawse," but when he begins uttering oaths in frustration at her silence, she reproves him for blasphemy and spars with him "for Goddys cawse."[56] In this she follows a practice adopted at the beginning of her public experiences of weeping. When she was "usyd to be slawndred & repreued, to be cheden [chided] & rebuked of þe world," Christ taught her "how sche schuld han [have] pacyens," enduring in silence rather than replying in kind.[57] Early in her wanderings, she rebukes the Archbishop of Canterbury's clerks for reckless oaths, but then she is vehemently rebuked in turn by a woman: "I wold þe wer in Smythfeld, & I wold beryn a fagot to bren þe wyth; it is pety þat þou our leuyst." In response to this threatening branding of her as a heretic who should be burned in public—a threat especially ominous in the Archbishop's palace— she, as at York, simply "stod stylle & answeryd not," refusing to explain or defend herself.[58] As a woman seeking to practice a holy life, Margery Kempe must correct in others what the clergy has taught her that scripture condemns, but she must also practice patient silence when her own practices, like correction and singular dress, are reviled, even when her life is threatened. Like the interrogated Jesus of the York plays, she rejects replying in the genres of speech her abusers use, threat and insult, but, unlike him, as he remains silent to bring about human salvation, she speaks in a good cause.

The practice of silently enduring abuse of oneself and speaking in God's cause also governs the reactions of William Thorpe when he endures inquisition presided over by Archbishop Thomas Arundel, aided by three of his clerks. *The Testimony of William Thorpe* purports to be an autobiographical account of a Wycliffite priest's combative exchanges with Arundel as the inquisitor on August 7, 1407, at Saltwood Castle. Thorpe presents himself as a humble itinerant preacher who formed his way of life under Wyclif and his circle at Oxford. The text's archbishop is a devilish and often furious opponent who seeks the blood of true followers of Jesus if he cannot compel them to abjure positions that the institutional church deems heretical. He is cast as Caiaphas, as Sarah Beckwith has observed, quite in line with Wyclif's condemnation of institutional enforcers as betrayers and persecutors of Jesus.[59] Like the Caiaphas of the York plays, he appears from the outset as a person of great worldly power at the center of things. (An earl's son, he had been elevated to the episcopate directly after his school days, had twice served as Lord Chancellor under Richard II, had helped to bring about Richard's fall, and had served as Archbishop of York before being moved to the more important southern province.) Arundel stands in the castle's "greet chambre and myche peple aboute him," in contrast with the isolated and marginalized Thorpe, whom Arundel describes as an outsider who has been traveling for twenty years "in þe norþ lond and in oþir diuerse contrees of Ynglond."⁶⁰ In Thorpe's case, as a dissident priest who has been investigated earlier by another bishop, the archbishop charges him to submit immediately to his correction and observe his ordinances, stressing his authority and Thorpe's position as a priest subject to it.

The *Testimony*'s editor, Anne Hudson, reads it as, in some ways, a saint's life, a text designed to offer religious instruction but even more to present "a model of behavior under inquisition, and encouragement to steadfastness."⁶¹ As an exemplary narrative, Elizabeth Schirmer has argued, "it becomes the perfect vehicle for a Wycliffite theology conceived not as a set of propositions to be adhered to or debated but as a life lived in imitation of the Word."⁶² Thorpe claims to have written down their exchanges "for þe edificacioun of al holi chirche" (27), displaying a confidence, Fiona Somerset observes, that all true believers will digest and profit from the verbal duels, even at the most learned and academic points, because of God's grace working in them.⁶³ In Thorpe's account of this hostile questioning, patient silence emerges as a key protective strategy for Wycliffites harried by authorities, quite in contrast to the diocese of Norwich heresy trials and other official legal accounts of inquisitions, which simply record the suspect's legal confessions, abjurations, and, sometimes, betrayals of coreligionists. These institutional accounts lack altogether the to and fro of inquisitorial dialogue, giving no sense that the interrogated resisted in any way, let alone by silence.⁶⁴ Yet Thorpe's silences remain unexplored by readers, even by Mark Amsler, who deals extensively with evasion and equivocation as he analyzes the *Testimony* closely in terms of linguistic pragmatics and Critical Discourse Analysis.⁶⁵

From the outset of the *Testimony*, Thorpe presents himself, in characteristic Wycliffite ideology, as an apostolic Christian who embraces persecution from tyrants and "louers of þis world" as a test of patience to be accepted "wilfulli and gladli wiþouten ony grucchynge" against God (26–27). These two conditions for suffering to be transformed by patience are ubiquitous, as we have seen, in late medieval treatments of the virtue, like those of Guillaume Peyraut and Guillaume de Deguileville. Only when suffering is voluntarily embraced and never protested can believers be, Thorpe insists, "pacient suers [followers] of Crist" (27–28). In his initial confession of faith to the archbishop, Thorpe recounts in detail the patient and silent sufferings of Jesus in his Passion, noting that he did so "wiþouten grucchynge" (31). True members of the church, he insists, are characterized by the same virtue, as they are "wilfulli, pacientli and gladli suffringe persecuciouns bi ensaumple of Crist chefli and of his apostlis" (31).⁶⁶ Indeed, it is this very imitation of a patient Jesus "contrarie to þe maners of þis world" (31) that impels the worldly to hate and hunt down true Christians. Later in the conversation, Thorpe explicitly presents verbal abuse—scornful words, slander, and threats—as a kind of adversity that Jesus endured with patience, an example for his followers. True pilgrims trusting in the transcendent (like the Jesus of the York trial plays), they are moving toward the bliss of heaven, in contrast with those who entertain themselves with pilgrimages to shrines (62–63). Thorpe himself comes to exemplify this patience in the face of verbal abuse at the end of the *Testimony* when the archbishop's clerks attempt to compel him to submit: "And þanne I was rebukid and scorned and manassid on ech side. And ʒit after þis dyuerse persoones crieden vpon me to knele doun to submytte me. But I stood stille and spak no word. And þanne þere weren spoke of me and to me many greete wordis [angry, vituperative, violent speech]; and I stood and herde hem curse and manasse and scorne me, but I seide no þing" (92–93). Thorpe's silence marks, of course, a pious rejection of the genres of speech used by his opponents, quite in keeping with his vehement rejection of oath-swearing in the midst of the exchanges. Similarly, it marks his refusal to retaliate with speech in kind that Wycliffite texts, like those approved by the hierarchy (Peyraut's *Summa de virtutibus*, for example), advocated for believers imitating Jesus, the silent sacrificial lamb. For example, a Wycliffite sermon for the Third Sunday in Lent, expounding Jesus's healing of the man born deaf, blind, and dumb (Luke 11:14), claims that staying silent may be virtuous "þorow þe vertu of pacience, as þei [somme men] þat wolen not answere to wickid wordis and repreuable þat ben seide to hem." Then, before recalling Jesus the sacrificial lamb of Isaiah 53:7, it quotes Psalms 38:14 as what the virtuous say to themselves, Englishing the verse as "I, as deef man, heerde not repreues seide to me, and I, as doumbe man, not openyng my mouþe to answere ony yuel worde aʒeyn."⁶⁷ Responding in this way, Thorpe finds the inquisitors' abusive and violent language, like their formulaic legal and theological language, a confining and damning prison he will not enter. His refusal to speak is accompanied by physical stillness, as Wycliffite Bible suggests of Jesus when interrogated. It renders "Ille autem tacebat" as "he was still" (Mark 15:61) and "Jesus autem tacebat" as "and Jesus was stille" (Matt 26:63), both where the high priest asks what answer he has to accusations by false witnesses.[68] Whereas "tacebat" indicates only holding the tongue in medieval insular Latin (*DMLB*, s.v. "tacere" [v.], 1–3), the Wycliffite translation may suggest lack of movement, as well as of speech, conveying a stability and integrity not affected by unsettling emotions in a threatening and potentially violent situation of seeming powerlessness. Thus, Thorpe's stillness serves, as does Jesus's in the York pageants, as a sign of steadfast suffering and fidelity to a transcendent cause that his examiners, entrapped, he believes, in a worldly institution, cannot seem to fathom. In these ways, it, amid their vicious speech, enacts the Wycliffite (and Wyclif's) binary vision of true apostolic Christians amid a worldly institutional church.

Thorpe's silent endurance of verbal abuse at the end of the text and at intervals throughout stands in sharp contrast with the expansive expositions of beliefs that make up most of the *Testimony*, as they do in Richard Wyche's letter reporting his interrogations by Bishop Skirlaw and his secular and clerical seconds in the duel. As Thorpe explains in the preface, what he offers his fellow believers is an account of "myn opposynge and myn answering," of the questions asked of him and his answers on the nature of the Christ's presence in the Eucharist, auricular confession, and so on. As Mark Amsler detects, this antagonistic and fraught exchange carries with it the tense dialogue of authoritative and often punitive teacher and student from grammar school through university disputations.[69] Throughout it, Thorpe has confidence that God will give him answers that witness to his beliefs but skirt the edge of what his examiners consider heresy. Yet silence is a key strategy for Thorpe. When the archbishop demands that he reveal the names of his fellow Wycliffites, he feels trapped, as Susannah did when falsely accused by the lecherous elders. He recalls her words, "Angwysschis ben to me [griefs beset me] on euery side," and, because of that, he "stood stille musynge and spak not" (33). Certainly, his silence recalls Jesus's silences before his interrogators in the gospels, but it functions quite differently. Whereas Jesus's silence in the gospels, as in the York pageants, never suggests hesitancy or uncertainty, Thorpe's silence becomes a temporary refuge as he gathers his thoughts until he can give reasons for refusing to betray others, reasons that he thinks might give Arundel pause. When Arundel, in response, threatens him with burning at Smithfield as an obdurate heretic, Thorpe once again stands still and silent. This time, however, he uses the silence to assess

Arundel's fitness to be obeyed by a true believer, separating his "inner man" from his interrogator. In David Aers's analysis of Thorpe's theology, Thorpe has "confidence that he could judge who was joined to Christ eternally by his perception of their current works."[70] Once Thorpe judges Arundel as neither a true bishop nor a true priest, his footing changes: he is still the apostolic Christian, the role that powers his resistance, but his interrogator is not just a church official framing him as a suspected heretic but a diabolic inveigler trying to corrupt him, too. As a result, he resolves to change tack: he will speak no more to Arundel or his clerks than is necessary or beneficial for himself ("þan me need bihoued" [36]) as the target of their verbal tricks. The earlier forthright confessions of faith are replaced by switching topics and by evasive, quibbling, and disputatious answers that manage not to falsify what he believes to be scriptural truth.[71] Therefore, silence serves Thorpe as a tool to evaluate his opponents and discern how to change the very nature of the exchanges. In fact, he falls silent when pressed to submit, aiming to put an end to all the verbal exchanges now that they have become fruitless. Similarly, Richard Wyche falls silent when he is pressed over and over again to sign a statement prepared by his inquisitors that he has already told them he will not sign at that time.[72] Whereas Thorpe's refusal to return in kind his inquisitors' threats and slander presents a patient integrity that his fellows can imitate, his strategic silences offer them a way to assess and take control of examinations. By following his pragmatic use of silence, they may escape "detection," the church's juridical process of identifying heretics. Through these two very different uses of silence, Thorpe finds a way, to paraphrase a Wycliffite sermon quoted by Anne Hudson, to hold his peace when abused but also to discern how to speak against anything that is false to, or dishonors, God.[73] Thus, he avoids falling into the treacherous taciturnity that Wyclif condemned and *Mum and Sothsegger* satirizes, the practice of "dumb dogs" coveting the tithes, goods, and status that the institutional church can confer.

When William Thorpe confounds his inquisitors by adroit, extended hedging on the doctrinal formulas they are using to detect suspected heresy, he seems utterly unlike the still Jesus of the York plays in his arena of judicial interrogations. Jesus speaks rarely and briefly. Yet when he speaks, he voices what later enables his avowed follower Thorpe to endure what his inquisitors inflict on him: trust in a transcendent God, in his graciousness and redemptive designs. This provides the ground for their patience, the end for which they willingly suffer. They are confident that they are participating, like Deguileville's pilgrim, in a redemptive way of life that will outlast their powerful adversaries. This confidence enables them to be immune to the supposedly natural values that fuel their hostile interrogators and so imprison them that they cannot imagine anyone rejecting their appeal: institutionalized power over others, high status, ostentatiously displayed wealth, and legal gamesmanship. They may have the institutional positions and means to threaten and inflict suffering on Jesus and on Thorpe, but they cannot break their patient endurance, integrity, and emotional control. In their endurance, silence plays a key role. As Jesus declares in his longest, most surprising (to his York audience) utterance, and as Thorpe accepts, speech is a divinely given gift that must be used in ways the Creator will judge as good. For both of them, that is in confessing faith and in teaching. Jesus refers his inquisitors to his teaching over the years of his ministry. Even Thorpe's most evasive arguments on pilgrimage or Christ's presence in the consecrated bread and wine are designed to witness to God's presence and promises to believers. Yet using speech according to the divine will also entails, for both of them, refusing to utter kinds of speech that they judge as evil and so subject to God's condemnation: their antagonists' threats of violence, boasts, legal wrangling, insults that delegitimize others, and games designed to mock them—all forms of speech that convey, as do their misconstruals of their supposed victims' silence, their low cunning, arrogance, and fear of displacement. Amid the whirl of their antagonists' coercive, arrogant, and malicious speech, their silences signal to others, the York audience and the Wycliffite reader or auditor, what kinds of speech they should detest and shun and what kinds of institutional and hierarchical power they should question. The institutions that bear down on these late medieval English witnesses of interrogations are also often controlled by corrupt, lordly, and violent men who subject others to their devices and desires. The patient silence that Jesus and his follower Thorpe practice may confuse their adversaries, enabling them to achieve their purposes: for Jesus, fulfilling God's redemptive design for all humankind by moving toward his condemnation and death; for Thorpe, escaping detection as a heretic without abjuring his beliefs. In this sense, they conquer those who are inflicting suffering on them and attempting to break them. Their steadfast patience, like their confessional speech, never converts their adversaries, who persist in their self-imprisoning fury and arrogance even when frustrated. Yet their larger audiences also have the opportunity to be affected by their patience silences: women, men, and children in the streets of York and devout Wycliffite readers and auditors. The actor playing Jesus in *Pilate II* may even have addressed the audience directly when he speaks of everyone's capacity and responsibility to use "spiritual speech" in accord with God's will.[74] And Thorpe begins his *Testament* by inviting the reader to learn from his conduct under interrogation. The York interrogation plays, in line with clerical moral texts, dramatize Jesus as an exemplar of patient silence to be imitated in the lives of believers, moving them to live with equanimity and integrity even when suffering is inflicted on them by the powerful in church and state. In this way, they can, as patient Christians with an eye to the transcendent and with a ready sense of when to refuse to speak, conquer their oppressors.

Chapter 5 turns to the silence of a branded social, rather than institutional, deviant. In Hoccleve's last extended work, now called the *Series*, his textual self, Thomas, has been avoiding the conversations among old associates in crowded city streets. He has feared that they, who customarily use speech only for easy after-work banter, would misconstrue his words, even his body language, as signs of the mental disorder that once seized him, a disorder that his comrades found socially unacceptable, a violation of the bonds that hold them together. Thus, although Thomas, like the York Jesus and William Thorpe, is subjected to the norms of oppressive power, silence becomes for him a strategy for self-protection, as often in Albertano da Brescia, who like Hoccleve and his Thomas, lived in tightly codified urban social groups.

CHAPTER 5

THE LIMITATIONS OF SILENCE IN SOCIAL LIFE

Thomas Hoccleve's "My Complaint" and "Dialogue"

As we have seen in the *Regiment of Princes*, Thomas Hoccleve is given to exploring not only the strategic values of silence for rulers but also its destructive misuses by royal advisers. In "The Complaint" and "The Dialogue," the first two segments of the *Series*, he explores in complex ways first why silence appeals to the acutely self-conscious and distrustful Thomas, the poet's textual self, ostracized by his former companions, snubbed by them in public, and dominated by fears of further social losses.[1] Yet Thomas is a creature of second, and third, thoughts. Silence no longer seems a protective shield to Thomas when he realizes that it, like speech, is an unstable sign of his inner self, susceptible to being misunderstood because of people's preconceptions. The only value that silence comes to have for him, then, is a moral one. It becomes the means to endure insults and slights patiently, a practice, of course, that Hoccleve urged Prince Henry to adopt when king and that the York Jesus, Margery Kempe, and William Thorpe embody. However, silence greatly increases Thomas's sorrow, as clerical moral writers warned it does, prompting him to write a complaint that voices his painful experience of social misunderstanding and rejection. Yet how can he justify making that experience public, breaking his silence, especially when a friend cautions him that breaking his silence will sabotage his honor, his social standing, by reminding others of his unsettling mental illness? Finally, I argue, Thomas realizes that his complaint is fundamentally a socially acceptable confession of faith; through it he becomes a social force again. Indeed, not to testify to God's benignity and power in healing him of his mental illness would constitute a sinful form of silence. No other Middle English poet explores more urgently or complexly the limitations—indeed, the failures—of fearful silence as a social strategy and a personal resource. Indeed, Thomas's shifting perceptions of protective silence form a basic dynamic of "My Complaint" and the first section of the "Dialogue," a dynamic largely overlooked by scholars focusing on fragmented subjectivity and bureaucratic culture (as we will see in part 2 below). First, we turn to fear as an emotion with ambivalent status in medieval moral writing.

Like the virtue of prudence as set forth in chapter 1, fear, although an emotion and not a settled disposition, drives agents to avoid something they see as harmful in the future. Unlike prudence, however, fear could lead to them losing, not gaining, what they eagerly desire. From the Stoics, moral writers inherited an understanding of fear as an unpremeditated subjective judgment that something imminent would be evil, followed by the urge to flee from it. As Simo Knuuttila and Barbara Rosenwein have set forth, the Stoics labeled fear, like many other emotions, as a *perturbatio*.[2] Seneca, as embedded in Thomas of Ireland's fourteenth-century *Manipulus florum*, proclaims that nothing is as pernicious or irrevocable as frantic fears ("limphatici metus") because the fearful envision an uncertain future, one that may never happen, one that is, in the present, a fictitious scenario ("fabula"). In fear, humans run away from what they conjecture, like soldiers who desert their fortress because they see a cloud of dust stirred up by cattle and conjecture that a mighty army is approaching. In reacting with fear, humans twist the great good of foresight (*providentia*), so central to prudent action.[3] Citing Seneca, Guillaume Peyraut urges Christians to remind themselves constantly that the imagined terrible events fear engenders ("pictura terribilium") may never happen. Therefore, such imaginings should not torment them and throw them off virtuous action (he writes to create aversion to sloth).[4] Weak minds, medieval moral writers held, may be shattered by fears that torment them, but the wise assess the future in ways that enable them to take effective action. So, Cicero distinguishes between the fear (*metus*) of the foolish, who withdraw from what seems evil, and the caution (*cautio*) of the wise, who withdraw only if reason advises.⁵

Despite the Stoic writings that late medieval moral writers appropriate, they also see fear as a natural aid for moral agents seeking to avoid what is evil and so pursue what is good. Just as in clerical writings about prudence and patience, love is understood as the root of moral action, leading agents to desire or feel aversion to an object. Fear, then, can come into play, helping the will to act more effectively in avoiding an imminent evil, just as hope does in achieving what is desired. Yet fear may become destructive if the cognitive power has wrongly estimated the future as evil, causing agents to lose what they desired and might have attained.⁶ Both enabling and destructive fears can lead agents to choose to be silent when they could speak. Let us turn to several fifteenth-century English texts by way of example. The *Speculum laicorum* urges Christians to be silent at times rather than speak in unguarded ways that might endanger themselves and others, say, by revealing and inflaming anger. Citing Cassiodorus, the *Speculum*'s compiler presents speech as the mirror of the speaker's character: "est quoddam morum speculum loquentis oratio." Fear, he argues, can be valuable, even necessary, in restraining people from speaking what they might later regret. As we saw in chapters 1 and 3, clerical writers absorbed this self-protective view of silence from collections of Roman *sententiae* and from Hebrew wisdom literature with their cautions against speaking too much.⁷ In the fifteenth century, popular lyrics often voice this caution. In "The Cok Hath Lowe Shoone," for example, Cato is cited in praising the man who "goth stille of wysdam & resoun," and fear serves to prompt the wise "To thynke mochyl [much], and seyn but smal [little]."⁸ On the other hand, English preachers often inveigh against those whose fear of shame if others learn of their sins inhibits them from confessing fully, just as, we have seen, clerical writers denounce those priests whose fear of loss of positions and goods inhibits them from rebuking the sins of the powerful and wealthy. The Oxford preacher John Felton, expounding Jesus's healing of a mute, mocks people who fear that a priest would react to their sins with horror and disgust. Priests have heard it all over and over again, he remarks drily.⁹ And a Wycliffite, preaching on the same lesson, condemns those who allow the devil's finger to stop their mouths: "Þey wyll not schryue [confess] hem ne telle her syn for drede of sclaunder and schame."¹⁰ In both sermons, those who choose not to speak the truth about themselves because of their fears of others' reactions forfeit the healing confession offers.

As Felton's and the Wycliffite's sermons suggest, late medieval English writers thought that individuals' fears of social rejection could instigate silences that worked against, even stood in the way of, what might benefit them. In social encounters, fearful silence could seem to them a necessary strategy if they were to avoid others' aversion to what they, as transgressors of social conventions (or, in a religious context, divine law), might say. In narratives, these fearful silences are adopted within the parameters of figures' social groups, held together and governed by certain mores, like the chivalric code of Malory's *Le Morte Darthur* and the norms for speech and silence imposed on unmarried noble women in *William of Palerne* and Lydgate's *Temple of Glass*. Hoccleve's Thomas of "My Complaint" and "The Dialogue" has been avoiding conversations with old associates in the crowded Westminster and London streets because he fears their aversion, even social slights. For them, his former mental disorder, which they suspect has returned, has placed him outside their norms for social life. So does his present emotional unease, which also makes him feel powerless to change the terms of social interaction.

Roughly half a decade after Hoccleve had finished the *Regiment of Princes* and achieved greater recognition as a poet, a mental breakdown of some sort descended on him, described in "My Complaint" as

> the wylde infirmitee
> Which þat I hadde / as many a man wel kneew,
> And which me out of myself / caste and threew. (C40–42)[11]

Although recovery came on All Saints Day of that year (probably 1416), his "darkness visible," as William Styron would call it, was all too visible, he tells us, to his colleagues in the Office of the Privy Seal and to the crowded social world of London scribes and officials in which he moved perforce.[12] Since he began work as a scribe in 1387, this social nexus had offered him constant companionship, in taverns (as he depicts comically in *La Male Regle*), in his lodgings, and in the "press" of the crowded streets of Westminster and London. In late 1419 or late 1420, several years after the illness had dissipated, Hoccleve began writing "My Complaint," an unsparing account of what his figure Thomas experiences as a result of the "wylde infirmitee."[13] By choosing the genre of complaint, Hoccleve returned to a standard dynamic of his poems: a statement of wrong followed by an appeal for remedy addressed to a potential benefactor or an intermediary, a genre that, as Wendy Scase has shown, emerged in legal complaint.[14] Indeed, complaints and petitions of various kinds appear throughout Hoccleve's *Formulary* of the 1420s, a collection of model French and Latin writs, petitions, letters, and warrants that he compiled for his successors at the Office of the Privy Seal to follow.[15] To "My Complaint," Hoccleve appended the "Dialogue," an often-heated debate between Thomas and a Friend over making "My Complaint" public and over Thomas's desire to undertake other poems in his old age. To these two texts, Hoccleve appended his expansive verse translations of two tales (with lengthy prose moralizations) from the *Gesta Romanorum*, a popular collection of Latin exempla first compiled in the mid-fourteenth century and remade in England somewhat over fifty years later (the Anglo-Latin *Gesta Romanorum*).[16] Between the tales, he inserted "Learn to Die," a translation of the first part of an *ars moriendi* by the German Dominican Heinrich Suese (Henry Suso). Conversations between Thomas and the Friend link the parts of this heterogeneous compilation of texts, with the Friend serving, as R. D. Perry has perceived, to represent how chance encounters and the needs of others organize the variable and open-ended collection.[17] Hoccleve himself penned a copy of the whole text (Durham University Library, MS Cosin V.iii.9), now called his *Series*, before his death in 1426.

Recent readers have been drawn to Hoccleve's representation of subjective experience in "My Complaint" and the "Dialogue," but oddly, especially given the great interest in the history of emotions, they have neglected fear as what impels the misunderstood Thomas to remain silent or speak rarely amid streets full of conversation.[18] At the same time, while scholars have examined closely the six manuscripts containing the *Series*, they have not considered how Thomas's silences relate to the strategies for politically effective silence advocated in *The Regiment of Princes*, even though the *Series* precedes or follows the *Regiment* in all five nonholograph manuscripts.[19] These five do not constitute full compilations of Hoccleve's works, for they all lack the other three extended poems—*L'epistre de Cupide* (*The Letter of Cupid*), *La Male Regle*, and the "Address to Sir John Oldcastle"—plus most of the occasional, petitionary, and devotional poems. Moreover, all five also contain texts by other writers, yet those texts are never inserted between the *Series* and the *Regiment*. So, scribes clearly chose to link the two closely.[20] Scholars' failure to examine silence in the two together is all the more striking because Thomas follows the moral imperative of the *Regiment*: Respond with patient silence to public insults. Moreover, in both major poems, the importance of maintaining, or at least not losing, reputation drives the strategies of silence, as of speech.

The prologue to "My Complaint," like the opening of the *Regiment*, presents all life as unstable, a fundamental condition that elicits in Thomas a melancholy awareness of loss and suffering. Whereas the distracted Hoccleve of the *Regiment* is troubled by the fall of Richard II, the Lancastrians' unsure grip on power, the old man's penury, and his own financial uncertainties, all linked as the results of Fortune's capriciousness, "my prolog" places Thomas in the natural world itself: the "broun season" of autumn. Rather than presenting change as the acts of an inscrutable and unpredictable agent, Hoccleve here has a sleepless Thomas see in leaves stolen from trees and "doun throwen undir foote" "Þat stablenesse / in this world / is ther noon; / There is no thyng / but chaunge and variance" (C1–10).²¹ Instability is simply a condition that affects all things material, a rich man's wealth as surely as summer's leaves. It is in this natural world of profound change, far from the spring promises of new beginning in Chaucer's "General Prologue" that Hoccleve parodies, that Thomas places not only his sudden sickness and equally sudden recovery but also the subsequent loss of his fellows' favor, imaged as an autumnal "dirke shour" pouring on him after the sun has ceased to shine. The metaphor, like the autumnal setting as a whole, presents loss of social standing as irresistible in its onset and overwhelming in its effect, much like the mental disorder that precipitated it. However, while Thomas's illness gave way to recovery in the natural cycle of loss and renewal, his standing among his former companions has not recovered. His life of urban companionship has, seemingly, reached an end, like the autumn leaves spurned underfoot and like death itself, which Thomas faces squarely as "euery wightes [man's] conclusioun" (C14). Hoccleve's parody of the "General Prologue," in which Chaucer depicts a communal response to the changing natural world, only underscores Thomas's isolation and vulnerability, as Spencer Strub has registered.²² Paralyzed and in despair ("my spiryt / To lyue / no lust [desire] hadde / ne delyt"), he feels "languor" so overwhelming that all he can do is keep it "cloos" (C22–32)—that is, endure it in silence. Far from a carefully chosen strategic device, as in the *Regiment*, silence results, at first in the complaint, from being overmastered by distressing emotions.

Thomas's reputation has suffered such change because, he believes, his illness removed it from his own control and then he, although healed, was walled off from others first by their refusal to alter their perceptions of him and then by their ostracizing silences. His social self has been constructed anew and anew by those who talked so freely and widely about his mental disorder while he was in a state of helpless self-alienation. His "wylde infirmitee"

> was so knowen to the peple / and kowth [known]
> Þat conseil was it noon / ne nat be mighte.
> How it with me stood / was in euery mowth, (C43–45)

As the double negative following a negative stresses, Thomas believes he had no power at the time to keep his disturbance as "conseil," knowledge private to the person involved in figuring out how to deal with it. Once his disturbed self was in the mouths of his fellows in London and Westminster, gossiping about him in the streets, they were loath to surrender that sense of him. Although God had restored his former self, "Men wolde it nat so / vndirstonde or take" (C65). Thomas castigates this refusal to acknowledge God's action as foolish, ignorant, and unmannerly conduct ("lewdenesse"):

> What falle shal / what men so deeme [judge] or gesse,
> To him þat woot [knows] / euery hertes secree [secret]
> Reserued is. / It is a lewdenesse
> Men wyser hem pretende / than they be;
> And no wight [person] knowith / be it he or she,
> Whom / how / ne whanne / God wole him visyte;
> It happith often / whan men weene it lyte [little think of it].
>   (C99–105)

For scribes and officials to think that they perceive the hidden inner life of others—their rushes of feeling, their emotions, and their thoughts—is to arrogate for themselves a prerogative that is solely God's as Creator and Ordainer of all life. Not only is such presumption unworthy and wicked (another sense of "lewd"), but it springs from a refusal to admit that God could strike them at any moment with any affliction (*MED*, s.v. "leuednes" [n. 1], a, b, c, d). It is to deny what the autumnal prologue has shown: that the material world is unstable and that they, embodied in that world, may experience devastating change. Yet as the first lines of "My Complaint" state plainly, they see that instability all day every day as God afflicts men "With los of good / and bodily seeknesse" (C38). Thus, although they consider themselves superior to a mentally unstable Thomas, they have willfully misconstrued his state and God's acts in his life, just as they have misconstrued what they see around them daily. Thomas mocks their former "prophecie," their foretelling of a certain future in which his malady would attack him again during the summer heat, something that has not happened over the summers since God restored his health. Such cocksure pretense denies God's power to act as He pleases and His grace to provide a remedy for human suffering (C96–98). It also fails to acknowledge that, as Shannon Gayk observes of a later passage, uncorrupted sight belongs to God alone, and their reactions are a matter of perspective.[23] Unwilling to admit God's power over both Thomas and themselves or the limits of their interpretation, they cling to their image of him as a "riotous persone," someone whose conduct is out of his own control and unsettling, given their conventions for interaction. In the crowds, they are accustomed to hail each other cheerfully, to assume intimacy, to exchange pleasantries, and to engage in small talk ("daliance"). For them, conversation is unfettered and recreative, springing from what John Burrow calls "*urban* companionship," the familiarity uniting "those working in the busy 'press' of a great town who actually happen to know each other."[24] Now that they suspect that Thomas is unsettling, they use silence and averted faces to estrange themselves from him, denying him entrance to their (and his former) social world when they encounter him in the streets: "The world me made / a straunge [distanced, estranged, hostile] contenance" (C70). They have appropriated as their own what Thomas desired to keep secret about himself, and that seems to justify using silence as a tool to exclude him from their conversation and company.

Later in the *Series*, Hoccleve returns the anguished plight of those who are helplessly cast out of the world to which they have belonged and unable to remedy their situation by speech. In his first translation from the Anglo-Latin *Gesta Romanorum*, the virtuous wife of Emperor Jereslaus is first deprived of her previous life by her dissembling brother-in-law at the Roman court, who leaves her naked and strung up to a tree in her husband's absence. Then, her good reputation, like Thomas's, is taken away by others whose acts are beyond her control. At the safe harbor of an earl's household, she, living incognito, has made a place for herself as a governess. The earl's steward, whom she has rejected as a lover, slays the earl's daughter in her charge, putting the bloody knife in her hand, material evidence she cannot contest effectively: "Giltlees, hir good loos [reputation] refte a wikked wight [man]" (line 315).[25] After she briefly protests her innocence, she is denounced as unnatural and traitorous by the earl and his wife. Then she chooses to be silent, a silence Hoccleve added, with much emphasis, to the tale he found in the *Gesta*: "And, sikirly, whereas þat no credence / May been had, wysdam conseillith silence" (lines 426–27).[26] The earl sees her as an "Vnkynde [unnatural, alien, barbarous] womman" (line 414) and banishes her. She is misunderstood as a transgressor of the conventions of civilized society, much as Thomas has been because of his supposedly disordered and disruptive state. Helpless to use words to change how others think of her and their decision to exile her, she assumes silence out of pragmatic wisdom, recognizing the limitations of speech given the brute fact of the bloody knife.

When Thomas, by contrast, overhears people in the crowd speak of him as mentally ill (or about to be so), he is so overmastered by woe and fear that he falls back on silence as the only means to protect himself from the further slights, ostracism, and isolation he fears. Paraphrasing a psalm of unjust abandonment (30:12–14), he fears that their silent aversion signifies that he "deed [dead] was / from hertes cheertee" (C81). Ceasing to treat him in a loving and compassionate way, they have also lost their esteem for him, esteem being another sense of "cheertee" (*MED*: s.v. "chierte" [n.], 3), one that Hoccleve invoked in the *Regiment* when he lamented the loss of public standing, friendship, and compassion that formerly honored veterans of the French war were experiencing in Henrician England.[27] As fickle as the English public, "many a wight [man] / aboute me dwellynge / Herde I me blame / and putte in dispreisynge" (C83–84). This loss of esteem and social standing, like the loss of company, seems irreparable to him. Because he is quaking "for the verray shame and fear" (C154), the physiological effect of imagining further losses and of the confusion and humiliation caused by those he has experienced, he decides that to speak in these fraught public situations will only harm him more:

Of long abydynge heere / I may repente;
Lest þat of hastinesse / I at the laste

Answere amis / best is / hens hie faste,
For if I in this prees / amis me gye [conduct myself wrongly],
To harm wole it me torne / and to folie. (C136–40)

Just as medieval moral texts advance taciturnity as a way of protecting the self from the harm that unconsidered speech might bring and just as Hoccleve, drawing on moral *sententiae*, had warned Prince Henry against voicing rash oaths and promises that he might not be able to fulfill, so Hoccleve's Thomas fears a hasty reply to whatever he overhears. Unconsidered speech might be foolish in his case because auditors might take it as a sign of mental disorder, of wild feelings, instead of simply emotional distress. Only if he adheres to injunctions to speak rarely and briefly, found both in clerical moral texts and sentential lyrics like "The Cok Hath Lowe Shoone," would people not think him unbalanced: "I may but [only] smal sayn / but [lest] men deeme that I raue" (C264).[28] Or whatever he might speak, Thomas says with the sad folk wisdom of a well-known proverb, "They wolden nat / han holde it worth a leek [of no value]" (C143). The sustained silence of a man in a difficult situation who wishes to protect himself becomes his default position: "Forwhy / as I had lost my tonges keye / Kepte I me cloos" (C144–45). The key of the tongue is a common image in clerical moral texts. Guillaume Peyraut uses the image in advising those who wish to speak with deliberation not to respond too quickly: "Ille qui non vult loqui nisi precedente cordis deliberatione, clavem oris habet in archa cordis" (He who wishes to speak only with deliberation beforehand keeps the key of his mouth in the coffer of his heart).[29] However, whereas Peyraut assumes that anyone can carry out a step-by-step process of thought ("cordis") and physiological response ("oris"), Thomas's situation is too dire for this. His silence is not born of the received classical and biblical wisdom that marks royal silence in the *Regiment*, silence authorized and highlighted by Latin *sententiae* in the margins. He is clueless and powerless, much as in the melancholy prologue, so overcome by fear of damaging further his social stature that he has lost the capacity for speech that might benefit him by conveying what he believes to be his settled state. Silence and flight from social encounters seem the only self-protective courses open to him.

Since his recovery, Thomas believes that he has practiced silence for another strategic reason than self-protection. Like the exemplary rulers of the *Regiment*, King David or Duke Pisistaris (and the exemplary ruler

Prince Henry promises to become), Thomas has resorted to patient silence to govern himself whenever he is wronged by others' slights:

> Syn I recouered was / haue I ful ofte
> Cause had of anger / and inpacience,
> Where I born haue it / esily and softe,
> Suffryng wrong be doon / to me and offense
> And nat answerd ageyn / but kept silence,
> Lest þat men of me / deeme wolde and seyn
> "See how this man / is fallen in ageyn." (C176–82)

While Thomas does not voice his anger toward those who have offended him, his silence, unlike that of exemplary rulers, seems born less of patience and commitment to a noble cause than of fear. If he succumbed to angry, retaliatory speech, others would misjudge his inner state once again, taking his anger, like his sorrow and haste amid the crowds, as a sign of emotional disorder. Thus, words have become for Thomas, the man who pens words all day for a living, unstable vehicles of thought and feeling. Whatever state he might be in, he fears, words would fail in what Augustinian sign theory, as transmitted by clerical writers on the ethics of speech, promised: that words, as material sounds uttered by a material tongue, were messengers (*nuncii*) conveying speakers' immaterial thoughts and emotions to others to whom they wish to make themselves known.[30] Thomas's silence, dictated by his own fears and the limitations of speech, can only be seen as a self-protective strategy, a means of damage control.

In his silence born of fear and in the anguish and uncertainty that accompany it, Thomas resembles the narrator Drede in John Skelton's curial satire *Bowge of Courte* (1498?), set like "My Complaint" in autumn, the season of mutability. Like Thomas, Drede is agitated and downcast as the poem begins, before he even begins dreaming. Drawn in a vision to the splendid merchandise on the ship of court, he is "mased" (bewildered) from the outset, deterred by Daunger (aloofnness), chief gentlewoman of the gloriously enthroned owner who looks on him with disdain (line 24).[31] Like Thomas again (and like Skelton at the Tudor court), he is both inside and outside a world he desires to be part of.[32] Desire advises him to overcome "drede" and speak, citing the ubiquitous proverb "Who spareth to speke, in fayth, he spareth to spede" (lines 90–91).[33] Yet he immediately is filled with distrust and fear of his fellow courtiers, all promised favor by Fortune but all given to trickery, dissembling, and deceit ("subtyle"). In the whirl of court intrigue, in which Drede repeatedly sees other courtiers looking at him askance and whispering, each asks for his trust and friendship, so that he will break silence and, as Favell (flattery) begs, "shewe to me your mynde" (line 165). He is advised by Suspicyon to adopt the opposite course, the self-protective circumspection and initial silence advocated by Albertano of Brescia and cautionary lyrics, like "The Cok": "The sovereraynst thynge that ony man maye have / Is lytyll to saye, and moche to here and see" (lines 211–12). This second line completes dueling proverbs that encapsulate the conflict in Drede between speech and silence (or infrequent speech), both of which, in folk wisdom, enable one to obtain what is desired.[34] In a state of anguish and indecision, Drede reveals nothing of himself as Dyssymulation warns him that he is plotted against and as he observes "Poyntynge and noddynge with the hede / And many wordes sayde in secrete wyse" (lines 421–22). Fear of his new companions drives Drede to such a pitch of anxiety and uncertainty (all three are senses of "drede") that, when he hears rumors of all colluding in his murder, he rushes to jump ship and awakes from his dream. Like Thomas, all that Drede, in his anguish, can resolve on doing is to flee from a desired, but uncertain and threatening, world.

Silence, Thomas discovers as he practices it, is not the secure refuge he expects it to be. First of all, not only is it, like words, an unstable sign in itself, but also it draws attention to the remaining signifiers of the face and body, which have become unstable, too. If he hides in his lodging from the crowds in the streets, escaping their surveillance, people will judge that he is in a worse state than he is (C190–93). Yet if he passes them without speaking when he fears he might damage himself with an outburst, they judge that he is so disordered that he does not dare to speak. So, his fearful silences lead to what he seeks to avoid: being misunderstood anew as in the grips of his former illness. Moreover, his very silence invites the curious onlookers, estranged by their own silences as well as his, to scrutinize his gestures and looks with the same presuppositions that they would use with his words:

> Men seide I lookid / as a wylde steer
> And so my look / aboute I gan to throwe.
> Myn heed to hye / another seide I beer.

"Ful bukkish [disturbed] is his brayn / wel may I trowe [believe],"
Seide the thridde [third]. (C120–24)

Whatever countenance Thomas assumes is a sign of psychic instability. Fixity in his features indicates emotional wildness, but so does glancing about. Even changes in his looks are seen as a sign of instability.[35] So are changes in his gait. As the metaphors used by his former companions convey (steer, roe deer), whatever look or gait Thomas assumes signifies that he is seized by an irrational animality that seems, in their primitive response, almost contagious ("al braynseek" [C127–33]). As Matthew Goldie explained several decades ago and as more recent research has developed, late medieval Englishmen attempted to detect mental disorders by observing others' countenances and behavior, whether they did so in legal inquisitions or, like Thomas's former companions, in informal social situations.[36] But the companions carry out this cultural practice with prejudicial assumptions, misjudging Thomas's inner state by visible signs, like users of the clipped or counterfeit coins Thomas speaks about to his Friend, who assume that the coins have their usual value, although, by weight of the gold and silver, they have less or none at all.[37] In response, as Julie Orlemanski writes in her acute study of the limitations of corporeal signs, "Even in face-to-face encounters Hoccleve cannot make his flesh signify properly."[38]

Hoccleve, from his earliest poetry (as we have it), had displayed a keen sense of how words, looks, and gestures are not reliable signs of the inner self. His generic male seducer in the L'epistre de Cupide promises to fulfill a woman's desire to "keepe al thyng secree [secret]" (line 33), but soon he boasts of his conquest to his companions.[39] Cupid, who is recounting women's laments, observes,

> Ful hard it is to knowe a mannes herte,
> For outward may no man the truthe deme;
> Whan word out of his mowth may ther noon sterte,
> But it sholde any wight [person] by resoun qweeme [please].
> So is it seid of herte, as it wolde seeme. (lines 36–40)

Not only the seducer's pleasing words but his piteous looks convince the woman that he will be faithful and discreet because she judges his emotions and intentions by her knowledge of herself, by her desire to be straightforward, faithful, and honorable. Like Thomas's former companions in "My Complaint," she reads his outward signs by her own character and the social conventions to which her class subscribes. (He seems woeful, as stricken lovers were expected to be.) But Thomas's experience of words and looks is more complex than that of the seducer. The "fals apparence" of the *L'espistre* is contrived by an artful deceiver, fully in control of his words and gestures (line 42). They may not signify what is in his thought and emotions, but that is due in part to his mastery of outward signs and of the conventions of love as constructed in love complaints. Similarly, Prince Henry is imagined in the *Regiment* as someone who uses both silence and speech as thought-out strategies for managing his reputation among his subjects; understanding what they expect of a ruler and well instructed by advisory texts, he can influence how they see him. The artful seducer achieves the success he seeks, as will, Hoccleve is confident, the prudent prince. By contrast, Thomas's considered efforts to resort to silence and alter his looks and gait not only fail to achieve a renewed social acceptance but aggravate the painful situation. Born urgently of fear, all Thomas's public signs fail to make clear to others the settled self he believes he is experiencing, and they bring to pass exactly what he feared: more misconstrual, more signs of rejection, more isolation. While his changing behavior and speech may in themselves play a role in unsettling others, his attempts to alter his facial expression and body language by posing in front of a mirror lead to the sad conclusion that men's blindness would prevent them from realizing that there "is no thyng repreeuable [objectionable]" in his countenance (C167). In this famous mirror scene, his looks may be malleable, as Ethan Knapp has stressed, even as malleable as those of *L'epsitre*'s artful seducer, but men's reading of them would be straightjacketed by their individual prejudices and the powerful herd's gossip.[40]

Although Thomas's mental state may no longer be as fractured as it was, with his "wit" (thought, consciousness) dispersed, his emotional state throughout "My Complaint" and the following "Dialogue" is far from settled. Yet modern readers have not explored how Thomas's fearful silences themselves have led, in part, to his troubled state. As so often, silence in medieval texts is well-nigh invisible to us now. At the end of the prologue, the immediacy of change and loss in the natural world of November triggers violent grief in Thomas:

> The greef aboute myn herte / so swal [swelled]
> And bolned [surged] euere / to and to so sore
> Þat needes oute / I muste therwithal.
> I thoghte I nolde [would not] / keepe it cloos no more
> Ne lette [leave; allow] it in me / for to eelde [age] and hore [grow
>   gray]; (C29–33)

Even before the narrative of "My Complaint" begins, therefore, Thomas alerts us to his resolve to abandon the silence he has adopted as a way of dealing with social misunderstanding and loss. His conventional metaphor of swelling conveys the power of disordered affect and emotions, as Strub has traced in fifteenth-century writing and throughout the *Series*.[41] He grasps that voluntary silence has been a temporary and limited strategy because the sorrowful emotions and thoughts it has cloaked become so intense over time that it cannot be sustained, with unvoiced grief growing as he grows old. Clerical moral writers, for all their advocacy of taciturnity, advise that silence should be limited in duration for this very reason. Before the compiler of *De lingua* turns to the destructive effects that taciturnity can have on others, he describes those it has on the silent themselves: "talium corda, tamquam ulcera sanie repletur, que dum foris claudunter, intus miro modo fervent, dolent, ac tumescunt, et sic graviter affliguntur" (the hearts of such people, as if wounds filled with pus, while they are closed up outwardly, inwardly burn, grieve, and swell and so are gravely afflicted).[42] The compiler takes this metaphor of putrefaction from Gregory the Great, the insistent advocate, as chapter 4 has shown, of patient silence; he quotes a passage from the *Liber regulae pastoralis*, as does Thomas of Ireland, among his *sententiae* on taciturnity.[43] Alive to the incessant and mounting suffering caused by unspoken sorrow, Gregory advises the sorrowful that they should realize that they do not need to suffer more than is expeditious. If the tongue speaks calmly of buried troubles, Gregory insists, grief would flow out of the tormented person's consciousness like putrefaction ejected from a wound, opening it to healing. For those clerical writers concerned with the pastoral care of others, even the patient silence of those who virtuously endure unjust injuries should be limited in duration. The sufferer needs to abandon taciturnity and find a voice, albeit a considered one. Likewise, Hoccleve's prologue and the first two poems of the *Series* as a whole present silence as a temporary and limited way of dealing with painful social loss, quite unlike the *Regiment*'s sustained advocacy of habitual taciturnity as a prudent strategy for governing effectively and for dealing with potential threats to political control.

How can Hoccleve's Thomas find a clear way both to convey his sorrows and to make his present state clear to his former companions, given to judging all signs, even his silence, in terms of his former mental disorder? How can he find a considered means to voice grief of such intensity, let alone its humiliating causes: painful social encounters and his own frustrated fumbling as he sought to end them? And how can he present his experience in a way that might be acceptable to those who misjudged and excluded him?

As in the later joints of the *Series* where Thomas must decide what to write or make public to what readers, in the "Dialogue," conversation with his Friend serves as a catalyst, prompting him to grasp how to make known his recovery and stability to his former companions. The silence imposed on him and the silence of writing itself are broken by longed-for social exchange. From the Friend's entry, he casts himself, and Thomas casts him, as an adviser. He addresses Thomas as "thou," the familiar pronoun, whereas Thomas addresses him as "ye," the formal pronoun that indicates superiority. As the *Regiment* underscores, Hoccleve's poetry exalts counsel from truth-speaking and faithful advisers as a means of reaching a firm and productive decision. In the "Dialogue," the Friend invokes, as Hoccleve does in the *Regiment*, the Hebrew wisdom tradition as he asserts the value of his counsel-giving: "Salomon bit [bids] / aftir conseil do" (D391; also D451–52). Moreover, Hoccleve had depicted himself in the *Regiment*'s long dialogue with the old beggar as an impoverished man and an uncertain poet in need of advice. When the old man suggests that Thomas write a poem addressed to the Prince, he resolves to settle his problems by doing so. In the "Dialogue," however, Thomas resolutely, even vehemently, rejects the Friend's counsel after he has read "My Complaint" to him. What the Friend advises is nothing other than the self-protective silence that Thomas has practiced since his recovery:

> If thow be wys / of þat mateere ho!
> Reherce thow it nat / ne it awake;
> Keepe al þat cloos / for thyn honoures sake. (D26–28)

"Keepe al þat cloos" echoes "I nolde keepe it cloos no more" in the prologue (C32), where Thomas resolves on voicing his social loss and suffering as a means of escaping his mounting sorrow. Now he trusts that writing, as carefully cast voicing of his experience, will make known clearly to his former companions what silence and gestures have failed to convey, made unstable in meaning by men's presuppositions and, to a degree, his own distress and self-distrust. Thomas sees his complaint, in Rory Critten's words, as a messenger "mediating between himself and the audience whose understanding and goodwill he seeks ... to regain."[44] In this, it is akin to his earlier *La Male Regle*, in which his closing appeal to have his stipend in arrears paid is justified by the proverb "the doumb man no lond getith," the common posture of his complaints.[45] To the Friend, on the other hand, the social expectations of easy, recreative verbal exchanges among the urban coteries are what matter when considering releasing the complaint as a statement of grievance and plea for remedy. To circulate it would be to revive memories of a disturbing disorder wholly out of keeping with their casual and comfortable social mores. So, if Thomas makes anguished experience public—indeed, anguish caused in part by the casual talkers' erroneous apprehension of the signs of his inner life—he risks further erosion of his social standing, his good name. "Honour" depends on conforming to the mores of the dominant after-work "press."

Throughout the *Series*, the Friend is the voice of caution, of considered thought based on transmitted wisdom, a keen sense of human limitations, and foresight governed by fears of harm and loss. Above all, like chapter 1's moral writers influenced by Stoicism, Roman popular morality, and Jewish wisdom literature, he distrusts impulsivity fueled by feeling and strong emotions. In this, he is not unlike Thomas himself when he withdrew from public conversation, fearing what he might utter in haste. In his advice, Holly Crocker has argued, lies an acculturated sense that masculinity entails "calm governance that suppresses any forms of imbalance."[46] Later in their dialogue, the Friend sets about advising Thomas on how to choose another writing project, a poem that would please Humphrey, Duke of Gloucester, Prince Henry's youngest brother, already a discriminating patron of literature. Rejecting any spur-of-the-moment response, he expansively renders in English a line from Geoffrey of Vinsauf's influential *Poetria nova* (ca. 1200):

Thow woost [know] wel / who shal an hous edifie [construct]
Gooth nat therto withoute auisament [consideration]

If he be wys / for with his mental ye [eye]
First is it seen / purposid / cast & ment [directed],
How it shal wroght been / elles al is shent [ruined, put to shame].
   (D638–42)

The Friend's amplification is stuffed with the language of caution. The mental eye, as John Burrow notes, is the third eye of prudence, the eye of foresight, as we have seen, that looks to the future.[47] What the Friend looks to avoid is future miscarriage in the course of composition, a shameful failure caused by a hastily begun and, so, faulty design. Geoffrey's image of carefully projected house building should serve as a "mirror" providing Thomas with the wisdom to escape "smert," annoyance and pain (D643–51). The Friend fears rashness and loss, in line with Cicero and Seneca, with the *Disticha Catonis*, with clerical writers on taciturnity, with Albertano da Brescia, and, not least of all, with the Hoccleve of the *Regiment*. His preventive medicine is to understand making poetry as an act of prudence, which should control the entire process:

For wel is he waar / or [before] he wryte or speke,
What is to do or leue / Who by prudence
Rule him shal, no thyge shal out from him breke
Hastily ne of rakil [rash] negligence. (D652–55)

While Thomas later accepts, in part, the Friend's counsel about a new poem, he immediately contests the "wise" cautionary course of withholding "My Complaint" from the public. Thus, he reverses the roles of counselor/tutor and pupil that the Friend initiated and that, Eleanor Johnson has argued, echo Lady Philosophy and the lamenting Boethius in the *Consolation of Philosophy*.[48] While the Friend claims that Thomas's illness is no longer in men's minds, Thomas knows what he has overheard, continued misjudgments of his state: "I woot what men han seid / and seyn of me" (D37). But he quickly reformulates why the complaint will not damage his honor, indeed what kind of voice he has assumed in the complaint. From the first lines of the complaint, it is clear that Thomas understands his infirmity as an act of God, the God who created a world given over to radical change. Yet, as the lord of "vertu," God is inherently a being not only of supreme operative power but also of the "benigne grace" that has restored Thomas's mental well-being (C52–54). Indeed, the very mutability of the world He has created allows the change from loss to recovery. In the "Dialogue," "Goddes strook [stroke]" becomes grounds for asserting that his illness should not lower his reputation in others' eyes, the lowering that he helplessly felt he could not contest earlier as former companions blamed him for the illness:

> Of Goddes strook / how so it peise [measure by weighing] or weye,
> Oghte no man thynke / repreef or shame;
> His chastisynge / hurtith no mannes name. (D54–56)

Because his illness was involuntary, Thomas argues, why should it affect how people regard his reputation? Had he chosen to be an extortioner, heretic, or coin clipper, it would be foolish of him not to keep silent about his crimes, even if he had amended: "And to reherce his gilt / which him accusith, / Honour seith nay / there he silence excusith [where he by means of silence pardons himself]" (D76–77). In contrast with the guilty and the sinful, Thomas has not voluntarily acted contrary to law, divine or human. So, why should he be as silent as the lawbreakers?

Aware of God's power and grace, Thomas is now in a position to reconceive what "My Complaint" might accomplish—indeed, what kind of writing he has been driven to compose in order to break his silence. Since God has afflicted him so publicly, Thomas claims, he is bound to acknowledge God's act of deliverance by his own public act of thanksgiving:

> Anothir thyng / ther meeueth [moves] me also:
> Syn þat [Since] my seeknesse / spred was so wyde
> Þat men kneew wel / how it stood with me tho [then],
> So wolde I now / vppon þat othir syde,
> Wist [known] were / how our lord Ihesu / which is gyde
> To al releef / and may alle hertes cure,
> Releeued hath / me synful creature. (D57–63)

As "My Complaint" discloses, Thomas's former friends have been so sure of their own perceptions that they have refused to register God's gracious act in restoring Thomas's wits: the "remedie / of þat / God of his grace hath me purueide" (C96–97). They have clung to what they observed earlier, denying God's power to heal fully and denying his grace to Thomas as a created, but frail, being ("synful creature"). For them and for Thomas, "My Complaint" can serve as "Open shrift" (D83). Robyn Malo has rightly called attention to Hoccleve's reenvisioning of penitential discourse throughout the *Series*, but she focuses on "open shrift" as Thomas's declaration of the truth about himself to others.[49] Yet "shrift" also means public acknowledgment of God's attributes, a vernacularizing of one key sense of *confessio* (*MED*, s.v. "shrift" [n.], 4). Public confession of faith in God's power, goodness, and attributes as manifested in His deeds is exactly what moral writers on silence urged believers to speak (or write). One of the three forms of *mala taciturnitas* is silence from ingratitude, writes Nicolas de Byard in his *distinctio* "Taciturnitas": silence when someone leaves unspoken praise of God and thanksgiving for benefits received (tacet a laude Dei et gratiarum actione per beneficiis acceptis). Every other creature recognizes a benefit given by the gracious Creator, but humans are more likely to thank each other than God, even if for a drink of water.[50] Late medieval English homilists were given to treating failures to give thanks for healing when they preached on Jesus's healing of a mute man, the lesson for the third Sunday of Lent (Luke 11:14–28). Their homilies often draw in Isaiah 43:21, as a priest does in declaring that Jesus healed the dumb man first of all so that he could praise God for his healing: "a man scholde ever ʒife [give] preysyng and lawde to God and þanke hym hyʒly of [greatly for] that he sendythe hym, as Ysaie seythe: *Populum istum formaui michi et laudem meam narrabit. Ysaie xliij*. Owre soveren sauiour Ihesu seythe be [by] his prophete: 'þese pepil I haue made after my lykenes and similitude, þat wythe theyre tongis scholde ʒife [give] me lawde and preysyng.'"[51] Another homilist, preaching on the same gospel lesson, quotes the same text from Isaiah to argue that praise also works to edify others.[52] Likewise, the recovered Thomas believes he is bound to break his silence in order to instruct others about God's power and goodness in a mutable world.[53] He resees his sickness and recovery as a "spectacle" of God's greatness (D93–96), a public marvel that is also a means of seeing (*MED*, s.v. "spectacle" [n.], 1 and 2). Recast as a confession of faith to those who have failed to discern God's grace in Thomas's life, "My Complaint" has communal and exemplary purpose even as it, as a complaint, makes Thomas's stabilized inner life known to those who had wronged him and could join him in restoring his social standing. In this, they would follow God, who has restored his sanity. Moreover, as David Lawton discerns, by writing in a voice both interior and public, Hoccleve hopes for a larger audience beyond his immediate coterie.[54]

Another dimension of "My Complaint" as a confession of faith emerges in its last segment, before the Friend enters. Unable to alter others' perceptions of himself, which they cling to even when his fellow Privy Seal clerks testify to his health, Thomas begins to read the lamentation of a man cast down by loss and grief. As Thomas appropriates the text to voice his own condition, the original is given in the margin in all the manuscripts: a Latin epitome of the *Synonyma* of Isidore of Seville, as J. A. Burrow has detected.[55] What David Watt posits about the *Series* as a whole is true of this final stage of "My Complaint": Thomas looks into many texts as "mirrors in order to learn what form his reform should take."[56] In response to the suffering man's complaint that his distress is unending, Reason urges him to endure it with patience. If the man would understand tribulation as a potential vehicle for purging him of sin, then he could replace impatient murmur, the characteristic sin of the afflicted, with a patient silence that refuses to "grucche and seye / 'Why susteene I this?'" (C365). Thomas embraces Reason's remedy of patient silent suffering as a means to reform the way he has conducted his life:

> For euere sythen [since] / set haue I the lesse
> By the peples / ymaginacioun,
> Talkynge this and þat / of my seeknesse,
> Which cam / of Goddes visitacioun.
> Mighte I han be fownde / in probacioun [when tested]
> Nat grucchyng / but han take it in souffrance [patient endurance],
> Holsum and wys / had be my gouernance.
> Farwel my sorwe / I caste it to the cok! [cast it away]
> With pacience / I hens foorth thynke unpyke [unpick]
> Of swich thoghtful disese and wo / the lok [lock],
> And lete hem out / þat han me maad to syke [sigh]. (C379–89)

Recasting his experience of disease as a vehicle for his spiritual welfare enables him finally to be free from oppressive thoughts and feelings, including fears for his future. Indeed, he hopes to regain the affection of his estranged comrades. Patient silence is no longer a self-protective shell amid the crowds but a carefully discerned choice as part of a new way of life directed to the transcendent and its transformative powers. For what Thomas has come to recognize as the sin that needs correction by God's chastising is nothing less than neglecting to acknowledge what transcends him. During his prosperity, he did not apprehend, honor, and seek to please God as the Creator of the mutable world, and, as a result, he did not grasp the limits of his control over the terms of his own life (C393–407).[57] Thus, Thomas's new understanding of patient silence as the stance of a reformed sinner crowns "My Complaint," obviating the need to express further the overwhelming sorrow that initiated it in the prologue. Even though the poem is not declared a confession of faith until the dialogue between Thomas and the Friend, it has already been transformed into a socially acceptable witness to God's power and benevolence. It conveys an exemplary decision to move beyond complaint as a declaration of grievance, to discover a remedy through reading and reflection, and to begin a new form of life.

From the melancholy autumnal prologue of "My Complaint" on, silence occupies important places in two poems in which generic conventions might seem to exclude it: a complaint, a form designed to voice grievance and petition others for a remedy, and a dialogue. Weighed down by the sorrows and fears of not only having lived through a period of mental illness but hearing others brand him as still, or about to be, in a state of disintegration, Thomas falls into silence, first of all, as a retreat from a convivial social world that makes clear it has no room for a disturbing person, even if he once was a companion. Silence becomes the self-protective strategy of a once mentally ill person with a morbid, but entirely understandable, sensitivity to the social misunderstanding, aversion, slights, and rejection that the mentally ill learn to expect. Why increase pain by attempting to make a healed self known against the stacked-up odds of social prejudice, others' defensive moves, and one's own emotional lability, grief, and self-distrust? Yet, however much it might seem necessary, self-protective silence born of fearful imaginings works in time against Thomas, as his former social world reads even silence with its own lens, fashioned during his "wylde infirmitee." Hiding away may prevent further social scrutiny and further injuries (though the mirror scene indicates how hostile scrutiny wounds even in isolation), but it inflames the pain of existing wounds. Yet this bottled-up sorrow itself prompts Thomas, as a well-read scribe, to read a religious and moral text that induces him to identify with a sorrowing man, then open himself up to the voice of another. Reason's voice replaces the judgmental, all-knowing voices of his former companions and overcomes the fear and sorrow their voices have elicited. Once freed from lamentation, grievance, and the weight of social scrutiny, Thomas can choose to live by a patience not dictated by avoiding further injuries but by the choice not to complain of his grievances to God. At the end of "My Complaint," Thomas is newly aware of the power of the transcendent to transform suffering into a new way of life, truer to human experience in a mutable world where healing and restoration may follow loss. Empowered by this, he can resist the prudential voice of the Friend, who counsels yet another retreat into cautionary silence dictated by the fear of others' imagined reactions and of further loss of reputation. Thomas has come to realize that he can break the conspiracy of social silence by choosing not only to escape its inflamed pains but also to make known to others his narrative of mental disintegration, sudden recovery, social ostracism, self-imposed silence, and discovery of a chastising but benevolent God whose power over all human lives in a mutable world makes Thomas's narrative exemplary. It may inform and comfort readers because they may very well encounter the same pattern in their own mutable lives. By breaking his silence with a complaint that records a remedy already achieved by himself, Thomas, the injured person, moves beyond the therapeutic writing that modern readers often stress to an ethical act of "communynge": he offers to God the healer and to others the writing he owes them. Thus, Thomas's transformed stance toward fearful, and even patient, silence marks his move from dwelling on the suffering caused by the oppressive social norms to discovering a way of living that benefits himself and others subject to the same mutable world and its Creator.

CHAPTER 6

WISE SILENCES IN THE LIFE OF LEARNING
Will and the Philosophers in *Piers Plowman*

Last among the nearly 250,000 words of the *Summa de vitiis* of Guillaume Peyraut are these of a wise man: "Ultimo ad commendationem silentii potest valere illud sapientis: 'Loquutum esse aliquando penituit, tacere vero numquam'" (Finally, the word of a wise man can be effective in commending silence: "To have spoken has grieved me sometimes; to keep silent, truly, never").[1] This *sententia*, the cap for Peyraut's chapter on silence and for his whole ninth tractate on sins of the tongue, presents taciturnity as a dimension of a pragmatic cautionary ethic that devolves from Roman popular morality and classical philosophy. Taciturnity, as the teaching of a wise man, is founded in his personal experience over time ("aliquando"). It grows out of contrasting types of conduct ("Loquutum esse" and "tacere") and the painful consequences of one ("penituit"). It is advanced as a calculated way of protecting oneself from a self-inflicted injury leading to regret, even sorrow. Few classical *sententiae* appear more frequently in clerical moral literature on silence. It is included, I have found, in fifteen moral texts of the late thirteenth to late fourteenth centuries (most compiled by Englishmen) lodged in English libraries.[2] Its uses, however, like its pervasiveness, have not been recognized by scholars of *Piers Plowman*, even though it, coupled with another Latin *sententia*, focuses and furthers Imaginatif's analysis of Will the Dreamer's failure to assess wisely when to speak and when to listen in silence and so achieve his purposes in learning. (Andrew Cole and Andrew Galloway argue that Imaginatif recasts the term "philosophus" so that it conveys anyone who loves wisdom and virtue, not an adept in pre-Christian or extra-Christian ideas.)[3] Will's impulsive speech squanders an opportunity to learn from a knowledgeable figure, Reason, and this loss moves him, under the guidance of a new instructor, Imaginatif, to understand the value of taciturnity. Thus, he moves in the opposite direction from Hoccleve's Thomas, who discovers the value of exemplary writing after fearful silences fail to address others' misperceptions and augment his own sorrow. The process of learning, as envisioned at the end of the third dream, is inherently a social one, governed by asymmetrical power relations, though between individuals, not, as in "My Complaint," between a group with inflexible mores and a vulnerable person. As so often in *Piers Plowman* (from Lady Holy Church on in passus 1), Will the seeker after a good life deals with an authority figure, in this case, two wise and knowledgeable figures, setting up relations akin to those between master and pupil in medieval schools.[4] The power to discover what the seeker desires rests in the formidable figure, who conveys only what they choose in the situation, although the seeker's understanding of his experience also matters greatly and the teacher has limits. These relations, enforced within the medieval schoolroom, were founded and promulgated, in part, by late antique and midmedieval sayings attributed to classical philosophers as purveyors of wisdom. To these we now turn.

Even more than the common distich "Nam nulli tacuisse nocet, nocet esse locutum," "Locutum esse" crystallizes the Roman popular strain in late medieval moral discourse on silence as set forth in this book's chapter 1. In medieval moral texts, this saying is tethered often to a specific *philosophus* who speaks in a social context. According to the *Alphabetum narrationum*, Arnold of Liège's widely disseminated collection of exempla,

> Xenocrates philosophus cum aliquando sederet cum quibusdam aliis obloquentibus et taceret, interrogatus cur solus non loqueretur, respondit: "Quia, inquit, dixisse me aliquando penituit et [siluisse] numquam."[5]

> When Xenocrates the philosopher was sitting once among some people who were speaking slander, he stayed silent. Asked why he

alone was not speaking, he replied: "Because," he said, "to have spoken has sometimes grieved me and to have kept silent, never."

In this anecdote, which originates with the *Facta et dicta memorabilia* of Valerius Maximus, what the philosopher practices and what he, an authoritative speaker of wisdom, commends is taciturnity as the inclination to silence: restraining the tongue and so keeping silent until a fit time when speech can benefit the speaker and/or others and does not inflict damage on either (as we saw in chapter 1).[6] In this situation, the practice of taciturnity keeps Xenocrates from engaging in speech that is damaging someone's reputation and (at least presumably) benefiting no one.

Xenocrates's initial silence and his *sententia* are recalled by John Lydgate in the encomium to poverty that halves his brief account of Troy in the *Fall of Princes* (ca. 1431–38). As a counterpoint to the glory, then the misfortunes, of Priam and Agamemnon, Lydgate appends to his source, Giovanni Boccaccio's *De casibus virorum illustrium* (ca. 1360), five stanzas on the Greek philosopher as poverty's disciple. (In Middle English, a philosopher could signify generally a wise man [*MED*, s.v. "philosophre"].) Because Zenocrates (in Lydgate's spelling) scorned superfluity of all kinds (in food, housing, and all fleshly lusts, as well as speech), he lived with equanimity amid prosperity and adversity, free from violent emotions and other kinds of turbulence that might disrupt the pursuit of learning wisdom. As a fitting climax to his praise of this way of life, Lydgate turns to Zenocrates's habits of speech, first recalling how his word was wholly trusted, even in courts of law, and then retailing the common anecdote:

He axed [asked] was among gret audience,
Whi he was soleyn off his daliaunce [taciturn]:
His answere was, that neuer for silence
Thoruh litil spekyng he felte no greuaunce.
Spech onavised causeth repentaunce;
And rakil [rash] tunges, for lak off refreynyng,
To many a man hath be ful gret hyndryng.[7]

The public situation ("gret audience") presents Zenocrates with the opportunity to display his commitment to avoiding superfluity so that silence emerges as a significant form of reasoned self-restraint, certainly a means of avoiding self-recrimination but also a means of maintaining integrity amid the pull of standard social behavior, reckless talk ("rakil," "onavised"), and indulgence in gossip or chat ("daliaunce"). Although Lydgate, like Arnold of Liège, sees both this initial silence and the pithy justification as acts of an exemplary wise man, keen to instruct the other speakers once challenged, he ties it to a seamlessly temperate life that has brought many "bexaumple" "to vertu fro vicious lyuyng."[8] Moreover, such taciturnity becomes the marked practice of a classical philosopher devoted to a life of learning. He has learned from his own experience and that of others; he has chosen one course over another on the basis of consequences; he has voiced that course in a wise saying that others can use to recall the value of carefully weighed silence.

The wisdom that Xenocrates exemplifies in clerical moral literature and in Lydgate resembles the Christianized prudence of Albertano da Brescia and Hoccleve. It looks to the future and to the likely consequences of actions being considered, so that the wise never suffer regret, let alone remorse, for what they have done. In the *Compendium morale de virtutibus*, Roger of Waltham begins his chapter on the wisdom (*sapientia*) that administrators should possess by recalling Cicero's words from the *Tusculanae disputationes*: "sapientis proprium est nichil quod penitere possit facere vel invitum" (It is characteristic of the wise man to do nothing he can regret or nothing against his will).[9] Later (in book 12 on tempering the mind), Roger develops a more comprehensive sense of wisdom. He quotes the urgent plea Seneca directs to himself as he expounds to his friend Lucilius the good that Stoics believe wisdom brings:

> Pocius id age ut michi viam monstres per quam ad ista perveniam. Dic quid vitare, quid appetere debeam, quibus animum labantem studiis firmem, quemadmodum que ad me ex transverso feriunt aguntque procul pellam, quomodo par esse tot malis possim, quomodo istas calamitates removeam que ad me irruperunt, quomodo illas ad quas ego irrupi. Doce quomodo feram erumpnam sine gemitu.[10]

> Rather act so that you may show me the way through which I should go to those ends. Tell me what I should shun, what I should desire, by which studies I might strengthen my failing mind, by what way I might push far away those things which strike at me sideways and

push me, how I could be equal to so many evils, how I might remove those calamities that have rushed in on me, how those into which I have rushed. Teach me how I might bear hardship without sighing.

Wisdom, again akin to prudence, directs humans toward what they ought to shun or desire. Unlike prudence, it focuses on how to remove calamities and, since it is always ferreting out causes, to do so in part by understanding when one is responsible for them and when they are inflicted by other forces. When difficulties are unavoidable, the wise learn to bear them with equanimity, not succumbing to vehement emotions, like grief or, as in this saying attributed to Publilius Syrus, fear: "Stulti timent fortunam, sapientes ferunt" (Fools fear fortune; the wise bear it).[11] In all these functions, *sapientia* operates like taste (*sapor*). As Robert Holcot explains this common analogy, based on etymology, "Denominatus est a sapore quia sicut gustus aptus est ad discernendum sapores ciborum, sic sapiens ad dinoscendum res et rerum causas" (The term was coined from taste because just as taste is suited to discern the flavors of foods, so the wise man to distinguish things and the causes of things).[12] Wisdom's work lies in discernment: discerning likely consequences, discerning how to bear any kind of fortune, and discerning how to remove calamities after discerning their causes.

According to medieval moral writers, learning wisdom is an intense and extended social process, depending on good relations between the wise man and the seeker—relations asymmetrical in status and power because of the teacher's greater wisdom and learning. For Robert Holcot, acquiring wisdom is an arduous process, requiring hard labor, just like digging gold out of the ground. Although only love (*amor*) has the power to initiate and sustain that process and although it requires a stable disposition, seekers must have the humility to realize in the first place that they are not wise and so must insistently ask for wisdom from others.[13] In medieval moral texts, silence is an essential part of this extended, demanding social process of learning wisdom, as it is of acquiring knowledge (*scientia*). So, silence—not merely taciturnity as an inclination to silence—was a discipline required by the famous teachers of antiquity. Hippocrates compelled his students to swear an oath to keep silent before he consented to teach them, according to Simon of Boraston and his slightly later contemporary Ranulph Higden, an anecdote transmitted by the influential *Collationes* of John Cassian, who uses it to illustrate his claim that silence suits the position of pupils ("convenit statui et conditioni discipulorum"). Servasanta da Faenza extends the discipline required by Hippocrates to self-restraint in other dimensions of life, like clothing and bearing, so that his pupils set aside superfluity and distraction of all kinds, just as Zenocrates did, according to Lydgate.[14] The philosopher Pythagoras was famous for demanding that his students observe silence for a set period (variously five and seven years). Hugues de Saint-Victor explains Pythagoras's practice in his introduction to exegetical and theological studies, the *Didascalicon*, an explanation included in Thomas of Ireland's *Manipulus florum*:

> Pictagorus hanc in studiis suis consuetudinem servasse legitur ut usque ad septennium iuxta numerum septem liberalium arcium nullus discipulorum suorum de hiis que ab ipso dicebantur rationem poscere auderet, sed fidem dare verbis magistri quousque omnia audivisset. Scolares vero nostri aut nolunt aut nesciunt modum congruum in discendo servare, et idcirco multos studentes, paucos sapientes invenimus.[15]

> We read that Pythagoras observed this custom in his schools: that no one of his students would dare to ask for reasoning about those things that were being spoken by him until a seven-year period was over, according to the number of the seven liberal arts, but was to place trust in the words of the master until he had heard all things. Truly, our scholars either do not wish to or do not know to observe the fit way in learning, and therefore we find many students, few wise ones.

The philosopher, the consummately wise man, insists on silence as a discipline that, over an extended period, fosters listening to and absorbing a whole body of teaching because the pupil trusts the master. Out of that attentive hearing grows wisdom. Otherwise, the entire process of teaching is futile, its students failing to acquire wisdom.

This silence required for learning that medieval moral texts attribute to classical philosophers is a far cry from the silence imposed by adepts in order to protect secret knowledge from the unwashed public. The Aristotle of the *Secreta secretorum* imposes silence on Alexander the Great about hidden knowledge of the natural world before he conveys it to him figuratively and only in part, silence so that the undeserving and unworthy ("immeritos et indignos") do not even glimpse the secrets. These heavenly secrets were revealed by an angel to Aristotle, and God has preelected Alexander alone (at least at this point) to receive them. John Lydgate's translation (*Secrees of Old Philisoffres*) defines the unworthy in terms of class: the commons "To whoom nat longith / to medle in no degree / Of konnynges [knowledge] / that shulde be kept secre."[16] Like Pythagoras, the Aristotle of the *Secreta* exacts silence as a condition of learning something of great value. Indeed, such a condition, as Karma Lochrie observes of the *Secreta*, both inflates the "intellectual capital" of hidden knowledge and makes the master indispensable.[17] However, Aristotle imposes silence in order to restrict even partial knowledge to an elite, defined, at least in part, by regal status, whereas the Pythagoras of moral texts does so in order to test commitment to the arduous, disciplined process of acquiring wisdom and to facilitate teaching it as an integral corpus.

Ancient philosophers, according to sayings woven into medieval moral writing, anchor their teaching about the value of silence in the body itself, more geared by nature and the Creator to listening than speaking. Xenocrates, reports Ps.-Caecilius Balbus, addressed a loquacious man in this way: "'Stulte,' inquit, 'audi melius: os unum a natura, aures duas accepimus'" ("Fool," he said, "listen better. We have received from nature one mouth, two ears").[18] The dictum itself, like so many from Roman popular morality that are recalled by clerical writers, derives wise conduct from observation of the natural world. It presents one course of action (talking excessively) as foolish, another (listening) as wise.[19] Given philosophers' advocacy of listening in silence during the process of learning, especially learning wisdom, it is not surprising that the capacity to observe silence is taken as a mark of a philosopher, of the wise man. The heading "Silencium signum est sapientie" (or a variant) introduces a *topos* in some clerical treatments of taciturnity, where it is sometimes attributed to Seneca.[20] On the flip side, fools are mocked for their loquacity. In the midst of a web of Jewish and classical authorities on the silence of the wise, Roger of Waltham records the biting rebuke "Si tacuisses, philosophus fuisses," a saying adapted from Boethius's *Consolation of Philosophy* that became proverbial in fourteenth-century England. Lady Philosophy recalls an exchange between a philosopher and someone who had assumed the title (*nomen*) "philosopher" in order to acquire glory. After insulting the pretender roundly, the philosopher adds that he would grant that he was a true philosopher if he were to bear patiently all his injurious words in silence. After a while, the pretender claims the title, but the philosopher responds with this: "'Intellexeram,' inquit, 'si tacuisses'" ("I should have realized that," he replied, "had you kept silent").[21] This saying is adapted by English writers to mock a person's pretensions to understand or know more than they do, pretensions shattered when they break silence. Experience teaches us daily, writes John Bromyard in the midcentury, that the wise speak less than others so that simply to speak little creates the impression that one is wise. A Paris student, he reports, was thought learned (*litteratus*) by his fellows because he was always silent, an illusion he broke by speaking up one day and so revealing he knew little or nothing. When a student who was present retails the incident to a fellow student, he claims cryptically that the speaker resolved a doubtful question. How can that be? asks the fellow. The doubtful question, the first replies, was whether or not he was learned, to which he adds mockingly, "Huic illud commune proverbium dici potuit: 'Si tacuisses, philosophus fuisses'" (For this situation that common proverb could be uttered: "If you had kept silent, you would have been a philosopher").[22] For Bromyard's student to label the saying a proverb is to mark it as grounded in wide experience and so add even more weight to the claim that the practice of taciturnity is part of wisdom.

Among the first words that Imaginatif speaks to Will the Dreamer in *Piers Plowman* are those of this taunting rebuke from Boethius. In his third dream, Will has been questing to learn what a good life entails. In this inward journey, he has encountered, interrogated, listened to, argued with, and parted ways with a series of figures representing faculties engaged in learning (Wit, Thought) and the sources of learning (Study, Scripture, Clergy). Finally, well along into an inner dream within the third dream, Will is granted by Kynde (nature and God as its creator) an encyclopedic vision of "Mydelerthe," a revelatory vision within the inner dream in which Reason governs all the animals, save humans, so that they live temperately, especially in their habits of copulation. Interrupting abruptly, Will passionately blames Reason (the foundational principles of the world as created by God) for humankind's reckless sexual abandon. Reason, in turn, rebukes Will for his speech, vanishing along with the Vision of Kynde itself and thus depriving Will of what he might disclose about the good life. In the midst of Will's wild grief, Imaginatif, the last interlocutor in the third dream, appears. The poet's personifications, as Katharine Breen has recently argued, are varied in type and experimented with in ways that stimulate thought and work to solve perplexing problems for the reader—and here for Will.[23] As a figure for the creative power that mediates between sense experience and cognition, Imaginatif does this, in part, by memory, recalling for Will authoritative, wise sayings from classical philosophers that might clarify his experience. To the "philosophus" dictum, Imaginatif adds from another text (he says "alibi") Xenocrates's rejoinder to the slanderers with which this chapter began:

> "Haddestow soffred [If you had endured]," he sayde, "slepyng tho [then] thow were,
> Thow sholdest haue yknowe þat Clergie can [knows], and conseyued mor þorw Resoun;
> For Resoun wolde haue rehersed þe riht as Clergie seide.
> Ac for thyn entermetynge [interrupting] her artow forsake:
> *Philosophus esses, si tacuisses. Et alibi: Locutum me aliquando penituit, tacuisse nunquam.*"[24]

Xenocrates's rejoinder is added in the C text of the poem, its final version (probably late 1380s to 1390), which, in addition to being "the poet's final word" (Kathryn Kerby-Fulton), develops the value of taciturnity and extended silence far more extensively, explicitly, and insistently than the B version does.[25] For these reasons, it is the text used throughout this chapter, save where the earlier B version serves as a contrast. In it, Imaginatif's augmented biting characterization of Will as a would-be philosopher / wise man speaks to Will's contentious rebuke of Reason and its bitter consequences: Will's losses and the grief they arouse in him. As a seeker, Will has failed to learn from Reason what he has desired to know during the whole of his third dream because he has failed to practice the silence or, at least, taciturnity that the philosopher practices and commends: restraining the tongue until speech can benefit, not harm, him as a speaker—the mode of moderation most suited to him as learner. What Imaginatif offers Will are the benefits of wisdom, as understood in clerical culture rooted in Jewish and Roman texts. He analyzes what has caused Will's losses, disclosing their roots in certain mental, emotional, and moral habits; then he offers Will the means and the power to react differently in the encounters with others from whom he might learn. The wise man's silence becomes the way forward for

Will, the way he can work toward his aims in this pivotal stage in his life of learning. For how to learn is, as Emily Steiner has underscored, a central concern of this third vision.[26] That Latin *sententiae* crystallize Imaginatif's pivotal rebuke and advice is not surprising. Latin, as Lawrence Warner demonstrates, was how medieval readers, sharing the poet's biblical, legal, and aphoristic knowledge, "were most likely to engage with *Piers Plowman*."[27]

As a result of Imaginatif's extended analysis (C.13.222–41), Will comes to embrace taciturnity, refraining from speaking for almost all of the poem's next passus (C.14). This newfound taciturnity and its causes have tended to escape modern readers, in part, of course, because silence, of its very nature, can be hard to notice.[28] Perhaps more importantly, the many impassioned and extended debates earlier in *Piers Plowman* dispose us to read the poem, especially the third dream, in terms of its "discursive hunger."[29] However, Imaginatif's two Latin dicta, along with others in this episode, with metaphor, and with allusion, insistently point to the moral discourse on silence and taciturnity that informs the whole episode, the end of the expansive third dream: Will's anguished response to the vision of Kynde and Reason's countering rebuke, as well as Imaginatif's speeches and Will's eventual silence. This discourse, as we have seen in Albertano da Brescia's treatises and in clerical texts, understands taciturnity and extended silences as a practice that must be learned by encountering exempla and authoritative sayings, as well as by reflecting on social experience. It presents virtuous taciturnity as a resource that benefits listeners and speakers. To read this episode in light of this shaping discourse is to understand not only why Imaginatif corrects Will as he does but why Will sees the silence of the wise as a practice essential to learning. Granted, this episode exemplifies to the nth degree how verbal combat shapes the poem's episodes, as Anne Middleton has established firmly. Yet the episode does not end in "discord or irresolution," as such episodes usually do, but in cooperative learning, made possible by Will's silence.[30] While catechetical language and its users in the poem may often fail to show Will how to change, as Ralph Hanna maintains, here Will is given both the wherewithal and the affective power to change his habits of speech as he grasps why silence might matter to him.[31]

The glorious encyclopedic vision of "Mydelerthe" that Kynde offers Will presents animals living temperately, especially in their sexual rhythms. Following the directives of Reason, in food and drink as well as in sex, animal after animal ceases to copulate once the female has conceived (C.13.143–50).

That Reason governs all the habits of animals in this way should awaken in Will love for their, and his, Creator, according to the traditional Christian exemplarism recently described by Rebecca Davis.[32] Should Will respond this way, the "myrour of Mydelerthe" would offer not just knowledge of nature and the embodied self but the affective power to strive to emulate the moderate conduct of animals, a power Will needs since his search for doing well has been disrupted for forty years by a life of overindulgence in Fortune's world. Yet the natural order and temperance of animals also point to intemperance in all dimensions of human appetitive life:

> Ther ne was no kyne kynde [species] that conseyued hadde
> That ne lees [did not lose] the lykynge of lost [lust] of flesch, as hit were,
> Saue man and his make [mate]—and þerof me wondrede;
> For out of resoun they ryde and rechelesliche [recklessly] token on,
> As in derne [dark] dedes, bothe drynkyng and elles. (C.13.151–55)

These lines, new in the C text and marked by harsh alliteration at the end, present human conduct as so driven by appetites that it becomes vehement, disorderly, excessive, and beyond reason and social approval ("derne"). This radical human difference causes a sudden shift in Will's "moed"—emotion but also disposition of will and frame of mind—away from his initial wonder at the harmonious, productive conduct of animals:

> Ac þat moste meuede me and my moed chaungede
> Was þat Y seyh [saw] Resoun sewen [accompany] alle bestes
> Saue man and mankynde; mony tymes me thouhte
> Resoun reulede hem nat, noþer ryche ne pore. (C.13.179–82)

Varied and detailed though the images of all nonhuman creatures are in the mirror, their example and Reason's role in ensuring their orderly conduct comes to matter to Will only in pointing up the human exception to Reason's rule. Will's aversion to reading natural variety and order in traditional Christian exemplarist terms forms part of the pattern of failure from frustrated desire that Nicolette Zeeman traces so brilliantly in passūs 8–12 in B (10–14 in C), as Will increasingly becomes identified more with *affectus*, the will as the power of desire or appetite, closely linked to the passions, than with *voluntas*, the rational will engaged in moral choice and moral action as it directs, seeks knowledge, intends, chooses.³³

In considering Will's response to Kynde's "myrour of Mydelerthe," neither Zeeman nor Davis reckons with how the C text enlarges and complicates Will's rebuke of Reason (only two lines in B but ten in C), which firmly fixes the culpability for human reckless conduct on Reason and extends that conduct beyond the bodily to the verbal:

> Thenne Y aresonede Resoun, and ryht til hym Y sayde:
> "Y haue wonder in my wit, so wys as thow art holden,
> Wherefore and why, as wyde as thow regnest,
> That thow ne reuledest rather renkes [humans] then other bestes?
> Y se non so ofte sorfeten [overindulge], sothly, so [as] mankynde;
> In mete out of mesure and mony tymes in drynke,
> In wommen, in wedes [clothing], and in wordes bothe,
> They ouerdoen hit day and nyhte and so doth nat oþer.
> Bestes reule hem al by resoun, ac renkes ful fewe.
> And þerfore merueileth me—for man is moste yliche [like] the, of
>   wit and of werkes,
> Why he ne loueth thy lore and leueth as þou techest?" (C.13.183–93)

Immediately, the poet sets up a sharp contrast between Will as an interpreter and Reason as the governor of nature. Will's confidence in his own astuteness, powers of reason, and wise judgment ("wit") creates, for him, his authority as speaker. So does his belittlement of Reason as an opponent whose fabled wisdom is merely the product of vulgar opinion ("so wys as thow are holden"). Will's rude and aggressive lowering of Reason firmly sets them in opposition, as, Zeeman has recently argued, insulting language does throughout *Piers*, sharpening the difference between the passionate, desiring protester and the aloof sustainer of norms.³⁴ This arrogance and belittlement recalls the monologue of Recklessness (C.12.90–13.128), which preceded and precipitated the "myrour of Mydelerthe." When Recklessness terminates his long-running contentious exchange over salvation with Clergy (in C.11–13), both the clergy and Christian learning rooted in revealed texts, Kynde presents the vision to Recklessness, as well as to Will, in order to aid Clergy by giving Recklessness visionary knowledge of the natural world. At the monologue's close, the poet's voice sharply marks Recklessness's speech with "in a rage aresende" (C.13.129), an alliterated "ironic oxymoron" that distances the reader from it.[35] It rises rashly from intense, somewhat hostile emotion (the only use of "rage" in the poem). The verb "aresonede," which carries a sense of vehement berating, even of calling to account and arraigning (as a sinner), further characterizes his speech as contentious fault-finding with only a show of reason (*MED*, s.v. "aresounen" [v.], 2a and b). Now the poet uses the verb a second time to introduce Will's berating of Reason, linking him firmly to Recklessness. In the second and third lines, Will, carrying alliteration from line to line ("regnest," "reuledest"), hammers home what he sees as Reason's responsibility for human reckless conduct. Reason is cast as a ruler whose power seems so great and whose scope seems so extensive that the human anomaly amid temperate animal life seems an utter failure of Reason's design—a far cry from what Will actually observed in the vision, where Reason simply accompanies all beasts: "Resoun Y sey sothly sewe alle bestes" (C.13.143).[36] Will erases all human responsibility for immoderate living, fixing it firmly in the powers and principles that shape the natural world.[37] He fails to turn inward, reflecting on his own bodily indulgences, as he might have good reason to do, given his forty years of riotous living in Fortune's world. Moreover, the center of Will's rebuke (wholly new in the C text) extends humans' "out of mesure" conduct, specifying excessive food, drink, clothing, and words, as well as sexual behavior. Will's emphatic climax to the catalogue, "in wordes bothe," conveys his understanding that passion-driven speech may become excessive, just as eating and dressing can, while it underscores ironically his own complicity in reckless speech as a form of "surfeiting." Will takes on the characteristics of Recklessness's diatribes: he is driven by intense emotion and so speaks rashly; he trashes the authority and wisdom of a supposed opponent of greater stature; he amplifies; he fixes the blame for what troubles him on others.

While Reason's reply shifts from the anomaly of human reckless conduct to divine forbearance with it, it also introduces taciturnity as the means by which Will can control his own immediate mode of recklessness. Taciturnity first involves avoiding unnecessary contentious speech:

And Resoun aresounede me, and sayde, "Reche þe neuere [Do not
  ever concern yourself]
Why Y soffre [put up with] or nat soffre—certes [truly]," he sayde,
"Vch a segge [each man] for hymsulue, Salamon vs techeth:

De re que te non molestat, noli certare." (C.13.194–97)

In this opening sentence, Reason's reference to Solomon and the *sententia* from Sirach (11:9) foreground Jewish wisdom, hard won by experience intently examined by the *sapiens*, as the antidote to Will's tendency to rebuke others impulsively and vehemently. In Sirach, human beings need—Will needs here—to turn attention to their own conduct, rather than that of others: "Do not contend in a matter that does not concern you."[38] A key *sententia* in moral discourse on contentious speech, it caps Peyraut's chapter on *contentio* as a sin of the tongue, offering a terse practical remedy to initiating or butting foolishly into quarrelsome exchanges, just as it does in the *Ars loquendi et tacendi* of Albertano da Brescia, where it authorizes the first point of the first chapter.[39] The Latin *sententiae* in *Piers Plowman*, as John Alford noticed, serve to pull into the poem from the original texts material immediately surrounding the sayings themselves.[40] The verse preceding Sirach 11:9 enjoins the wise to listen rather than speak first; the verse before that, to shun blaming harshly before inquiring into a matter; all three occur amid injunctions to speak with humility and self-restraint.[41] Why Reason puts up with humans behaving recklessly while ordering the lives of nonrational animals is something, Reason contends, that Will cannot know, and so that should not be subject to disputatious, let alone reproving, speech. To counteract the impulse for it, John of Mirfield, like other moral writers, advises adopting taciturnity: "Precipue, igitur, secundum consilium Anastastii episcopi, 'Linguam suam custodia taciturnitatis obsepiat, ne in litigium contenciosa fervescat'" (Especially, therefore, according to the advice of Athanasius the bishop, "The guard of taciturnity should hedge in one's tongue lest it, contentious as it is, burn hot in dispute").[42]

Reason is the suitable figure to commend discerning judgment of words before they are uttered and to do so to Will. Throughout moral discourse on speech, as chapter 1 sets it forth, reason is presented as a "pedagogus" that should guarantee that speech conveys considered thought. That is its God-given function.[43] As the *Book for a Simple and Devout Woman* (first half of the fifteenth century) reasons, "For þe tonge is messanger of reson, as Sent Austyn seiþe, forþi þe tonge oweþ [ought] so to be ladde wiþ skile [reason], þat hit ne smyte into no worde wiþowte forlokynge and skile." For verbal sin rises when someone "ne recceþ neuer what he speke"—that is, from the recklessness, the neglect of attentive, reasoned assessment, that drives Will's speech, as it does that of Recklessness.[44] Moreover, the widely disseminated *Speculum vitae*, on which Ralph Hanna has demonstrated that the poet drew, sees Reason's work of discerning what to speak as part of its role in enabling humans to achieve temperance in all of life and so to adhere to the example of all other creatures (the example the "myrour of Mydelerthe" provides Will and Recklessness).[45] In the *Speculum*'s closing section on Wisdom, "Sobrenes" or "Temperancia" may be achieved in speech, as in food and drink, by, as Jewish wisdom literature advocates, observing "right Mesure," calculating correctly what is the virtuous mean in any matter.[46] In speech, this "right Mesure" is achieved, according to the section "Mesure in Wordes and Speche," when the wise man "with al his myght" weighs words "In þe balaunce of Resoun and Skille [sense of what is fitting] / And of Discrescioun, and noght of Wille." This painstaking process not only prevents verbosity but edits out any words that might become the "cause of mykill [much] ille, / Of motes, of stryfs" (legal wrangling and verbal conflict), words that have adverse consequences for the speaker and others.[47] Yet "mesure," central to moral life in *Piers Plowman* since Lady Holy Church commends it to Will in the first passus (C.1.35), is what Will angrily accuses Reason of failing to enable humans to achieve.

Reason may bid Will to practice the wise discipline of taciturnity, checking the impulse to loquacity and contentious fault-finding, but what can enable him to do so? Before Reason closes by enjoining verbal restraint, he lays the ground for it in God's very "soffrance" (patience, forbearance) for all that is amiss in human conduct, enacted "in ensaumple þat we sholde soffren alle" (C.13.200). Throughout Guillaume Peyraut's treatise on the sins of the tongue, he recommends patient endurance of what is troubling or painful as a way to avoid contentious or grumbling speech.[48] As Reason's French proverb emphasizes with its internal rhyme and repeated words, avoiding evil, especially angry, speech goes hand in hand with forbearance: "*Bele vertue est suffrance; mal dire est petite vengeance. / Ben dire e ben suffrer fait lui suffrable a bien venir*" (C.13.204–5) (Derek Pearsall's translation: "Patience is a fair virtue, evil speaking is a petty vengeance; / Gentle speech and forbearance bring the patient man to a good end").[49] Restraint guarantees the good outcomes that the wise seek. From all of Reason's sources of authority—Jewish wisdom conveyed in Latin as well as popular morality in French and God's example of "soffrance" in English—he draws his conclusion: "'Forthy' [For that reason], quod [said] Resoun, 'Y rede [advise] thow reule thy tonge euere, / And ar [before] thow lacke [find fault with] eny lyfe, loke ho [who] is to preyse" (C.13.206–7). Restraint is rooted in the ethical self-reflexivity, the rigorous examining of one's own conduct ("loke ho is to preyse") in the lens of wise authorities, that Will has failed to practice in his reckless rebuke of Reason. In humans, patient forbearance with others only becomes possible when one recognizes, as one of the limitations of life in the natural order, the inevitability of "lac," of sin and, as Zeeman has argued, of the loss and suffering that sin brings.⁵⁰ As Reason explains, humans cannot create themselves differently than they are, however much they might long to be "lacles" (C.13.208–13). As in Roman popular morality and Jewish wisdom literature, to push against such a natural condition is pointless ("For is no creature vnder Crist þat can hymsulue make" [C.13.209]). This rudimentary wisdom is underscored, at Reason's climax, by the closing schoolboy's *sententia* from the *Disticha Catonis*: "*Nemo sine crimine viuit!*" (No one lives without sin [C.13.213]).⁵¹ For Will to reflect on his own failures at living as he longs to and to accept the limitations of human life would enable him to forbear with others, following the example of the Creator. Thus, at the very end of Will's inner vision, Reason instructs him in how to practice moderation in the uniquely human gift of speech, just as he directs the animals of "Mydelerthe" in moderate conduct, the vision that Will failed to read reflexively. In doing so, Reason speaks in the forms of distilled Jewish, classical, and folk or experiential wisdom, forms notably absent from Will's rebuke: *sententia*, distich, proverb, and example.

For all of Reason's arguments from instructional texts in multiple ethical traditions, his pedagogue's roadmap for Will is incomplete, limited by his stern reasoning and admonitions, so at odds with Will's passionate response to what he observes. What can move Will to desire, then undertake, the arduous work of ethical reflection that makes wise taciturnity possible? After the grim distich about the inevitability of sin and failure, Reason vanishes abruptly. With him vanishes Will's inner dream, with its promise of disclosing Dowel in a fuller and more immediate way than the third dream itself. With it, Will has also lost the vision of Kynde, with the opportunity it offers him to feel the wonder and love for the Creator that might move him to follow the example of the animals' moderate behavior. Moreover, Will's failure to be a self-critical interpreter of the natural world he inhabits drives home his need to learn from wise and knowledgeable interlocutors, to experience learning anew as a social enterprise.

In one of the poem's more "surprising arrivals," an unidentified figure, later revealed to be Imaginatif (the narrator's synthesizing imaginative power), shifts the ground of learning away from verbal restraint rooted in "soffrance" and a sense of human limits.[52] As his use of the philosopher's dictum "*Locutum me / aliquando penituit, tacuisse nunquam*" suggests, although Imaginatif, like Reason, turns to taciturnity guided by a classical and Jewish wisdom, he will use it differently: to discern further the causes of Will's emotionally immediate loss and sorrow, to help him bear both, and to teach him how to remove both in his future of learning. As the creative power that works with sense experience and cognition, operating in part by memory, Imaginatif weds Will's experience of loss and sorrow to Latin dicta from the wise, to biblical exemplum, and to aversive metaphor.[53] Imaginatif's fresh use of the exemplary and the figurative, absent from Reason's bare-bones instruction (save for the example of God), has the potential to mesh more readily with Will's experience because medieval epistemology, as Zeeman has noted, asserts that figures in speech or text pass directly to the inner senses to be processed, just as sensory experiences do.[54] This full rhetorical arsenal, characteristic of moral discourse on taciturnity as a remedy for destructive acts of speech, works to awaken aversion to unconsidered speech while it presents taciturnity as a practical moral discipline of the wise that will further the learning Will seeks. As such, it offers a remedy for the quicksilver contemptuous and disputative speech that he shares with Recklessness, the product of unexamined emotions, distrusted in both Stoic-inflected and Jewish wisdom. Unlike Reason's more theological discourse and his rebarbative rebuke, which only elicits Will's shame and grief for losing his revelatory dream (C.13.215–18), Imaginatif's more comprehensive and forceful rhetoric has the power to appeal to those emotions in Will that will enable him to embrace that remedy.[55] His unexpected appearance in itself serves, as Zeeman has explored in other disruptive moments in *Piers*, to sharpen his difference from Reason and to suggest new workings of the mind, new forms of insight.[56]

Imaginatif first develops the causes of Will's overwhelming sorrow along the lines of moral discourse on taciturnity:

"Haddestow soffred," he sayde, "slepyng tho thow were,
Thow sholdest haue yknowe þat Clergie can, and conseyued mor
 throw Resoun;

For Resoun wolde haue rehersed þe riht as Clergie seide.
Ac for thyn entermetynge her artow forsake." (C.13.222–25)

Imaginatif's assessment that Will's quick and passion-driven intervention in the scene has caused his loss reflects Jewish wisdom, which insisted that responding immediately (as Will could have) results in confusion: "Qui prius respondet quam audiat stultum se esse demonstrat et confusione dignum" (He who answers before he listens shows himself a fool and worthy of confusion) (Prov 18:13). The *Paradisus animae* (Paradise of the soul), a treatise on the virtues from the first quarter of the fourteenth century or earlier, uses this *sententia* to reprove those who speak impudently, recklessly, and clamorously ("proterve et clamorose loqui") rather than asking questions of others or listening to them. Sometimes they even speak as if they knew what was in the thoughts of another, as Will has done.[57] Such excessive speech, Guillaume Peyraut claims, injures and offends others, whereas silence removes angry quarrels and, by nourishing "iusticia," orderly and harmonious social relations, fosters amicable exchanges.[58] Recall that the *Speculum vitae* counseled that observing "right Mesure" in words prevents verbal wrangling ("motes" and "stryfs") and, as that faithful translation of the *Somme le roi*, *The Book of Vices and Virtues*, adds, gives others "no þing to undertake [blame, chide] ne [nor] to reproue hem [speakers] wiþ."[59] Forbearing to speak ("Haddestow soffred") would have prevented the rebuke that Will suffers, just as it would have prevented Reason from breaking off contact with Will.

It is at this point that Imaginatif voices, one after the other, the two classical *sententiae* that feature regularly in medieval discourse on silence from the mid-thirteenth century on. The first, "*Philosophus esses, si tacuisses*" (C.13.225a), is used, we have seen earlier in this chapter, to confirm that speaking readily what one does not securely know betrays pretension and a lack of concerted wisdom.[60] A fascinating, nearly contemporaneous use of the saying may reflect the influence of Imaginatif's somewhat-mocking use here. The sustained Latin lyric, "Heu! quanta desolatio Angliae praestatur" (Alas! How great the desolation of England is now), a satire of Wycliffite opponents at Oxford in 1382, concludes with twenty-two stanzas mocking those who defended the poverty of the mendicant orders. After rehearsing the torturous and deceptive reasoning of one of them, Peter Stokes, a stanza concludes with a tart couplet: "With an O and an I, si tunc tacuisses / Tu nunc stulto similis philosophus fuisses."[61] In both texts, while, as in Bromyard's

Paris anecdote and in Boethius's *Consolatio*, the saying exposes the folly of someone who pretends to be wise, it also subverts fruitless and deceptive reasoning (more heavy-handedly in the lyric with its "nunc stulto similis" [like a fool now]). Moreover, in context in *Piers*, it works, as a past conditional statement ("if you had kept silent, you would have"), pointing to the sources of wisdom that Will has forfeited: a more fully revelatory experience of the vision of "Mydelerthe," Reason's conversation, Clergy's knowledge, and their corporate understanding of the natural order and its moral significance. "*Locutum me / aliquando penituit, tacuisse nunquam*" (C.13.225a–b), added in the late 1380s revision of the poem, does more than commend taciturnity again through another *sententia* from the wise men of antiquity. As a product of what Ralph Hanna calls "the poet's fundamentally commentative imagination," which still ruminates on texts even as the poet revises the poem, the newly added *sententia* stresses the deep regret that precipitous speech can cause—regret, in Will's case, for loss of vision with its opportunity for fuller and more immediate knowledge.[62] It invites Will to grasp that a wise man would have avoided the emotional consequences of precipitous speech. As a second dictum remembered by the poet, it glosses the first by adding what is involved in the wisdom that Will lacks. The wise assess, as part of a classical ethic of caution, the consequences of different ways of responding in a situation, and thus they avoid harming themselves by precipitous speech.

Imaginatif takes one step further in his analysis of Will's speech. He identifies it also as temerarious theological disputation through the biblical exemplum of Adam's speech to God:

> Adam, þe whiles he spak nat, hadde paradys at wille;
> Ac [But] when he mamelede [babbled] aboute mete and musede
>   for to knowe
> The wisdom and the wit of God, he was pot out of blisse.
> Rihte so ferde Resoun by [Reason behaved toward] the for thy
>   rude speche,
> And for thow woldest wyte [know] why of [the reason for] Resones
>   preuete [secrets].
> For pruyde and presompcioun of thy parfit lyuynge
> Resoun refusede the and wolde nat reste with the,
> Ne Clergie of his connynge kepeth þe nat shewe [did not wish to
>   instruct you]. (C.13.226–33)

A. V. C. Schmidt finds the biblical exemplum "rather ill-suited" because "Adam's sin was not to speak (about the fruit) but to *listen* to what Eve said."[63] However, Adam "mamelede aboute mete" in his only words in Genesis 3: "Mulier quam dedisti mihi sociam dedit mihi de ligno et comedi" (The woman whom you gave me as a companion gave me from the tree and I ate; Gen 3:12). In moral discourse on deviant speech, Adam's speech is the original excuse for sin, itself a sin of the tongue. For Thomas of Chobham, subdean of Salisbury in the early thirteenth century, this proud refusal to accept culpability becomes the reason why God ejects Adam from paradise—not listening to Eve, not consenting to eat the fruit, not eating, not violating God's commandment (for Thomas, all acts that bring other punishments).[64] Moreover, Adam's words call into question "the wisdom and wit" of God in creating Eve as Adam's companion and helper. Adam thinks ill of God, complains about His creation, and presses Him for His reasons ("musede": *MED*, s.v. "muse'" [v.], 2, 3, 7). In these ways, his speech is akin to Will's "rude" speech complaining about Reason's failure to govern, seeking Reason's reasons, questioning Reason's wisdom, and, powering all that, evading his own culpability. Beneath Will's "out of mesure" rebuke of Reason, his excess in speech, lies excess in intellectual appetite. Like Adam's uncontrolled babbling, Will's springs from a willful striving to know what is beyond what God allows humans to know: the reason for human failures and human limitations, especially in the form of "out of mesure" acts. The first degree of "Mesure" in the *Speculum vitae*, the mode of self-control that makes "Mesure in Wordes" (the third degree) possible, lies in understanding the truth of things "Withouten any musyng of Wytte [intellect]." "Musyng," in both the *Speculum* and Imaginatif's speech (Reason's, too), becomes excessive when it is directed to knowledge that is beyond human powers to grasp: "Oboun [Above] mans skille [reason] and vndirstandynge."[65] Like Adam seeking to grasp "The wisdom and the wit of God," Will has sought to "wyte why of Resones preuete."

Will's form of ungoverned disputation with Reason differs from the unlearned frivolous and blasphemous theological questioning condemned by Study as a false mode of learning earlier in the third dream (C.11.35–77). Will's questioning arises from fundamental anguish: Why do the natural order and its Creator allow humans to act recklessly and excessively? However, he is akin to Study's disputers in his rash, proud, and presumptuous speech ("For pryude and presompcioun of thy parfit lyuynge"). Pride is the passion that drives humans to seek to search into divine matters beyond their powers, according to Pierre le Chantre in his influential *Verbum abbreviatum*, shaped by his concern with the proper mode of theological disputation in the Paris schools of the late twelfth century. Such excessive inquiry, issuing in "temerarius" disputation ("rash," "unconsidered," and "unadvised" but also "arrogant" and "spoken out of turn or above one's position"), is for Pierre a form of folly.[66] This line also recalls Will's chosen companion, Pruyde of Parfit Lyuynge, when Fortune fetches Will and takes him to the "lond of longyng" (C.11.168–77) early in the inner dream. Alluding to Will's dissolute life here further subverts his moral and intellectual stature as a proud arraigner and questioner of Reason. Instead of acknowledging his own sexual recklessness, he has offloaded responsibility for all human sexual intemperance onto Reason, much as Adam did in casting the responsibility for his acts onto God—and Will has done so because of pride in his way of life and his intellect. Such arrogant and temerarious speech blocks the way in which moral writers maintain that wisdom can be learned: by humbly recognizing what one does not know and then inquiring of others. Thus, to reread Will's unwise speech in terms of Adam's is to add to the classical fix on adverse emotional and cognitive consequences the Jewish and Christian fix on the genesis of speech in pride and in the intellectual appetite, a dimension of the will. The common ground lies in the sense of human limitations found in both traditions: the destructive power of turbulent emotions, the limits of human powers, and the folly of kicking against the way things are constituted.

Throughout Imaginatif's speech, he stresses the harsh consequences of Will's rash rebuke of Reason. When he compares Will's loss of Reason's presence, and therefore Clergy's knowledge, to Adam's loss of paradise ("blisse"), he is not indulging in an extravagant analogy since Will has just acknowledged to himself that the inner dream was the means of "grace / To wyte what Dowel is" (C.13.217–18). The metaphor that Imaginatif then develops, "in the strongest reproach ever used towards the Dreamer by any of his interlocutors," recalls Will's own complaint about humankind's excessive drinking ("In mete out of mesure and mony tymes in drynke").[67]

> For lat a dronkene daffe [fool] in a dykke [ditch] falle,
> Lat hym lygge [lie], lok nat on hym til hym luste [he desires] to ryse.
> For thogh Resoun rebuke hym thenne, recheth he neuere [he never cares];

> Of Clergie ne [nor] of Kynde Wyt [natural reason] counteth he
>   nat a rusche;
> To blame hym or to bete hym thenne, Y [I] halde hit but synne.
> Ac when Nede nymeth [picks] hym vp, anoen he is aschamed,
> And thenne woet [realizes] he wherfore and why he is to blame.
>   (C.13.235–41)

The fall of a person into a ditch because of uncontrolled actions is a staple of discourse on taciturnity and silence, where it drives home, in a metaphor from quotidian life, the protective power of silence as a wise practice that prevents the ruinous consequences of precipitous speech. "Silencium servare est foveam obturare in quam multi cadunt ac ruunt perniciose" (To observe silence is to block the way to the ditch into which many fall and tumble down ruinously).[68] However, moral writers use the metaphor to move others to embrace silence as the means to avoid such a ruinous fall; they play on a sense of danger. By contrast, Imaginatif crafts the metaphor so that shame becomes the aversive emotion that, together with Will's potent grief for loss, works change, making Will aware of what has caused his error and then leading him to acknowledge it: "Why ʒe worden [speak] to me thus was for Y aresonede Resoun" (C.13.245).

While this shame, as readers have stressed, has the power to affect Will and move him to self-reflexivity, it grows out of Imaginatif's advocacy of cautious taciturnity, cast differently by Imaginatif than by Reason, but cast by both in terms of Roman and Jewish wisdom, with its keen sense of human limitations and the givenness of the world.[69] What does this reiterated advocacy of taciturnity actually do for Will as a speaker associated with Recklessness and a speaker engaged in the social process of learning? After all, Will cannot regain what he has lost. Gone is the Vision of Kynde with its potential to transform Will's affections, thinking, and conduct. Gone are most of his recent interlocutors: not just Reason but Scripture and Recklessness before him. However, Imaginatif remains with Will, and although Will has failed repeatedly, in Zeeman's reading of the third vision, "to respond in desire and actions to the teaching received," he does so in this, his last opportunity in the dream.[70] In fact, passus 13 ends with Will silently reverencing Imaginatif, saluting him with the respect expected of inquirers—a reaction far from his recent response of berating a teacher of great knowledge and status—and then choosing to follow him so he does not lose the company of this new instructor.

To follow Imaginatif entails for Will as a learner more than adopting taciturnity as a pragmatic way to prevent loss and painful regret, a remedial way that involves reflecting on speech acts, completed and potential, in terms of wise sayings and exempla. Taciturnity also opens him to the attentive, extended, and receptive listening that may enable him to learn what he eagerly desires, the listening championed by the philosophers' tradition of learning, transmitted by late antique and medieval materials. From now on in this dream, Will speaks only to further Imaginatif's discourse. Before Imaginatif's long integrative discourse on the value of learning from books and from nature, Imaginatif, as "the power of the soul that discerns significant relationships in the succession of events," looks back throughout Will's experience in the third dream to synthesize an understanding that to do well is, in no small part, not to misspeak:[71]

> Y haue folewed the, in fayth, mo then fourty wynter,
> And wissed [taught] the fol ofte what Dowel was to mene,
> And conseyled the for Cristes sake no creature to bygile,
> Noþer to lye ne [nor] to lacke, ne lere [teach] þat is defended [forbidden],
> Ne to spill [waste] no speche, as for to speke an ydel,
> Ne no tyme to tyne [waste] ne trewe thyng tene [anger]. (C.14.3–8).

Imaginatif's catalogue reads largely as an analytic summary of Will's speech at the end of the third dream: rebuking, pushing to acquire knowledge beyond his reach, misleading, wasting speech, angering interlocuters. Moreover, "spill no speche" recalls, as Schmidt notes, an earlier characterization of Dowel by Wit [Intellect]: "Ne spille speche ne tyme" (C.10.187). This echo further ties Imaginatif's long-term counsel about speech to Will's search for Dowel, to what Will must do to do well.[72] In these ways, the new passus marks Will's verbal excesses as speech left behind. Then Will's habits of speech change radically. In the entire passus, he speaks only one line to answer Imaginatif's rhetorical question (C.14.109) and three lines (late in Imaginatif's monologue) to call attention to a seeming contradiction in his disquisition on the salvation of non-Christians (C.14.199–201). Because of Will's newly acquired taciturnity, the third dream ends with Imaginatif instructing him on how learning derived from revelation (Clergy) relates to knowledge of nature (Kynde) when humans attempt to understand salvation—what Will's precipitous rebuke of Reason prevented him from learning after he had witnessed Kynde's vision of "Mydelerthe." Like the philosophers who demanded silence from their disciples, often for years, Imaginatif has been able because of Will's taciturnity to deliver a comprehensive body of thought on matters that had vexed Will through much of the third dream. What was lost when the inner dream was ruptured by Will's speech has now been restored. Will has altered, or at least largely controlled, the emotional, mental, and moral habits that had obstructed his learning. With this new knowledge, the arc of speeches and vision stretching back to Recklessness's diatribe, with its vehement rejection of the salvific value of Clergy's learning, now comes to a fruitful end.

In addition to this synthesis of how humans may reliably learn about fundamental religious and ethical matters, Imaginatif redirects the object of Will's inquiry as Will listens in silence. After he explains Dowel as, in large part, not misspeaking, he introduces Charity as Dobet (C.14.9–29), revealing to Will the fundamental nature of what he has been seeking throughout the third dream. Charity, he proclaims, is the source of patience, peace, and the life of innocent poverty, the central concerns of the next dream. In passus 15, the first of the new dream, Will accepts Patience as his guide. *Piers Plowman*, as Vance Smith declares, is ungraspable as a whole because "its several parts, its multiple dreams, each aim for a totality that is broken and disrupted by the poem's other parts."[73] While it is risky to ask if Will's newfound taciturnity before a teacher and guide extends into this dream, how could we avoid considering if there is a fundamental shift from Will the disputer to Will the listener after Will awakes from the third dream?

Patience becomes Will's companion at the Feast of Conscience, when he is tempted to dispute with and expose the gluttonous Doctor of Divinity, who has been preaching about penance recently but battens on the richest and rarest foods at the table:

> "Y schal iangle to [dispute with] þis iurdan, with his iuyste [juste] wombe,
> And apose [confront with a question] hym what penaunce is and purgatorie on erthe,
> And why a [he] lyueth nat as a lereth [teaches]!" "Lat be," quod Patience. (C.15.93–95)

Will conveys his vehement, even visceral, disgust with "iurdan," a bulbous glass vessel or a chamber pot, and by "iuste wombe," probably a belly like a large-bottomed vessel (a potbelly). He characterizes the speech that his emotion is about to generate as verbose as well as disputatious (*MED*: s.v. "janglen" [v.], 1a, 1c). Such emotionally driven speech would return to his old ways, even if his sense of the Doctor's inconsistent life as a mendicant preacher is valid. But when Patience counsels him to refrain from speaking then and let the Doctor suffer his own penance with indigestion, "Y seat stille, as Pacience wolde" (C.15.108). Although Will needs a check on his would-be rash speech, he heeds Patience and bides his time, asking his question of the Doctor tersely only when Patience nods to him. He even ceases to speak at the banquet when Conscience, as host, asks Patience to beg him to be still because he has begun to dispute the Doctor's answer. As a result of this new silence, he hears Piers Plowman and Patience speak on the nature and value of patience, then chooses (along with Conscience) to follow Patience as a teacher and companion (as he did Imaginatif before). In the episodes that follow, Will lets Patience and Conscience question Activa Vita and Activa Vita prompt Patience's extended catechesis on poverty. Will is a wholly silent listener. When a new "ledare" appears, Liberum Arbitrium, Will is curious but first asks Patience if he can speak and then formulates, step by step, terse questions that all trigger informative answers. Among those is Liberum Arbitrium's great discourse on Charity, instigated by Will and shaped in part by his pivotal questions at intervals (from C.16.286 into the sight of the Tree of Charity in C.18). Thus, talking about doing well in much of the third dream gives way, after Imaginatif's tutoring of a taciturn Will, to listening well and learning well in C's vast fourth dream, a new way of questing in which impulsive and disputatious questioning has little, if any, place for a pilgrim living with others in voluntary poverty. Love, not so much the Jewish, Greek, and Roman ethic of cautious speech and careful listening, drives this new phase of learning in a new dream that ends with discourses on love. Love, after all, is what the fourteenth-century philosopher and theologian Robert Holcot insists must initiate and sustain humans in the arduous process of acquiring wisdom (recall his metaphor of digging gold out of the ground laboriously), just as, we saw in chapter 1, clerical writers claim that it should be the driving force in making prudent choices. That love, for Holcot and for Will, entails the humility to realize in the first place that they are not wise and must seek wisdom from others.[74]

From Imaginatif's appearance to his vanishing, Will's taciturnity becomes more than an act done out of self-interest and learned from the cautious wise: not wasting words, not rebuking, not provoking anger in others, and not experiencing the harsh consequences of loss, shame, and grief. It lies even further from a self-imposed penalty, like that of the famous philosopher Secundus, who, discerning that his harsh speech led to his mother's death, chose a life of unbroken silence, sustained even when he was threatened with death by the emperor Hadrian.[75] Although, like Secundus, Will has learned the wisdom to perceive the cause of his calamity and has come to understand that silence is practiced by those who seek wisdom, he perceives that taciturnity furthers learning in dialogue with others by fostering listening. Blaming others in a state of vehement emotion "undermines the life of learning," in Emily Steiner's words, but taciturnity as the inclination to stay silent while an august teacher is speaking makes learning possible for the inquirer.[76] For the thirteenth-century friar Nicolas de Byard, taciturnity involves a reverence and seemliness (*honestas*) toward an informed speaker that enables one to learn what one ardently desires. Such a taciturn listener, he writes, is akin to a sick person listening, without creating a disturbance, to a physician or to a pilgrim hearing avidly news of their homeland. The taciturn person adheres, Nicolas continues, to the wise injunction "Audi tacens, et pro reverentia accedet tibi bona gratia" (Hear in silence, and, because of your reverence, good grace will come to you; Sirach 32:9).[77] Such silence springs from a will directed toward obtaining what is good, understanding that as a gift from someone somewhat more informed. It creates an attentive and receptive attitude.[78] Will has already practiced the taciturnity of a *sapiens* by hearing out Imaginatif's harsh, probing analysis of his rebuke of Reason, then by tersely acknowledging the truth of that analysis. Certainly, Will's far more extended taciturnity in passus 14 shows that he has accepted and put into practice what Imaginatif, and, less efficaciously, Reason, enjoined on him at the end of 13 so that he can avoid "out of mesure" speech and its bitter consequences. More profoundly, though, it shows that he understands and desires taciturnity as a positive habit of temperance, an act of patiently restraining emotions, thoughts, and words in which, as a learner engaged in exchanges with others, he lives as Lydgate's

Zenocrates does. To read the final exchanges of the third dream alongside moral discourse on the taciturnity of the wise is to grasp that although taciturnity sometimes may elude us as readers of episodes crammed with avid and often contentious speakers, Will's need for it as a quester for knowledge, and its newfound value for him, matter.

POSTSCRIPT
Literary Invention, Power Differentials, and Ethical Multiplicity

Imaginitif's classical dicta on taciturnity take us back to the first two chapters of this book, where feelings are distrusted, foresight is valued, and silent analysis of situations protects public figures from committing to dangerous courses of action and thus avoiding loss of reputation and support, foolish commitments, verbal contention, and even violence. For Albertano da Brescia's fellow civic leaders in Italian communes, for clerics engaged in teaching and rebuking others, and for the king of Hoccleve's *Regiment of Princes*, silence in the forms of initial circumspection and then, sometimes, sustained silence creates (to quote Cheryl Glenn again) "a strategic position of strength." Yet Albertano's imagined readership, his daily companions in communal legal life, are already in positions of power, as are the late medieval clergy as preachers, catechists, and confessors (and some, like Roger of Waltham, royal officials), as will be Prince Henry when he becomes king. For them, silence serves to sustain and augment power they already possess or soon will. The same is true of the courtier bishop Mum in chapter 3, a high liver at court, a companion of clerics who bilk laypeople and mayors who manipulate a legal system that already favors the rich over the poor. Yet the three following chapters present figures who are outcasts, subject to the oppressive power of the great: Jesus before the high priests, King Herod, and the Roman governor; William Thorpe before the notorious inquisitor Archbishop Arundel; the anguished social pariah Thomas in the "My Complaint" and "Dialogue"; Will the Dreamer seeking wisdom from authoritative teachers, one of whom has rejected him because of his reckless speech. The taciturnity and sustained silence advocated by the people with power, a senior lawyer and influential clerics, and, often, promoted for the powerful, also becomes crucial for these outcasts, enabling them to achieve what they seek in seemingly impossible situations. Silence as a strategy gives religious dissidents power over adversaries with institutional clout. It enables Jesus and Thorpe to preserve their integrity, confound and resist their inquisitors, and achieve their aims: the salvation of humankind for Jesus and survival without betraying the truth or his fellow Wycliffites for Thorpe. It enables Will, who has lost the opportunity to discover what he seeks through a revelatory dream, to learn how to learn and even to acquire something of what he sought from an exalted teacher. It initially seems to protect a disturbed and distrusted Thomas from a ruling clique, and when it fails him, it does so, in part, for reasons moral writers warned about. How can moral writing on silence inform texts with figures in such radically different situations, possessing various levels of status, driven by different emotions, holding different intentions and purposes, achieving such different ends?

Medieval moral discourse on silence is always hybrid, woven from multiple cultural and, so, ethical strands. Sometimes it seems monologic because of this very multiplicity, a segment of a master discourse drawn from Roman popular morality, "Greek" philosophers, Jewish wisdom books, the New Testament, patristic writings, canon law, and medieval exempla. For example, David Lawton contrasts the Parson's "totalizing" discourse with the plurality of voices and their "free play" in Chaucer's *Canterbury Tales*. And just before the Parson, the Manciple's parody of pastoral discourse on taciturnity, as explored by me and by Lawton, captures the annoying "completeness," stultifying all-wise authority, and arid prescriptiveness that late medieval moral writing can be seen to possess.[1] Yet imaginative writers can also be stimulated by its multiple strands, discovering in them ways of imagining how silence works and what it achieves or forfeits in specific public situations. Even when one strand seems dominant in a text, others present new dimensions. For example, Hoccleve's political advice about circumspect silence as a critical resource for a ruler relies heavily on classical and Jewish *sententiae* and exempla, yet it cites canon law to authorize the obligations of ruler and advisers, and it grounds prudent political actions in love, as medieval clerics do. Moreover, his *Regiment* turns to the destructive silences of royal advisers by laicizing, in effect, material designed originally to deter clerics from abandoning their obligation to check and correct the evils of the powerful and wealthy. The subversive *Mum and the Sothsegger*, of course, develops this strand of self-serving and self-protecting silence with far more detail and wit, tying it to Roman popular morality, with its appeal to avoiding the consequences of speaking against one's interest. By its devastating critique of this way of life, even in the voice of Mum himself, it repudiates comprehensive clerical textual materials on silence, replacing them with strictly biblical and canonical authority, as John Wyclif had done in his later treatises that condemn the silence of greedy and pusillanimous clerics.

The ways in which multistranded moral discourse can stimulate or assist literary invention can be seen most sharply in Hoccleve's "My Complaint." At first, Thomas, fearful that any type of conversation will alienate further his skittish former companions, takes to the nth degree silence as self-protection: he abandons even calculated speech after initial circumspect taciturnity. Yet he discovers that silence is an uncertain sign, sure to be misinterpreted as stemming from mental illness because of preconceived judgments. Then he settles on seeing his silence as a form of the virtuous patience amid rejection and insult that patristic and medieval writers celebrate. What impels Thomas to abandon silence forms another strand in moral discourse: the overwhelming pain silence causes if it is sustained too long, even in the virtuous. Thomas's way out of the silence that has failed him in multiple ways enacts a quite different imperative of discourse on silence: do not remain silent if healed by God but proclaim His redemptive acts. Altogether these shifting stances toward silence, these various ways of understanding both its strategic value for a vulnerable outcast and its limits and adverse consequences, provide shape and complexity to "My Complaint" and the beginning of the "Dialogue." These strands of discourse on taciturnity Hoccleve knew, as his sentential glosses on the *Regiment* demonstrate.

Lest this *postscriptum* turn into a *scriptum*, I will rest with this paragraph. Our current fascination, as medievalists, with feelings and emotions (an important dimension of this book) can lead us to miss or dismiss the importance of the rational and pragmatic in medieval literature. Hybrid moral discourse had another value for imaginative writers. It helped them to fuse the spontaneous and the calculated, the affective and the rational, experience and written authority. This fusion, where Roman scrutiny and pragmatic self-interest lie alongside Christianized emotions, like charity and greed, allows writers to explore how silence works in public life. In the court, royal or judicial, reasoned calculation matters for actors striving for favorable outcomes for themselves and, at times, others: the king's restraint as he listens to advice, Jesus's efforts to resist degraded institutional speech and ensure his death, Thorpe's efforts not to implicate others or fail to proclaim what he believes to be true, Mum's failure to report popular unrest or reprove violent magnates. Yet these actors are sustained by powerful emotions: the king by piety toward God and his people, Jesus by love for humankind, Thorpe by fear of missteps, Mum by greed and fear of the displeasure of those on whom he depends, Will by sorrow for the loss that his impetuous speech has caused. Moral discourse on silence, because of its hybridity, embraces all of these dimensions of human experience, of human choices within radically different situations and their outcomes. In this way, hybrid cultural discourse has multiple resources for writers, as for their intended readers—and more power, more appeal. To miss how such a multistranded discourse shapes texts is akin to missing silences in those texts: it limits our reading, blinding us to key shifts in emotions, intentions, perceptions, choices, and strategies. More broadly, it can also keep us from grasping that for many medieval writers, the pragmatic and the emotional had ethical dimensions.

NOTES

INTRODUCTION

1. John of Mirfield, *Florarium Bartholomei*, London, British Library, MS Royal 7.F.11, fol. 217r^a. Six copies of the *Florarium* survive in British libraries, along with four sets of extracts from it, while six additional copies are attested to (Sharpe, *Handlist*, 284). See also Étienne de Bourbon, *Tractatus de diversis materiis predicabilibus*, Oxford, Oriel College, MS 68, fol. 157v^b (the wise man is Socrates); extracts from *Pera peregrini*, Oxford, Bodleian Library, MS. Laud misc. 389, fol. 171r^a (Socrates); and Bromyard, *Summa praedicantium*, vol. 1, fol. 450r (the wise man is Solon). This is one of two extant British manuscripts of the *Tractatus*. (Because Bloomfield and his associates were unaware of this Oriel College manuscript, they list only one in *Incipits*, 423.) One full copy of *Pera peregrini*, a set of *distinctiones* (ca. 1350), survives, and another is attested to; but this manuscript of about 1400 is the sole witness to these extracts (Sharpe, *Handlist*, 244). John Bromyard's *Summa* survives in full in three manuscripts (Sharpe, *Handlist*, 221).

2. Goffman, *Forms of Talk*, 121–22.
3. Jaworski, *Power of Silence*, xii.
4. Johannesen, "Functions of Silence," 29–30. See also Jensen, "Communicative Functions of Silence."
5. For the difference in medieval texts between feeling as affect and emotion as scripted and performed feeling, see Burger and Crocker, introduction to *Medieval Affect*.
6. Suarez-Nani, "Faire parler le silence," 271.
7. Jaworski, *Power of Silence*, 3.
8. Saville-Troike, "Place of Silence," 11–17; Jaworski, *Power of Silence*, 73.

9. Saville-Troike, "Place of Silence," 16–17.
10. On the performative nature of silence, see Dauenhauer, *Silence*, 3–5.
11. On shifts in footing, see Goffmann, *Forms of Talk*, 140–54.
12. Benhabib, *Situating the Self*, 23–67; Gadamer, *Truth and Method*, 214–341; Gadamer, "Hermeneutics as Practical Philosophy," 108–13.
13. Even more than *distinctiones*, treatises on the Sins of the Tongue or general treatises on speech, like the thirteenth-century anonymous *De lingua*, treat taciturnity and silence as a way to avoid transgressive speech in general and specific sins of the tongue. See the survey of these texts, Middle English and Latin, in Craun, *Lies*, 10–24.
14. John of Mirfield, *Florarium*, fol. 217r^a. The two questions, with the wise man's answers, are transmitted to the late Middle Ages as separate anecdotes in the tenth-century collection of wise sayings wrongly attributed to Caecilius Balbus, where the first silent man is identified as Zenocrates and the second as "Salon" (Ps.-Caecilius Balbus, *De nugis philosophorum*, ed. Woelfflin, 26 ["De taciturnitate"]). As in the *Florarium*, both questions and answers appear as an anecdote in the extract "Tacere" from the *Pera peregrini*, fol. 171r^a. See chapter 6 for many late medieval versions of the second question and answer, which originate in the *Facta et dicta memorabilia* of Valerius Maximus.
15. John of Mirfield, *Florarium*, fol. 217r^a. *Disticha Catonis*, ed. Boas, 1.12. Other clerical moral writings that cite this saying as authoritative are the *Verbum abbreviatum* of Pierre le Chantre (364) and Thomas of Ireland's *Manipulus florum* (Taciturnitas 2 [accessed June 11, 2024]). It may be found in

the twelfth-century *Florilegium morale Oxoniensis* (Oxford, Bodleian Library, MS. Bodley 633, fol. 69r).

16. The role of emotions in assisting agents to achieve what they desire is developed by Rosenwein in *Generations*, 149–65; and by Knuuttila, *Emotions*, 359–65.

17. From canon law and *pastoralia*, I develop the general obligation of fraternal correction and distinguish it from disciplinary correction by clerics in *Ethics and Power*, chap. 1.

18. On the fundamental ways in which late medieval moral thought evaluated acts, see the essays on "Ethics" in Pasnau and Van Dyke, *Cambridge History*, 457–535; see especially Porter's "Action and Intention" and Kent's "Virtue Theory." For a more through discussion, see Kent's *Virtues of the Will*.

19. Burnley, *Chaucer's Language*, especially chap. 4.

20. Gower, *Confessio Amantis*, ed. Macaulay, 3.417–75.

21. Gower, *Confessio Amantis*, ed. Macaulay, 3.674–75, 680–81.

22. *De lingua*, Cambridge, Trinity College, MS B.15.35, fol. 187r. *De lingua* survives in twenty manuscripts in British libraries (Craun, *Lies*, 19n37.).

CHAPTER 1

1. *Disticha Catonis* 1.3; "Eine Nordenglische Cato-Version," ed. Förster, lines 61–64.

2. Oxford, Bodleian Library, MS Canon Latin Classical 72, fol. 64r:
Virtutem primam, id est, precipuam et excellentem. *Compescere linguam*, id est, sedare et refrenare. "Virtus autem est habitus mentis bene constitute" qua aliquis bene vivit et nullus male utitur . . . enim taciturnitas maxima est ceterarum virtutum et primum locum obtinet post Deum. Vnde Virgilius: "Exigua est virtus prestare silencia rebus / Et contra gravis est culpa notanda loqui." Et hic est *proximus ille Deo*, id est, vicinus. *Qui scit tacere ratione* secundum racionem quia sicut hostium quondam clauditur, quondam aperitur, ita ad tempus debet os loqui uel tacere. Vnde dicitur "Omnia tempus habent" et alibi "Et locus et tempus rebus conveniunt" et alibi "Quam potes extingue uiciose crimina lingue de prudencia." Prudencia est omnium rerum distinctio, discriminatrix cum cautissima circumspeccione.

This definition of virtue may be found in Boethius and becomes crucial in the twelfth-century moral philosophy of Peter Abelard, John of Salisbury, and Alan de Lille (Nederman, "Nature," 93–108). The couplet is from Ovid's *Ars amatoria* 2.603–4, but Ovid has "tacenda," not "notanda," as do medieval florilegia, like the *Flores philosophorum et poetarum* (1.9, 273) and the *Polythecum* (3.278).

3. Hazelton, "Christianization of 'Cato,'" 161, 165.

4. Morgan, *Popular Morality*, 1–2, 43–47, 102–5, 168–69, 228.

5. *Disticha Catonis* 4.20.

6. *Disticha Catonis* 1.12.

7. The *Florilegium* survives in a single manuscript in the Bodleian Library, Oxford: MS Bodley 633. Sayings about taciturnity appear especially in fols. 66v–71v.

8. Powell, *Albertanus*, 65, 67. *De arte* survives in British libraries in two Latin manuscripts of the thirteenth century, seven of the fourteenth, and fifteen of the fifteenth, according to the census by Navone ("La doctrina") and that of Graham ("Albertanus").

9. Albertano da Brescia, *De arte*, ed. Sunby, 94. See also Albertano's *De amore* 1.2. One manuscript of *De amore* from the thirteenth century survives in British libraries, as do six of the fourteenth century and ten of the fifteenth, according to Navone ("La doctrina") and Graham ("Albertanus"). For the verse from James, ubiquitous in clerical writing on speech, see, for example, Guillaume Peyraut, *Summa de vitiis*, Lyon, Bibliothèque municipale, MS 678, fol. 137v[b]. An unpublished inventory compiled by Siegfried Wenzel, Richard Newhauser, and Edwin Craun records thirty-eight manuscripts of the *Summa* in

British libraries, plus a number of abbreviated versions and fragments.

10. Albertano, *De arte*, 95. From Cicero, *De officiis* 1.38.

11. Albertano, *De arte*, 93. Rosenwein explains why Cicero evaluated *cautio* as a good emotion in *Generations*, 18–19.

12. Powell, *Albertanus*, 37–50.

13. Demarco, "Violence," 153–55.

14. Blenkinsop, *Wisdom and Law*, 17, 25; Grizzard, "Scope of Theology."

15. Albertano, *De arte*, 95–96.

16. "Si autem verbum, quod dicere velis, dubium appareat, utrum bonum effectum habiturum sit an non, silere debes potius quam dicere.... Sapienti enim magis expedit tacere pro se, quam loqui contra se, quia paucos vel neminem tacendo, multos loquendo circumventos vidimus" (Albertano, *De arte*, 97–98; cf. Albertano, *De amore* 1.2). See "Pamphilus, de Amore," ed. Garbaty, 120, lines 335–38. The distich is a slight variant of *Disticha Catonis* 1.12.

17. Albertano, *Liber consolationis et consilii*, ed. Sundby. The *Liber* survives in British libraries in one manuscript of the thirteenth century, five manuscripts of the fourteenth, and eleven of the fifteenth (Navone, "La doctrina"; Graham, "Albertanus").

18. Albertano, *De arte*, 115; Albertano, *De amore* 1.2.

19. Albertano, *De arte*, 94, 102–3; Albertano, *De amore* 1.2. The *sententia* he attributes to Augustine actually comes from a homily of Gregory the Great: *Homiliae in Evangelia* 1.18 (ed. Était, 140). The *sententia* is also included by Thomas of Ireland in the *Manipulus florum* (Iniuria 1 [accessed September 9, 2021]). This fourteenth-century florilegium survives in nineteen manuscripts in British libraries, largely from that century (Rouse and Rouse, *Preachers*, 313–405).

20. "His denique auditis circa praedicta, exercitatione intentissima et frequenti usu te ipsum exerceas—nam exercitatio ingenium et naturam saepe vincit, et usus omnium magistrorum praecepta superat—ut valeas doctrinam dicendi et faciendi in promptu habere" (Albertano, *De arte*, 119).

21. Caxton, *Good Manners*, fol. Div. The proverb: "And therfore Cathon sayth to his sone / my sone thou oughtest to flee noyses and stryues. for moche people haue had harme by spekyng but by beynge styll & not to speke fewe or none haue had ony harme." This translation of Jacques Legrand's *Livre de bonnes moeurs* of 1410 was made by or for Caxton in 1486; three other English translations from the century also survive.

22. Caxton, *Curtesye*, lines 141–47.

23. For example, "Proverbs of Alfred," 131–32; "Proverbs of Salamon," 179; *Dicts and Sayings*, 15–16, 98–99. The *Dicts* was translated from the French by Sir Stephen Scrope and also by Anthony Woodville, Earl Rivers, whose translation was the first book published by William Caxton.

24. "Consail and Teiching," 198, 200–201. This long monitory poem is printed as part of *Ratis Raving*, a Scottish text of the fifteenth century. The circumstances also appear in poems on circumspect speech that do not mention silence, like "Think Before You Speak," lines 57–60, also from the fifteenth century.

25. Roger of Waltham, *Compendium morale de virtutibus*, Oxford, Bodleian Library, MS Fairfax 4, fol. 166v. The *Compendium* survives in sixteen manuscripts in British libraries, according to Bloomfield et al., *Incipits*, 455; and Newhauser and Bejczy, *Supplement*, 298–99. Étienne de Bourbon, *Tractatus*, fol. 157r[a]. *Speculum laicorum*, Oxford, Bodleian Library, MS Bodl. 474, fol. 154v. Welter records sixteen manuscripts of all or parts extant in British libraries (*Speculum laicorum*, ix–xix), and Bloomfield et al. add two more (*Incipits*, 125). John of Mirfield, *Florarium*, fol. 216v[a]. *Alphabet of Tales*, ed. Banks, 475; one manuscript survives.

26. Peyraut, *Summa de virtutibus*, fol. 68v. This widespread Augustinian definition is also given by Thomas of Ireland in his list of *sententiae* on "Providentia sive Prudentia" in *Manipulus florum* (Prudencia 1 [accessed August 5, 2021]). The Augustinian definition is Englished in *The Book of Vices and Virtues* (ca. 1375), whose writer/translator grasps that Augustine

understands the four cardinal virtues in terms of what love does: "þe loue of þe herte þt wisely forsakeþ al þat may greue hire, and cheseþ al þat may helpe hire to haue þat sche loueþ, þat is God" (ed. Francis, 124–25). The *Book*, a fairly faithful translation of the widely read and translated *Somme le roi* of Laurent d'Orléans, survives in three manuscripts (*Book*, xlvii–lii).

27. "Docet enim Tullius secundo rethorice quod prudentie tres sunt partes: memoria, providentia, et intellectiva. Memoria est per quam animus repetit illa que fuerunt. Intellectiva est per quam ea prospicit que sunt. Providentia per quam futuri aliquid videtur antequam sit. . . . In omni ergo specie providentie deus occurit diligentibus, docens quid eis expedit recordari, quid meditari, quid prestolari" (Robert Holcot, *Super Sapientiam*, fol. tiv). For a similar version of the three parts of prudence, see Thomas of Ireland, *Manipulus florum* (Prudencia 2 [accessed August 5, 2021]). On the Christianization of the cardinal virtues from late antiquity on, see István Bejczy's comprehensive, but rapid-fire, *Cardinal Virtues*.

28. Roger of Waltham, *Compendium*, fols. 47r and 46r. His first sentence comes from Cicero, *De officiis* 1.23. Martin of Braga, *Formula*, 239.

29. Peyraut, *Summa de virtutibus*, fol. 70r.

30. *De lingua*, fol. 187r.

31. Extracts from *Pera peregrini*, fol. 170v[b].

32. Pierre le Chantre, *Verbum*, ed. Boutry, 362. The *textus prior* survives in eight thirteenth- and fourteenth-century manuscripts in British libraries (ix–xli). For the circumstances that should restrict speech, see also Peyraut, *Summa de vitiis*, fol. 138v[a]; and Nicolas de Byard, *Distinctiones theologicae*, Oxford, Bodleian Library, MS Bodl. 563, fol. 157r[a–b] ("ex defectu sapientie," "ex defectu eloquentie," "ex defectu vite" [all of the speaker]; "propter indignationem," "propter repulsionem," "propter contemptum" [all of the listener]); and *Summa fratris Alexandri* 2.2.3.3.2.1.2.2 (ed. Brothers of the College of St. Bonaventura). Nicolas's collection is extant in five British manuscripts of the thirteenth and fourteenth centuries, according to Bataillon ("Tradition," 247–48).

33. Bromyard, *Summa praedicantium*, vol. 1, fol. 453v[a]. On the swan's neck as a metaphor for discreetly weighing thought and emotion before speaking, see Craun, "Aristotle's Biology," 298–99.

34. *Speculum laicorum*, fol. 155r.

35. Craun, *Lies*, chap. 2.

36. *Book of Vices*, 282–83. The *Book* paraphrases Proverbs 17:14, often used in clerical texts on silence: "For as Salamon seiþ, 'Who-so letteþ go þe watre at his wille & habundauntliche, he is ofte cause of plee [contention, discord, litigation] and grete strif'" (283). For this verse, see also *De lingua*, fol. 187r; and John of Wales, *De vita religiosa*, fol. 267v. The compilation is extant in seven manuscripts in British libraries, according to Swanson's *John of Wales*, 236–56.

37. *Speculum laicorum*, fol. 154r.

38. "Est enim quedam dulcedo sermonis qui irrepit et blanditur et non aliter quam ebrietas vel amor secreta producit" (Roger of Waltham, *Compendium*, fol. 166v). Ovid, *Ars amatoria* 2.603–4.

39. Simon of Boraston, *Distinctiones*, Oxford, Bodleian Library, MS Bodl. 216, fols. 139v[b]–140r[a]. The *distinctio* is titled "Tacere." The *Distinctiones* survives in ten manuscripts in British libraries (Sharpe, *Handlist*, 610), and the same *distinctio* appears in Worcester Cathedral MS F. 128, fol. 111v[a–b], attributed to Ranulph Higden. Only two manuscripts of Higden's *Distinctiones theologicae* survive, both at Worcester, but four more are attested to (Sharpe, *Handlist*, 454). The anecdote can also be found in *Alphabet*, 98; and a version is told by Jacques de Vitry, where the ruse is the husband's (*Exempla*, ed. Crane, 98).

40. Millemete, *Nobility*, 43–47.

41. *Governance of Kings*, 355. For the Latin original, see Colonna, *Regimine* 3.2.17.

42. Peyraut, *Summa de vitiis*, fol. 150v[a–b]; *De lingua*, fol. 159v.

43. Roger of Waltham, *Compendium*, fol. 166r.
44. Peyraut, *De eruditione* 5.2; also his *Summa de vitiis*, fol. 151v[a]; and the *Speculum laicorum*, fol. 153v.
45. John of Mirfield, *Florarium*, fol. 216v[b]; Guillaume Peyraut, *Summa de vitiis*, fol. 150v[a]. The *sententia* is also included, among several on silence, in the extract "Sapientia" from the *Pera peregrini*, fol. 159r[a].
46. *Book for a Simple and Devout Woman*, ed. Diekstra, 299. It survives in two manuscripts (3–8).
47. Roger of Waltham, *Compendium*, fols. 75v–76r; also Peyraut, *Summa de vitiis*, fol. 152r[a]; and *Speculum vitae*, ed. Hanna, vol. 2, lines 15428–29. The *Speculum* survives in forty manuscripts in British libraries (Raymo, "Works," 7:2479).
48. Roger of Waltham, *Compendium*, fol. 62v. In addition, the *Speculum laicorum* illustrates patience in response to contumely with the silence of King David (fol. 125r). The incident is recounted in 2 Samuel 16.
49. Casagrande and Vecchio, *I peccati della lingua*, 443.

CHAPTER 2

1. For the constraints on Hoccleve's speech as a royal clerk, see Simpson, *Reform*, 209–11; Knapp, *Bureaucratic Muse*, chap. 1; and, especially, Perkins, *Hoccleve's "Regiment,"* chap. 1. Meyer-Lee contrasts Hoccleve's struggle to overcome constraints with Lydgate's confident reliance on the authority of the learned monastic tradition (*Poets and Power*, 88–94).
2. Burrow lays out the references that date the poem in *Thomas Hoccleve*, 18. Seymour describes forty-two of the forty-three manuscripts of the complete or nearly complete *Regiment* in "Manuscripts."
3. Kirby, *Henry IV*, 86–237.
4. Hoccleve, *Regiment of Princes*, ed. Blyth. All citations to the *Regiment* are to this edition by line in the text; citations of Blyth's notes are to the page in the notes.
5. Perkins, *Hoccleve's "Regiment,"* 85–86.
6. Patristic *sententiae* are rarer in Albertano's treatises than in pastoral moral texts and in Hoccleve's *Regiment*.
7. On the Aristotelian tradition of political analysis in medieval literature, see Simpson, *Reform*, 221–23.
8. Griffiths, "In Bookes Thus Writen," 93, 103.
9. The words are Knapp's in *Bureaucratic Muse*, 2. Strohm, *England's Empty Throne*.
10. Ferster, *Fictions of Advice*, chap. 8.
11. Scanlon, "King's Two Voices," 227.
12. *Liber regalis*, ed. Wickham, 82–83. I am indebted to a reader for the press who suggested that I look at the *Liber's* section on preparation.
13. It is worth noting that Thomas Aquinas, perhaps under the influence of Aristotle, considers the prudence of a ruler (*prudentia regnativa*) as the most fully realized type of prudence because a ruler, like prudence, directs and commands (*Summa theologica*, 2a.2ae.50.2). I was directed to this section of the *Summa* by Burrow, "Third Eye of Prudence," 41.
14. What Giancarlo remarks about mirrors for princes as a whole holds true of this section on prudence: "the narrative strategy of the *Fürstenspiegel* actually assumes, as the practical condition of its own efficacy, what it ostensibly seeks to produce as its end: the good prince already possessed of good principles" ("Mirror," 42).
15. Focusing on lying, I set forth the destructive personal and communal consequences that clerical moral writings trace to an unruly tongue in *Lies*, 25–47. For the economic, social, and political value of good repute and the consequences of losing it, see the essays in Fenster and Smail, *"Fama."*
16. Scanlon, "King's Two Voices," 238.
17. Green notes in his excellent chapter "Truth and Treason" that the memory of Richard II might work to enable Prince Henry, when king, to avoid "repeating a predecessor's mistakes" by seeming to break oaths (*Crisis of Truth*, 235).
18. Hoccleve's gloss: "Melius est quod aures hominum sint sitibunde ad regis

eloquia quam suis affatibus satientur, quia saturatis auribus anima etiam saturatur, et cetera" (*Regiment*, ed. Blyth, 222). This gloss warning against loquacity in a king also appears in a brief political tract, *De quadripartita regis specie*, probably compiled in the late fourteenth century (34).

19. Perkins, *Hoccleve's "Regiment,"* 133.
20. Perkins, *Hoccleve's "Regiment,"* 17.
21. It has become easy for scholars to miss the extent of Jewish and Christian scriptural material in the *Regiment*, given the current bent to treat Hoccleve as a secular poet finding ways to carry out writing verse outside the church. For this bent, see Perkins, *Hoccleve's "Regiment"*; Knapp, *Bureaucratic Muse*; and Tolmie's searching article "The Professional."
22. Scanlon, "King's Two Voices."
23. Pearsall, "Hoccleve's *Regiment*," 389–91.
24. Scattergood argued that policy recommendations point to 1463 as the year in which the *Active Policy* was written ("Date"), but, more recently, Meyer-Lee has reviewed the possible date in light of historical events of the 1460s and very early 1470s (*Poets and Power*, 151–53).
25. *Secreta secretorum*, ed. Steele, 45, 49, 135.
26. Caxton, *Game*, ed. Adams, 23. Egidio does not even develop silence as a strategy to avoid speaking untruths in his chapter on truth and lying (*Egidius de regimine* 1.2.29).
27. Ashby, *George Ashby's Poems*, ed. Bateson. All references are to this edition by line number.
28. John Scattergood gives codicological, poetic, and thematic reasons for reading the *Dicta* as part of the *Active Policy* ("Date," 171–76). Only one manuscript of the *Liber* survives in British libraries, so I have not included it as a source in this study.
29. Glenn, *Unspoken*, xix.

CHAPTER 3

1. Barr and Ward-Perkins, "Spekyng," 255. Horobin has traced the writer to the vicinity of Bristol on the basis of relict spellings and alliterative techniques ("Dialect").
2. In Barr's introduction to her edition of *Mum*, she identifies Wycliffite concerns in the poem (introduction to *"Piers Plowman" Tradition*, 26–27), and, in *Signes*, she examines its Wycliffite terms (104–8).
3. Craun, *Ethics and Power*, 120–31.
4. Some scholars who have explored the *Mum*-poet's satire of bureaucratic and legal culture: Grady, "Generation"; Steiner, *Documentary Culture*; Yeager, *Lawmen to Plowmen*.
5. *De lingua*, fol. 187r. Casagrande traces how *mala taciturnitas* was developed as a sin in the twelfth century in "La *mala taciturnitas*."
6. *Summa fratris Alexandri* 2.2.3.3.2.1.3. To support its claim that taciturnity may be a sin, the *Summa* paraphrases Pope Gregory the Great, the great authority on pastoral care: "Discrete pensanda sunt tempora, ne . . . cum [lingua] loqui utiliter potest, semetipsam pigra restringat" (2.2.3.3.2.1.1). From Gregory the Great, *Moralia*, ed. Adriaen, 1:7.61.
7. On these types of culpable taciturnity, see Nicolas de Byard, *Distinctiones*, fol. 161v[b]–62r[a]; and Casagrande, "La *mala taciturnitas*."
8. Roger of Waltham, *Compendium*, fol. 105v; from *Corpus iuris canonici*, ed. Friedberg, vol. 1, C.11 q.3 c.86 (col. 667). See also *Summa fratris* (3.2.1.1.8.4); and *Floretum* (London, British Library, MS Harley 401, fol. 303v, the sole manuscript). Simon of Boraston states succinctly in the entry "Tacere" in his *Distinctiones* that clerics must fulfill the terms of their office and speak in defense of the truth: "Ubi vero incumbit persone ex officio vel veritas periclitatur, tacere est viciosum" (fol. 139v[b]).
9. "Video non nullos ita personam potentis accipere vt requisiti ab eo pro fauore eius non dubitent in causa proximi rerum negare" (Roger of Waltham, *Compendium*, fol. 105v). From Gregory the Great, *Moralia*, 3:29.16.
10. Pierre le Chantre, *Verbum abbreviatum*, 357–58. Although the extract "Tacere" from *Pera peregrini* does not mention the

powerful, it begins by proclaiming that any priest who decides not to correct a sinner is a "mercenarius" seeking only his own goods (fol. 170v[b]).

11. Rosenwein, *Generations*, 33, 234–35. For a fuller account of fear in medieval moral writing, see chapter 5 below.

12. Nicolas de Byard, *Distinctiones*, fol. 161v[a–b]. See Roger of Waltham, *Compendium*, fol. 105v; *De lingua*, fol. 187r; Pierre le Chantre, *Verbum abbreviatum*, 358–59.

13. Roger of Waltham, *Compendium*, fol. 105v; John of Mirfield, *Florarium*, fol. 216v[b]. See Nicolas de Byard, *Distinctiones*, 157r[a]; and *Corpus iuris canonici*, D.43. c.1 (col. 153).

14. Roger of Waltham, *Compendium*, fol. 106r; *Book for a Simple and Devout Woman*, 298. On the consequences of priests' taciturnity, see also *Floretum*, fol. 303v; and Peyraut, *Summa de vitiis*, fol. 151r[b].

15. "Qui enim proximorum mala respiciunt et tamen in silencio linguam premunt, quasi conspectis vulneribus, usum medicaminis subtrahunt et eo mortis auctores fiunt, quo virus, quod poterant curare, noluerunt" (*De lingua*, fol. 187r). See also *Summa fratris Alexandri* 2.2.3.3.2.2.2. From Gregory the Great, *Liber regulae pastoralis* 3.14.

16. Roger of Waltham, *Compendium*, fol. 105v; see also Pierre le Chantre, *Verbum abbreviatum*, 354–55.

17. Casagrande and Vecchio, *I peccati*, 443.

18. Wyclif assigns causes to treacherous taciturnity in *Tractatus de ecclesia* (430) and in *De veritate* (1:318).

19. Wyclif, *Tractatus de mandatis*, 404–5. Much of this entire discourse on *proditoria taciturnitas* from *De mandatis* appears verbatim in the *distinctio* "Taciturnitas" in the *Floretum* (fol. 303v), compiled after Wyclif's death.

20. Wyclif, *De veritate*, 316. Even in an Assumption sermon on what virtues are pleasing to the Virgin, Wyclif interposes damnable silence as a vicious extreme of taciturnity, a vice "magis culpabilis in prelatis" that entails omitting the preaching, correcting, and exhorting incumbent on people in the pastoral office (*Sermones*, 2:151).

21. Wyclif, *De veritate*, 318–20. Wyclif quotes the same decretal on failing to preach or defend the truth as did Roger of Waltham.

22. Wyclif, *De veritate*, 318.

23. Hoccleve attacks Wycliffites not only in "To Sir John Oldcastle," his remonstrance against the prominent "Lollard Knight" and rebel, but in many of his other political poems (however brief), especially those written after the coronation of Henry V.

24. *Governance of Kings*, 151–52.

25. Hoccleve, *Cy ensuyte la male regle de T. Hoccleue*, in *"My Compleinte,"* lines 279–80 (lines 185–288 for the entire invective).

26. Blyth gives the gloss on page 230 of his edition. Thomas of Ireland includes the *sententia* in his entry on flattery in the *Manipulus florum* (Adulacio 3 [accessed October 5, 2021]), although he concludes it slightly differently: "quem credit habere propicium."

27. In "Before and After Wyclif" (141), Somerset refers to the maxim, included at the time of Pope Gregory IX among the legal principles derived from Roman law in a new supplement to the *Decretals*.

28. On the consequences of prodigality, see, for example, Peyraut, *Summa de vitiis*, fol. 67r[b].

29. *Corpus iuris canonici*, 1:2. C.11 q.3. c.80 (col. 665). This canon is quoted in the *Floretum*'s entry on "Taciturnitas" (fol. 303v). Kerby-Fulton observes that Hoccleve's citations from canon law should alert us to a "pastoral sensibility" in the *Regiment* and other poems, a cast of thought derived from his clerical training and frustrated desire to serve as a priest in a benefice (*Clerical Proletariat*, 83–96 and chap. 3).

30. All citations of *Mum and the Sothsegger* in the text are by line to the Barr edition.

31. Nuttall, *Lancastrian Kingship*, 41–42.

32. Barr, introduction to *"Piers Plowman" Tradition*, 42–43. See also Dean's justification for including the Latin lines in the text of his edition (introduction to *Mum and the Sothsegger*, 79). As Lawrence Warner demonstrates, readers of *Piers Plowman* added Latin lines in the margins of some manuscripts of the poem, engaging with it in a way that those who were literate in Latin were likely to do (*Myth*, chap. 2). It is possible that the Latin lines in the margin of *Mum* were added, at some stage in the poem's transmission, by a reader or readers who shared the poet's knowledge of law and the Vulgate. However, the poem's survival in a single manuscript reduces this possibility considerably, pointing to a limited readership.

33. *Corpus iuris canonici*, vol. 1, D.86 c.3 (col. 298).

34. *Materials for the History of Thomas Beckett*, 5:270.

35. The errant, in William's case, were pertinacious heretics. William of Ockham, *Dialogus* 1.4.34. "Facientis culpam" also appears in two manuscripts of the widespread Latin *Gesta Romanorum*, which give a story about wise men offering a king advice about the cause of his people's misfortunes. After glossing the first man's enigmatic third reply with a dictum of St. Augustine that not to prohibit illicit doings is to consent to error, the text adds "Facientis culpam" (the whole sentence). The Latin version is included by Herrtage in his edition, *Early English Versions*, 97–98. The "Facientis" *sententia* is also included in a section on correction in the catechetical treatise with the incipit "Vani sunt omnes homines in quibus non est scientia" (London, British Library, MS Lansdowne 385, fol. 80r). Five copies of "Vani sunt" survive in British libraries (Sharpe, *Handlist*, 761). John Bromyard quotes it, too, in his entry "Correctio" as he concludes elaborate arguments for the responsibility to reprove sin (*Summa praedicantium*, vol. 1, fol. 161v), as does Thomas of Ireland in the *Manipulus florum* (Correctio 5 [accessed September 23, 2021]).

36. Fraternal correction, a practice repeatedly invoked in the poem, requires that the corrector begin by speaking in private to the offender in order to protect his reputation. See Craun, *Ethics and Power*, 125–31.

37. Interestingly, the English commentary on the *Disticha Catonis* with which chapter 1 began qualifies the distich the narrator connects to Mum by insisting that speech, as well as silence, is essential to political life. Silence, just like speech, may both harm and benefit the community, so those in public life must observe carefully the circumstances under which they speak. Speech harms only when it does not suit the time or the place (fol. 65r).

38. For example, sayings from Martin of Braga's widely read *Forumla honestae uitae* and the earlier anonymous *De moribus* were usually attributed to Seneca in medieval moral texts.

39. The priest's exclusive knowledge of canon law is noted by Helen Barr in her edition (*Mum and the Sothsegger*, 320).

40. I am very much indebted to Barr's informed analysis of Mum's legal stratagems in her notes to the edition (*Mum and the Sothsegger*, 329–30); her monograph *Signes* carefully unfolds the meanings of the poem's legal diction.

41. Barr notes in her edition (*Mum and the Sothsegger*, 326) that this maxim of canon law is underlined in the sole surviving manuscript.

42. In Barr's edition, she sees Mum serving Mum as inconsistency in personification (*Mum and the Sothsegger*, 328–29), whereas Day and Steele, in their edition, posit that the poet seems to have forgotten that Mum is speaking (*Mum and the Sothsegger*, 120).

43. Scase, *Literature and Complaint*, 104–5.

44. "Qui ergo potest contradicere, et non contradicit, peccat, et videtur fautor esse, secundum illud Gregorii" (Matthew of Paris, *Historia Anglorum*, 146). The poem's editors have not been able to find a source for the *sententia*, but, as I have demonstrated above, clerical writers cited, even

quoted, Gregory's works often when treating *mala taciturnitas*, notably the culpable failures of clerics to correct the powerful. See especially Gregory's *Liber regulae pastoralis* 3.13 and 14 (cols. 70–73).

45. For an example of rejecting a pragmatic, self-regarding Roman morality for one commanded by a religious text, see Study's contrast of love as the ground of theology and human action with a distich of "Cato" that advocates craftiness in deceiving others, who will deceive you if they can (Langland, *"Piers Plowman": A Parallel Text Edition*, vol. 1, *Text*, B.10.183–208). All references to the text are to this edition by version, passus, and line.

46. It is important not to miss the limits that the poet sets to truth-telling: after his dream, the narrator lambasts the commons at length for complaining themselves about the king, seizing a role that knights of the shires have and should play (lines 1388–1509). For institutional restrictions on the truth-telling, given the poet's royalist and aristocratic ideology, see Revere, "Advise or Consent," 146–48.

47. Latin dicta of all kinds are used by late medieval English poets in the various ways. Cannon shows that they incorporated schoolboy aphorisms into their poems (*From Literacy*).

48. Blamires, *Chaucer*, 13 and 18.

CHAPTER 4

1. *Pilgrimage*, ed. Henry, 50–51.
2. *Pilgrimage*, 51.
3. In *Lies*, chap, 3, I set forth pastoral teaching about murmur and then explicate *Patience*.
4. *Pilgrimage*, 51.
5. *Pilgrimage*, 53.
6. Thomas of Ireland, *Manipulus* (Paciencia 2–4 [accessed August 6, 2021]).
7. Gregory the Great, *Homiliae in Evangelia* 2.35.4 (ed. Était, 324). Quoted in *Speculum laicorum* (fol. 125r), in Thomas of Ireland's *Manipulus* (Paciencia 2 [accessed March 25, 2020]), in Peyraut's *Summa de virtutibus* (fol. 93r), and in the *Liber pharetrae* 2.33. The anonymous *Liber* survives in four manuscripts in British libraries, according to Bloomfield et al., *Incipits*, 222; and Newhauser and Bejczy, *Supplement*, 167–68. Hanna writes of the ubiquity of these and two other "definitions" of patience in "Commonplaces," 67–68.

8. Gregory the Great, *Homiliae in Evangelia* 2.35.9 (ed. Était, 329). Quoted in Thomas of Ireland's *Manipulus* (Paciencia 2 [accessed August 6, 2021]), in the *Liber Pharetrae* (2.33), and in Bromyard's *Summa praedicantium* (vol. 1, fol. 165r^a).

9. Thomas of Ireland, *Manipulus* (Paciencia 2 [accessed August 6, 2021]). The dictum is also quoted by Albertano da Brescia (*De amore* 4.13) and by Peyraut (*Summa de virtutibus*, 93r). Chaucer Englishes the dictum in "The Parson's Tale" (*Riverside Chaucer*, "The Parson's Tale," line 660).

10. "Nullum vestrum ad odium proximi contemeliosa verba commoveant, nulla periturarum rerum damna perturbent. Si enim fixa mente mansura damna pertimescitis, damna rerum transeuntium gravia non putatis; si aeternae retributionis gloriam conspicitis, de temporali iniuria non doletis. Tolerate ergo adversarios vestros, sed ut fratres diligite quos toleratis. Aeterna praemia pro damnis temporalibus quaerite" (Gregory the Great, *Homiliae in Evangelia* 2.35.9 [ed. Était, 330]).

11. Cicero, *De inventione* 2.54, 330. Quoted by Thomas of Ireland (*Manipulus*, Paciencia 5 [accessed August 6, 2021]), by Peyraut (*Summa de virtutibus*, fol. 93r), and by the author of the *Fasciculus morum* (ed. and trans. Wenzel, 620). See Hanna, "Commonplaces," 70–71.

12. "Ille autem uere est patiens, qui et aduersis atteritur et tamen ab spei sue rectitudine non curuatur. . . . In hoc itaque mens iusta ab iniusta discernitur, quod omnipotentis Dei laudem et inter aduersa confitetur, quod non cum rebus frangitur, non cum casu gloriae exterioris cadit" (Gregory the Great, *Moralia*, 2:11.47). Quoted by Thomas of Ireland, *Manipulus* (Paciencia 2 and 3 [accessed August 6, 2021]).

13. Gregory the Great, *Moralia*, 2:20.74–76.

14. Guillaume Peyraut, *Summa de virtutibus*, fols. 95r and 93v; Gregory the Great, *Homiliae in Evangelia* 2.35.5 (ed. Était, 325).

15. For Gregory's close association of mildness with patience, see *Homiliae in Hiezechielem Prophetam*, ed. Adriaen, 2.5.14.

16. "Patientia dominatur homo sibiipsi. Luc.xxi. 'In patientia vestra possidebitis animas vestras.' Hoc dominium attenditur in hoc quod ipsa cohibet hominem interiorem ab illicito appetitu vindicte. Cohibet similiter exteriorem: linguam enim cohibet a contumelia: manum a violentia" (Guillaume Peyraut, *Summa de virtutibus*, fol. 94r). The condition of the persecutors is described on fol. 95v.

17. Burnley, *Chaucer's Language*, especially chap. 4. Barbara Rosenwein explains the value Cicero placed on *constantia* (consistency) in *Generations*, 18–19.

18. Guillaume Peyraut, *Summa de virtutibus*, 93v. Ps.-Gilbert, *Distinctiones*, Oxford, Bodleian Library, MS. Bodl. 4, fol. 74r. This set of *distinctiones* survives in one more manuscript in British libraries (Bloomfield et al., *Incipits*, 30).

19. *Disce mori*, Oxford, Jesus College, MS 39, fols. 109–10. It is extant in one other manuscript (Raymo, "Works," 2263–64). See also the *Speculum spiritualium*, which develops the moral commonplace, stated, for example, in Chaucer's "The Parson's Tale," that patience is so utterly at odds with wrath that it alone has the power to heal the wrathful and end strife (fol. ixva–b; *Riverside Chaucer*, "The Parson's Tale," lines 653–76). The *Speculum* survives in ten manuscripts of the fifteenth century (Bloomfield et al., *Incipits*, 512).

20. On Caesar's patient endurance of insults, see Roger of Waltham's *Compendium*, fol. 63r.

21. For the silence of Hezekiah's messengers, see *De lingua* (fol. 187r) and the *Floretum* (fol. 289r); for Mary Magdalen and the woman taken in adultery, see the *Floretum* (fol. 289r) and the entry "De silencio et taciturnitate" by Nicolaus de Hanapis in *Liber de exemplis*, Oxford, Bodleian Library, MS Bodl. 107, fol. 74v. The *Liber* is extant in twelve manuscripts in British libraries (Bloomfield et al., *Incipits*, 77). The *Floretum* and Nicolaus's collection contain other biblical exempla of patient silence.

22. *Memoriale credencium*, ed. Kengen, 92–93. The *Memoriale* survives in four manuscripts and another four contain fragments of it (Kengen, 3–11).

23. Psalm 140:3 is quoted in *De lingua* (fol. 188r), in Pierre le Chantre's *Verbum abbreviatum* (363), in the extracts from *Pera peregrini* (fol. 170v^b), and in *Speculum laicorum* (fol. 154v). Psalm 38:2 is quoted in the *Speculum spiritualium* (fol. ixvb), and in the *Speculum laicorum* (fol. 154v).

24. *De lingua*, fol. 187r–v. Chaucer's Dame Prudence also urges the vengeful Melibee to imitate the patience of the silent Jesus (*Canterbury Tales* 7.1502–4).

25. The phrase "textual imitations of past theatrical performances" is King's in her cautionary essay "Medieval English Religious Plays," 541. King reminds readers that the York Register containing the pageants, written by a city functionary in the 1470s, is "an unfinished quality-control document, written with the intention of recording and regulating performance, if probably compiled from the playbooks owned by the various contributory guilds." It does not necessarily present scripts. For the status and purpose of the Register, see *York Plays*, ed. Beadle, 1:xi–xxvi.

26. The intervening pageant (32) that I do not treat dramatizes the remorse of Judas. Jesus never appears.

27. Robinson, "York Realist."

28. In *York Mystery* Cycle, King explores connections between the York pageants and both the liturgy and political and judicial conflicts, especially those over the execution of Archbishop Scrope by Henry IV. Walker's excellent introductory essay on medieval drama, "Cultural Work," analyzes how late medieval plays raised questions and provoked thought about current issues at the same time that they conveyed cultural

paradigms and norms. Lipton has recently explored how collective witnessing in courts of law positioned the York audience to be witnesses affected communally by what they experienced during the pageants (*Cultures of Witnessing*).

29. Beadle, "Verbal Texture," 170.

30. Woolf, *English Mystery Plays*, 256.

31. Clopper, "Tyrants."

32. Forest-Hill suggests that the York spectators would have been drawn into an adversarial relationship with Herod and the other threating lords to the extent to which they had suffered abusive and disruptive behavior by lords, secular and ecclesiastical (*Transgressive Language*, 51–57).

33. All references for the York interrogation pageants are by pageant number and lines in *York Plays*, ed. Beadle, vol. 1.

34. Wright, "Acoustic Tyranny."

35. Beadle explains the significance of Pontus in legendary biographies of Pilate in *York Plays*, 2:256–57.

36. Beckwith, *Signifying God*, 104.

37. Lipton, *Cultures of Witnessing*, 87.

38. Beadle, *York Plays*, 2:243; Beckwith, *Signifying God*, chap. 6. Examining over seventy-five years of contested kingship in which the citizens of York were often unwillingly entangled, Tinkle concludes that when Caiaphas and Anna, and later Pilate, charge Jesus, a legitimate king, with treason, they call into question, in the eyes of the York audience, their system of justice and their own legitimacy ("York's Jesus"). Pageants 20 ("Conspiracy and Capture") and 21 ("Buffeting") of the Towneley plays develop Caiaphas and Anna even more fully than York as corrupt late medieval churchmen, ecclesiastical lawyers using the law to promote their power and status. Caiaphas even perversely cites the canon law maxim "Qui tacet" (on the force of this maxim, see page 52) to claim that Jesus's silence is a sign that he is guilty of the charges voiced by the Tortorers as witnesses (*Towneley Plays*, ed. Stevens and Cawley, 21, 207–8). (All other references are to this edition by play and line.) In so doing, he twists a maxim about the complicity in those who are observing, but not reporting, others' crimes into a tool to condemn Jesus: by not speaking, Jesus incriminates himself.

39. The vernacular version of Isaiah 53:7 comes from a Wycliffite sermon on Luke 11:14–28 for the Third Sunday of Lent; it has been edited by Cigman, in *Lollard Sermons*, 169. Beadle comments on the rope as a prop recalling the silent lamb led to slaughter in *York Plays*, 2:247. Peyraut uses the verse to commend silence through the example of Jesus before Herod and Pilate in the *Summa de vitiis*, fol. 151v^b.

40. The glossator of the Wycliffite short commentary on Luke explains Jesus's silences during the inquisitions as patient submission leading to sacrifice: "Whanne he helde silence as an innocent lomb he ȝaf pacience to be sacrifisid for al þe floc" (Bodleian Library, Oxford, MS. Bodl. 243, fol. 107v^a–v^b).

41. The Caiaphas of the Towneley "Buffeting" mocks the obscurity of Jesus's birth by questioning how he could be "a lord of name" when he is neither booted nor spurred and thus not a member of the knightly class. In contrast, he, as "A lord in degré," has knights waiting on him (21, 211–27). Thus, as in the York interrogation pageants, he works to deny Jesus any social standing, revealing his own obsession with status and his inability to think of any claims on allegiance Jesus might have that lie outside institutions.

42. The refusal to retaliate by uttering injurious words is one of the two reasons given by Nicolas de Lyre in his gloss on Isaiah 53:7, with its image of the silent lamb carried to the slaughter: "'Et non aperuit os suum,' et cetera, verbis recalcitrando et iniurias pro iniuriis reddendo, sed magis coram false accusantibus tacendo" (*Bibliorum sacrorum*, vol. 4).

43. Billington, *Social History*, 18–19. On pages 4–13, she presents evidence for popular games revolving around a king of fools, but she also argues that Jesus must be seen here as a Paulinian fool, someone who rejects worldly wisdom for the wisdom of God, which seems folly to the world (16–17, 19).

44. A late fourteenth- or early fifteenth-century sermon from a priest's

notebook preserved in Lambeth MS 352 and edited by Holly Johnson in *Good Friday*, 206.

45. Kolve, *Play Called Corpus Christi*, 182–84.

46. *Cursor mundi*, ed. Morris, 12639–56. Alexandra Johnston notes that Jesus's discourse on speech also does not appear in any other English cycle play or in any of the poetic analogues to the York trial pageants ("His langage," 185–86). Beadle gives an exegesis of the gospel passages that shape this discourse in *York Plays*, 2:300.

47. King, *York Mystery Cycle*. Davidson had traced earlier how iconography of the Passion and of Patience might have shaped the emotional responses of the York audience, though he stressed personal, rather than communal, response (*Creation to Doom*, 97–115).

48. Tiner points out that both witchcraft and sorcery are crimes under ecclesiastical law that the secular arm may punish ("English Law," 142–43). Although Caiaphas and Anna are clearly compiling a list of crimes that Jesus may be punished for, witchcraft first surfaces as their explanation of his miracles.

49. A. Johnston, "His langage."

50. *Metrical Life*, ed. Sauer, lines 1132–59.

51. *Metrical Life*, lines 2534–51. William of Nottingham paraphrases Jerome on why Jesus did not exculpate himself when Pilate invites him to do so: "nec crimen per responsionem diluens dimitteretur et crucis ultilitas differetur" (Commentary on *Unum ex quatuor*, Oxford, Bodleian Library, MS Laud misc. 165, fol. 533r[b]). So does Thomas Aquinas in the *Catena in Matthaeum*, in *Catena Aurea* 404. Three Wycliffite commentaries ("Glossed Gospels") of the late fourteenth to early fifteenth centuries give Jerome's reasoning in the vernacular; the short exposition of Matthew translates it thus: "lest he, puttynge awey þe cryme bi answere, were delyuerid of þe justise and þe profit of þe cros were delaied" (London, British Library, MS Additional 41175, fol. 98r[b]). See also the commentary on Mark (15:15) in the same manuscript (fol. 155v[b]) and the longer commentary on Matthew

(Oxford, Bodleian Library, MS Laud misc. 235, fol. 252v). The *Cursor mundi*'s account of the Passion also observes that Jesus, despite Herod's yearning for a miracle, "answerd him noght" because any such sign would have prevented his antagonists from killing him (lines 16183–90 in the Cotton manuscript).

52. Jesus's steadfastness is also emphasized in the Chester cycle; Herod describes him as a menacing warrior: "Such a scalward [stalwart man] never before me stood, / so stowt and sterne is hee" (*Chester Mystery Cycle*, ed. Lumiansky and Mills, 16.1, lines 181–82).

53. Woolf, *English Mystery Plays*, 257.

54. Walker, "Cultural Work," 87.

55. Craun, *Ethics and Power*, 132–42.

56. *Book of Margery Kempe*, ed. Meech and Allen, 120.

57. *Book of Margery Kempe*, 2. We might expect Richard Rolle to use silence, as Margery Kempe does, when he records in *Melos amoris* the abuse he suffered during his wanderings, criticized by monastics for his erratic life and by clerics and the wealthy for advocating secular reform. But he does not.

58. *Book of Margery Kempe*, 36.

59. Beckwith, *Signifying God*, 99.

60. *Testimony*, ed. Hudson. 29. All following references are to this edition by page.

61. Hudson, *Premature Reformation*, 221. Hudson carefully weighs evidence for the historical accuracy of the *Testimony*'s events and references in her introduction to *The Testimony*, in *Two Wycliffite Texts*, xlv–liii. She examines it as "in some senses a substitute saint's life" on lvi–lix. Jurkowski has more recently studied a document recording Thorpe's arrest and a wealth of related material that confirms details in his narrative ("Arrest of William Thorpe").

62. Schirmer, "William Thorpe's Narrative Theology," 270.

63. Somerset, "Vernacular Argumentation."

64. See *Heresy Trials*, ed. Tanner.

65. Amsler, *Medieval Life*, 183–202. Because of Critical Discourse Analysis's

focus on power differential, unsaid ideology, and strategies of dissent, it might seem useful in examining the silences of the *Testimony*. However, its major proponents have no interest in silence because they focus on how discourse analysis could transform society, politics, and economics (e.g., Norman Fairclough's *Critical Discourse Analysis* and Robin Wooffitt's *Conversation Analysis and Critical Discourse Analysis*).

66. Thorpe's embrace of the patient and silent Jesus as an exemplar for himself and "true" Christians is similar to what the Good Friday sermon from the long Wycliffite cycle advocates, as Gayk characterizes it in her penetrating reading of Passion sermons: "The sermon holds up Christ's humanity as a model of a life of radical faith, emphasizing Christ as an example of non-violence, verbal restraint, and passive resistance to ecclesiastical authority" ("Form of Christ's Passion," 248).

67. *Lollard Sermons*, ed. Cigman, 168–69.

68. Wycliffite New Testament in Bodleian Library, Oxford, MS Ashmole 1517, fols, 39v and 25r. This manuscript contains the later version.

69. Amsler, *Medieval Life*, 187.

70. Aers, *Sanctifying Signs*, 96.

71. Mark Amsler, whose *Medieval Life of Language* I read after submitting a typescript of this book to the press, examines adeptly Thorpe's strategy of switching topics (194–98).

72. "Trial of Richard Wyche," ed. Matthew, 534, 540.

73. Hudson, *Premature Reformation*, 158.

74. For when direct address may have been used in late medieval English plays, see Steenbrugge, *Drama and Sermon*, 87–114.

CHAPTER 5

1. "Textual self" is a term characterized usefully by Sobecki in "Authorized Realities": "the context-dependent and situated narrative self," which, as "an extension of Hoccleve's biological, indexial self," is subject to the same conditions he is (539–41). See also his *Last Words*, 13–15.

2. For emotions as *perturbationes* in Stoic thought and particularly for fear as subjective evaluation, often mistaken, that something in the future is evil, see Knuuttila, *Emotions*, 47–71; and Rosenwein, *Emotional Communities*, 32–41.

3. "Nec miror ista sic ire, utrumque pendentis animi est, utrumque futuri expectatione sollicitum. Maxima autem utriusque causa est quod non ad presencia aptamur sed cogitaciones in longinque premittimus. Itaque providencia, maximum bonum condicionis humane, in malum versa est. . . . Plura sunt que nos terrent quam premunt et sepius opinione laboramus quam re. . . . Nulli tam perniciosi tam irrevocabiles sicut limphatici metus sunt" (Thomas of Ireland, *Manipulus*, Timor 3 [accessed August 8, 2021]). From Seneca, *Ad Lucilium* 5.8; 13.4, 8, and 9.

4. Peyraut, *Summa de vitiis*, fol. 71r^b.

5. Cicero, *Tusculan Disputations* 4.6.13.

6. Rosenwein, *Generations*, 149–65; and Knuuttila, *Emotions*, 359–65.

7. *Speculum laicorum*, fol. 154r. The compiler is quoting Cassiodorus's *Epistolae variae* 5.22.3 and 6.9.3–4. In his entry "De timore," the compiler, following Augustine, conceives of fear in cautionary terms as spiritual flight to prevent losing what one loves (fol. 204r).

8. "Cok Hath Lowe Shoone," 2:813, lines 1 and 9–10. The poem may be attributed wrongly to Lydgate.

9. John Felton, *Sermones*, Oxford, Oriel College, MS 10, fol. 291r^b. His sermons are extant in twenty-nine manuscripts held in British libraries (Sharpe, *Handlist*, 243–44). Felton is preaching on Luke 11:14–28, the *lectio* for the third Sunday of Lent.

10. Bodleian Library, Oxford, MS Hatton 96, fol. 105r.

11. Hoccleve, *Complaint and Dialogue*, ed. Burrow. All references are to this edition by line in the text, where "C" signifies "My Complaint" and "D," "Dialogue." I have chosen this edition because Burrow uses Hoccleve's scribal practices in the holograph of the *Series* to help to reconstruct, from the five other manuscripts, "My Complaint" and lines 1–252 of the "Dialogue," missing

because the first two quires of Hoccleve's holograph of the *Series* have been lost.

12. From a trove of documents that Mooney has discovered were penned by Hoccleve in the Office of the Privy Seal, she has argued persuasively that his illness fell in 1416, a period of scribal inactivity in which his Easter annuity was collected not by him but by several of his fellow clerks ("Some New Light," 301-7). William Styron wrote *Darkness Visible* (1990) after his recovery from a bout of depression; he took the title from *Paradise Lost* 1.63. Richard Lawes has attempted to describe Thomas's infirmity in terms of modern psychiatry, even resorting to *Diagnostic and Statistical Manual* diagnostic criteria ("Psychological Disorder," 217-28).

13. Burrow discusses the date when Hoccleve began writing "My Complaint" in his edition, lvii-lx. He settles on late 1419 because of references to events in the *Series*, but Sobecki dates "My Complaint" to late 1420 because, he argues, its composition was triggered by the death of Hoccleve's colleague and friend John Bailey on November 11, 1420 (*Last Words*, 65-100). However, he regards the date for the first draft of the *Series* as uncertain ("Authorized Realities," 555).

14. For the source of the complaint genre in legal complaint, see Scase, *Literature and Complaint*, 5-41.

15. On the contents and purpose of the *Formulary*, see Burrow, *Thomas Hoccleve*, 4-6; and Knapp, *Bureaucratic Muse*, 29-36.

16. The date and composition of the original *Gesta* and the Anglo-Latin version are examined in *Anglo-Latin "Gesta,"* ed. and trans. Bright, xvii-lxxxiv.

17. Perry, "Logic of Incompleteness," 74.

18. Stressing that Thomas describes his illness as a dispersal of self, Knapp explores how Thomas, as a melancholic, seeks, and fails, to overcome a fragmented self (*Bureaucratic Muse*, 163-79). Spearing and Willian trace how subjectivity, once stable selfhood is displaced by madness, is subjected to others and how the very construction of the "Dialogue" from literary fragments dissolves the inner life of Thomas (*Medieval Autographies*, 181-207.). Taking an entirely new tack, Appleford has recently linked Thomas's "disordered subjectivity" to ascetic self-fragmentation in the Office of the Dead ("Sea Ground"). See also the earlier essay of Goldie, who stresses differences within Thomas's inner self ("Psychosomatic Illness"); see also Atkinson, "'Why Þat Yee Meeued Been.'"

19. Watt's *Making* examines the manuscripts with an eye to reform, ecclesiastical and personal, while Critten is interested chiefly in the reception of Hoccleve's poetry in *Author, Scribe, and Book*.

20. The five manuscripts containing both the *Regiment* and the *Series* are described by Burrow in his edition (introduction to *Complaint and Dialogue*, xi-xvii).

21. Knapp describes the prologue as a dark rewriting of Chaucer's "General Prologue" (*Bureaucratic Muse*, 164-65), as does Langdell ("'What World,'" 281).

22. Strub, "Hoccleve," 131-32.

23. Gayk is writing about the mirror scene (*Image*, 67).

24. Burrow, "Autobiographical Poetry," 238.

25. Thomas Hoccleve, *Fabula de quadam imperatrice Romana*, in *"My Compleinte" and Other Poems*, ed. Ellis, 160-95. All references are to this edition by line.

26. Anglo-Latin "Gesta," 644-45. Schieberle has recently identified Hoccleve's hand in part of the *Gesta*'s "Chaste Empress" and elsewhere in London, British Library, Harley 319 ("A New Hoccleve Literary Manuscript"), and Sobecki has established that this is the copy of the tale that Hoccleve translated for the *Series* ("Authorized Realities"). Harley differs from the edited *Gesta* in phrases only so I rely on the edition for comparison.

27. Thomas in the *Regiment* sees the disgraceful change in the way veterans are treated as analogous to his own experience as a government clerk whose annuity has not been paid as promised:

> Allas! I see routhe and pitee exylid
> Out of this land. Alaas, compassioun!

O fikil world, allas thy variance!
How many a gentil [noble] man may
  men now see
That whilom [formerly] in the werres
  olde of France
Honured were and holde in greet
  cheertee
For hir prowesse in armes, and plentee
Of freendes haddde in youthe, and now,
  for shame,
Allas, hir frendshipe is crookid and
  lame! (*Regiment* 862–63, 869–75)

28. See, for example, Peyraut, *Summa de vitiis*, fol. 151v[a]; the *Speculum laicorum*, fol. 153v; "Cok Hath Lowe Shoone," lines 1–16.

29. Peyraut, *Summa de vitiis*, fol. 151v[a].

30. Craun, *Lies*, 26–37.

31. Skelton, *Bowge of Courte*, in *English Poems*, ed. Scattergood. All references are to this edition by lines in the text.

32. John Scattergood examines Drede in relation to Skelton's position at court in "Insecurity," and Greg Walker writes of Skelton's continued interest in the "political centre," no matter how close or far from it he was ("John Skelton").

33. Whiting and Whiting give many instances of the proverb (*Proverbs* #S554, page 537) in collections, in love poems, and in hortatory speeches in narratives, like Desire's.

34. Whiting and Whiting give many references to the proverb (#H264, page 275) in proverb collections, narratives, letters, and carols. In *The Prouerbes of Wysdom*: "Here and se and be styll; Thou may the sunner haue thi wille" (lines 99–100).

35. In an illuminating essay on discernment, Raby explains the problems medieval scientists saw in physiognomy as a means of knowing others ("Tasting Thomas Hoccleve," 210–14).

36. Goldie, "Psychosomatic Illness," 28–29. See also Hickey, "Legal Personhood." Turner presents more extensive evidence for medieval English legal opinions of insanity and ways of discerning it in *Care and Custody*, chaps. 2 and 3.

37. Readers have been puzzled by the longish passage on clipping and counterfeit coins in "Dialogue" (lines 99–196). Yet, coming just after Thomas has determined to circulate "My Complaint" (D92–98) so that others, deceived by his silence, may grasp what he believes to be the truth, it serves as an extended analogy to his own experience. Clipping and counterfeiting are acts of "vntrouthe," acts through which the appearance of coins comes to misrepresent their true, diminished, value. Coley, who is broadly interested in relations between verbal and monetary exchanges, focuses on how clipping can take coins out of exchange because merchants may refuse them. He then reads this as an analogy to Thomas being removed from verbal exchanges by his own choice and the slights of others (*Wheel*, 137–43).

38. Orlemanski, *Symptomatic Subjects*, 219. I differ from Orlemanski in understanding the onlookers' comments to fall in the years after Thomas's recovery as part of a continuing experience, like their prophecies of his illness returning in summers. Whereas she links the initial statement of his "wylde infirmitee" (C40–41) to their voices (C120–33), I believe that the stanzas that fall in between— Thomas's recovery, their persistent false prophecies, and the torment they cause him (C50–98)—distance their comments from the bout of illness, as do the ones generalizing about how "God hurte now can / and now hele and cure" (C112). Moreover, Smyth, in her study of time in Hoccleve, concludes that the former friends see Thomas's illness in cyclical terms, while he sees his illness, his recovery, and their misinterpretation in episodic time (*Imaginings of Time*, 137–43).

39. Thomas Hoccleve, *L'epistre de Cupide*, in *"My Compleinte" and Other Poems*, 93–111. All references are to this edition by line. *L'epistre* is Hoccleve's translation and adaptation of Christine de Pizan's *L'Epistre au Dieu d'amours*.

40. Knapp elegantly unpacks Hoccleve's analogies to artistic representation in *Bureaucratic Muse*, 170–71.

41. Strub, "Hoccleve."

42. *De lingua*, fol. 187r.

43. *Liber regulae pastoralis* 3.14; Thomas of Ireland, *Manipulus florum* (Taciturnitas 1 [accessed August 8, 2021]).

44. Critten, *Author*, 53.

45. Hoccleve, *Cy ensuyte la male regle de T. Hoccleue*, in *"My Compleinte,"* line 433. All references are to this edition by line.

46. Crocker, "Engendering Affect," 74.

47. Although Burrow notes in his edition (Hoccleve, *Complaint and Dialogue*, 104) that the poet's eye may be read as the third eye of prudence, his note surely rests on his earlier article "The Third Eye," 42.

48. E. Johnson, *Practicing Literary Theory*, 208–9.

49. Malo, "Penitential Discourse."

50. Nicolas de Byard, *Distinctiones*, fol. 162r^a.

51. *Late Fifteenth-Century Dominical Sermon Cycle*, ed. Morrison, 1:128–29. The full text of the cycle survives in four manuscripts.

52. Philip Repingdon (?), *Sermones*, Oxford, Bodleian Library, MS Laud Misc 635, fol. 133r^b. Ten copies of this collection survive; eleven more are attested to in catalogues and other records (Sharpe, *Handlist*, 437–38).

53. Thomas's reseeing his healing as an act of God and his decision to make it known to others accord with the motto on Hoccleve's seal as reread by R. F. Green and Ethan Knapp: "VA:MA:VOLUNTEE," an injunction to turn the will to God ("Thomas Hoccleve's Seal").

54. Lawton, *Voice*, chap. 3.

55. Burrow's edition provides notes relating the Latin glosses to the version of the epitome closest to what Hoccleve used, a version Burrow found in an early fifteenth-century manuscript (Hoccleve, *Complaint and Dialogue*, 83–86).

56. Watt, *Making*, 11.

57. Thomas's recognition of the limits of his life in an inexorably changing natural world emerges more fully in the middle of the "Dialogue," where he tells the friend that he knows life is brief and death is nearing for a man of his age (fifty-three), that life inevitably brings sorrow and torment, extinguishing any sweetness it had, that his body is weakening, and that he is losing his eyesight and mental agility (D246–90).

CHAPTER 6

1. Peyraut, *Summa de vitiis*, fol. 152r^b.

2. In addition to Peyraut's *Summa* and the *Alphabetum narrationum* (note 5 below), I found this *sententia* in these texts: Simon of Boraston, *Distinctiones*, fol. 139v^b; Holcot, *Super Sapientiam*, fol. Viiira; extracts from *Pera peregrini*, fol. 171r^a; Roger of Waltham, *Compendium*, fol. 166v; Étienne de Bourbon, *Tractatus*, fol. 157v^b; John of Mirfield, *Florarium*, fol. 217r^a; *Speculum laicorum*, fol. 154r; Thomas of Ireland, *Manipulus* (Taciturnitas 2 [accessed August 5, 2021]); *Summa fratris Alexandri* 2.2.3.3.2.3; "Vani sunt," fol. 64v; Higden, *Distinctiones theologicae*, fol. 111r; Ps.-John of Lathbury, *Distinctiones* (London, British Library, MS Royal 11.A.XIII), fol. 92r^a; Vincent de Beauvais, *Speculum historiale* (in *Speculum quadruplex*, vol. 4), col, 121. Five manuscripts of the Ps.-John of Lathbury survive in British libraries (Sharpe, *Handlist*, 284), as do seven of the *Speculum* (Kaeppeli, *Scriptores*, 4:440–46). The dictum is also found in the tenth-century collection of Ps.-Caecilius Balbus, *De nugis philosophorum*, where it heads sayings on taciturnity (26.1), as well as the *Florilegium morale Oxoniensis* of the twelfth century (fol. 67v), where it is ascribed to Xenocrates.

3. Cole and Galloway, "Christian Philosophy," 136–38.

4. On relations between schoolmaster and student in early education in medieval England, see Orme, *Medieval Schools*, 128–86.

5. Arnold of Liège, *Alphabetum narrationum*, ed. Brilli, 405. (I have emended "soluisse," surely an error in the edition, to "siluisse," following Oxford, University College, MS 67, fol. 108v.) The exemplum lies side by side with ones from the *Vita patrum* and contemporary France, all under the heading "Silentium." The *Alphabetum* survives in English libraries in six fourteenth-century manuscripts of

proven or likely English provenance (described on xcv–cii).
6. Valerius Maximus, *Facta et dicta memorabilia* 7.2.ext.6, in *Memorable Doings and Sayings*, 2:118–19.
7. Lydgate, *Fall of Princes*, vol. 1, Book 1, lines 6217–23.
8. Lydgate, *Fall of Princes*, vol. 1, Book 1, lines 6194–95.
9. Roger of Waltham, *Compendium*, fol. 8v. Cicero's *sententia* is also quoted by Vincent of Beauvais in his *Speculum doctrinale* (in *Speculum quadruplex*, vol. 2, col. 437) and by John of Wales in his *Compendiloquium* 5.2 (in *Summa*, fol. 213v), a work that survives in four manuscripts in British libraries (Swanson, *John of Wales*, 236–56).
10. Roger of Waltham, *Compendium*, fol. 178r; from Seneca, *Ad Lucilium epistulae morales* 117.21.
11. Publilius Syrus, *Sententiae*, in *Minor Latin Poets*, 1:100.
12. Holcot, *Super Sapientiam*, fol. niira. Isidore of Seville's etymology from *sapor*, close to Robert's wording, is quoted by Thomas of Ireland (*Manipulus*, Sapientia 4 [accessed December 13, 2021]). Like Holcot, John of Wales derives *sapientia* from *sapor*; he then defines it as "recta estimatio rerum cum vero sapore," adding that its work is "omnia enim distinguere" (*Breviloquium de sapientia sanctorum* 1, in *Summa*, fol. 235v). He also defines wisdom, in part, as knowledge of the causes of things: "sapientia est nosse diuina et humana et eorum causas" (fol. 233v). This *Breviloquium* survives in seven manuscripts lodged in British libraries (Swanson, *John of Wales*, 236–56).
13. Holcot, *Super Sapientiam*, fol. niiva.
14. Simon of Boraston, *Distinctiones*, 140r[a]; Higden, *Distinctiones theologicae*, fol. 111v[b]; Cassian, *Collationes patrum* 14.9. "Ypocrates antequam doceret discipulos adiurabat et eos iurare cogebat de silencio seruando, de sermone modesto et raro, de incessu plano et habitu honesto et optimis moribus" (Servasanta da Faenza, *Liber de exemplis*, Oxford, Bodleian Library, MS Bodl. 332, fol. 250v). Four manuscripts of this Franciscan work survive in British libraries (Bloomfield et al., *Incipits*, 119).
15. Thomas of Ireland, *Manipulus* (Taciturnitas 2 [accessed August 5, 2021]); from Hugues de Saint-Victor, *Didascalicon*, 53. The last sentence is included in the extracts from *Pera peregrini* after Pythagoras's mandated period of silence (fol. 171r[a]). For that period, see also Holcot, *Super Sapientiam* (fol. Viiira); Higden, *Distinctiones* (fol. 111v[b]); John of Wales, *De vita religiosa* (in *Summa*, fol. 268r); and the *Glossa ordinaria* on Eccles 3:7 (*Bibliorum sacrorum cum glossa*, vol. 3).
16. *Secreta*, 40–41; Lydgate and Burgh, *Secrees*, lines 519–23.
17. Lochrie, *Covert Operations*, 95–96 and 102–6.
18. Ps.-Caecilius Balbus, *De nugis*, sec. 27 ("De loquacitate"). Also Bromyard, *Summa praedicantium*, vol. 1, fol. 452v[a] (from the entry "Loquutio"), and, worded slightly differently, the extract "Tacere" from *Pera peregrini*, fol. 171r[a]. Robert Holcot conveys the same physiological argument for the importance of silence: "Nam geminas aures nobis Deus; os dedit vnum" (*Super Sapientiam*, fol. viiira). In the later *Dicts and Sayings*, Diogenes addresses a loquacious man: "thou hast ij eris and thow hast bot oo mouthe; wherefore thou shuldist bi the halfe more hire than speke" (72).
19. This physiological argument is of a piece with the late medieval work of deriving an ethic of speech, together with one of taste, from Aristotle's biological writing, work I have examined in "Aristotle's Biology."
20. The *sententia* is attributed to Seneca by John of Mirfield, *Florarium*, fol. 216v[b]. See also Holcot, *Super Sapientiam*, fol. viiira; and extracts from *Pera peregrini*, fol. 159r[a].
21. Boethius, *Philosophiae consolatio*, 2.pr, 7. Quoted by Roger of Waltham, *Compendium*, fol. 166r; and by Holcot, *Super Sapientiam*, fol. niiirb. Alford regards the dictum as proverbial in the fourteenth century, citing several British texts (*"Piers Plowman,"* 70). So familiar was it among the literate that the surgeon John Arderne

Anglicizes it in a treatise on the fistula in the anus when he advises young surgeons on their speech: "For a wiseman seith, 'It semeth more to vse the eres than þe tunge'; And in an-oþer place, 'ȝif thou had bene stille thou had bene holden a philosophre'" (*Treatises of Fistula in Ano*, 6–7).

22. Bromyard, *Summa praedicantium*, fol. 450r^b–v^a. The entry is "Loquutio"; the section deals with the silence of the wise.

23. Breen, *Machines*, chap. 7.

24. Langland, *"Piers Plowman": A Parallel Text Edition*, vol. 1, *Text*, C.13.222–25b. All references to the text are to this edition by version, passus, and line.

25. Kerby-Fulton, "Pedagogy," 217. Derek Pearsall observes that the revisions make explicit "what was enigmatically implicit in B" and give "the argument great vehemence and directness" ("Poetic Character," 165).

26. Steiner, *Reading "Piers Plowman,"* chap. 4.

27. Warner, *Myth*, 53–54. Warner makes this statement before he records evidence of Latin lines that readers added to the margins of the manuscripts of *Piers*. Through extensive documentary research, Robert Adams and others have identified William Rokele, a priest from the gentry class, as a likely candidate for the author. "William Langland" is a name constructed from the text and several ascriptions, including one by John Bale. The William Rokele whose well-to-do family Adams and others have traced would have had the resources for an extended education. See especially Adams, *Poet*; Galloway, "Parallel Lives"; and M. Johnston, "Clerical Career." With the poet's long-given name and personal history in doubt, I refer to him simply as "the poet."

28. In *World of Echo*, Adin Lears considers the poem's consistent interest in hearing, but she focuses on the material and aural aspects of sound of all kinds (94–115).

29. Middleton, "*Piers Plowman*," 96. The term "discursive hunger" is also Middleton's (101).

30. Middleton, "Narration," 98. Recently, Zeeman has stressed the "conceptual divisions and narrative gaps that are opened up by the poem's verbal and narrative oppositionality" as she argues for the poem's "conversionary potential" in the Christian work of pastoral care with a diverse laity ("Pastoral Care," 436).

31. Hanna, "*Speculum vitae*," 128.

32. Davis, "*Piers Plowman*," chap. 3. For Reason as the principles of divine order in the created world, see Alford, "Idea of Reason," 201–6.

33. Zeeman, "*Piers Plowman*," 64–224.

34. Zeeman, *Arts of Disruption*, chaps. 5 and 6.

35. The term "ironic oxymoron" is Schmidt's in Langland, *"Piers Plowman": A Parallel-Text Edition*, vol. 2, *Introduction*, 611. As Pearsall has observed, C revisions have already distanced the reader from the speech by giving it to Recklessness instead of the narrator, as in B, and by extending it with such passages as Recklessness's "outrage at the good fortune of the penitent thief" ("Poetic Character," 161).

36. By contrast, in Will's brief rebuke in the B text (11.373–74), Reason simply fails to follow behind or accompany ("sewest") humans, preventing misdeeds from overtaking them, a limited power to check.

37. Kruger explores how Will represents here "the general human tendency" to misunderstand sin and "exonerate individual volition" from complicity in it ("Mirrors," 88).

38. For a general study of the Wisdom books as an intertext for *Piers Plowman*, with similar themes, styles, and purposes, see Davlin, "*Piers Plowman*."

39. Peyraut, *Summa de vitiis*, fol. 148v^a. Albertano da Brescia, *De arte*, 94; see also his *De amore* 1.2. Sirach 11.9 is also used to authorize avoiding contentious speech in the chapter "De contentione et inimicicia" of the fourteenth-century catechetical collection beginning "Vani sunt," fol. 69r.

40. Alford, "Role of Quotations."

41. Sirach 11:7–8: "Priusquam interroges, ne vituperes quemquam; Et cum interrogaveris, corripe iuste. Priusquam audias, ne respondeas verbum; et in medio sermonum ne adiicias loqui." The *Glossa ordinaria* explicates "Priusquam audias" by

defining the person who speaks before listening as someone who desires to be thought learned before learning or to pronounce on causes of things before discerning them: "Qui prius respondet quam audiat; id est, qui doctor esse desiderat antequam discat. Vel aliorum causas iudicare priusquam dignoscat stultum se esse demonstrat" (*Bibliorum sacrorum*, vol. 3). This fits nicely Will's rebuke of Reason as Imaginatif sees it.

42. John of Mirfield, *Florarium*, fol. 116v[a–b]; the entry is titled "De loquacitate." The *sententia* occurs in monastic rules and prescriptive advice: in the ninth-century *Codex regularum* of Benedict of Aniane (col. 668) and earlier in the anonymous *Exhortatio ad monachos*, sometimes ascribed to a Pseudo-Athanasius (col. 73).

43. Étienne de Bourbon, for example, writes of how God intended speech to function as part of the created order: "Deus ... dedit pedagogum rationis sine quo non debet quidquam loqui uel quidquam procedere" (*Tractatus*, fol. 153v[a]).

44. *Book for a Simple and Devout Woman*, ed. Diekstra, 263, 264.

45. Hanna, "*Speculum vitae*," 122–25. The *Speculum* (third quarter of the fourteenth century) was one of three Middle English works derived from the influential catechetical treatise *Somme le roi* by Lorent d'Orléans, which also spawned ten English translations in the fourteenth and fifteenth centuries. So, the *Speculum*'s advocacy of moderation in speaking may be found in many other texts.

46. *Speculum vitae*, vol. 2, lines 14965–74.

47. *Speculum vitae*, vol. 2, lines 15376, 15393–94, 15428–29 (from the section on the third degree of "Sobrenes," "Mesure in Wordes and Speche").

48. Peyraut, *Summa de vitiis*, fols. 139v[b]–40r[a], 142r[a], 148r[b].

49. The translation is Pearsall's in Langland, "*Piers Plowman*," ed. Pearsall, 231n.

50. Zeeman, "*Piers Plowman*," 4–8, 238–41.

51. *Disticha Catonis* 1.5. Cannon notes in his fascinating study of how the process of learning Latin in grammar schools shaped the composition of late medieval English poetry that the poet refers to the *Disticha* more than any other authority, often at climatic moments (*From Literacy*, 129).

52. The term "surprising arrivals" is Wood's in *Conscience*, 7.

53. Karnes, *Imagination*, 179–206; Carruthers, "Imaginatif"; Minnis, "Imaginatif."

54. Zeeman, "*Piers Plowman*," 179–80.

55. As Hanna notes, writing about the next passus, the similitudes that Imaginatif employs function "at a level fundamentally fortuitous and emotive, one of affective desire," firmly distinguishing his discourse from that of Reason ("Langland's Ymaginatif," 88).

56. Zeeman, *Arts of Disruption*, especially 374–76.

57. Ps.-Albertus Magnus, *Paradisus animae*, 494–95. Two manuscripts of the *Paradisus* survive in British libraries (Bloomfield et al., *Incipits*, 507–8). For temerarious speech and its destructive effects, see also *Floretum* (fol. 115r); *Rosarium theologie* (London, British Library, MS Harley 3226, fols. 73v–74r); and Roger of Waltham, *Compendium* (fol. 166r).

58. "Item silentium pacem facit; unde Isaiah 32[:17]: 'Erit opus iusticie pax et cultus iusticie silentium.' Silentium quasi quedam cultura est iusticie. Sicut ex nimia loquela sequitur frequenter iniuria tam Dei quam proximi, sic ex silentio iusticia nutritur, ex qua uelut ex quadam arbore fructus pacis colligitur. ... Multe lites et ire [remouentur] ex obseruatione silentii" (Peyraut, *Summa de vitiis*, fol. 152r[a]). I have emended the last verb on the basis of three *pecia* exemplars; "remanent" in Lyon 678 is untenable. See similar material in *De lingua*, fol. 187r–v.

59. *Book of Vices and Virtues*, 282; Laurent d'Orléans, *Somme le roi*, 388.

60. In Roger of Waltham's *Compendium morale*, this *sententia* appears along with, though not immediately next to, "Me esse locutum pluries penituit; tacuisse

numquam," with both used to confirm the same point: that taciturnity shows a person wise (fol. 166r).

61. "Heu! quanta desolatio Angliae praestatur," in *Political Poems*, ed. Wright, 1:262. Since Scase sees a possible reference to Piers the Plowman in the stanza following this, the *sententia* may be taken to refer to Imaginatif's use of it ("Heu!," 34). Kerby-Fulton thinks that the "Heu" poet may be using this *sententia*, in addition to the naming of Piers, to position his poem in the tradition of *Piers Plowman* (*Books Under Suspicion*, 184). However, she considers the *sententia* uncommon because she relies on John Alford's listing of only one other use (in John Bromyard's *Summa*).

62. Hanna, *Patient Reading*, 297.

63. Langland, *"Piers Plowman": A Parallel-Text Edition*, vol. 2, Introduction, 2:612 (Schmidt's emphasis).

64. On excuses for sin as a sin of the tongue, including pride as the root, see Craun, "'It is a freletee.'" "Tercium peccatum erat cum vocatus ad penitentiam confiteri noluit, set se excusat. Et tunc primo eiectus fuit a paradyso" (Thomas of Chobham, *Sermones*, 73).

65. *Speculum vitae*, lines 15198–202.

66. In his chapter "De temeritate disputationum et temerariis disputationibus," Pierre le Chantre writes, "Licet autem stulti pereant, magis tamen insipientes qui de celestibus supra vires et supra ea que sufficiunt ad salutem inquirunt, qui vespis set pugionibus Dominum Iesum exagitare videntur" (*Verbum abbreviatum*, 29). He later attributes such speech to "superbam et curiosam disputationem nimis inuestigando" (34). The *Speculum vitae* also attributes lack of "Mesure" in theological thought to pride (lines 15220–21). As Newhauser has demonstrated, pride is linked by Augustine, and moral writers after him, to *curiositas* as a vice: "that disturbance of the human will which led to an intemperate desire" for knowledge of the natural world and "which treated the divine mysteries as if they fit into these categories [of knowledge]" ("Augustinian *vitium curiositatis*," 106–7). In its excessively eager desire to know, intemperate *curiositas* is associated with loquacity by monastic writers (Newhauser, "Towards a History," 573), just as it is in the third vision of *Piers Plowman*.

67. Langland, *"Piers Plowman": A Parallel-Text Edition*, vol. 2, Introduction, 613.

68. *De lingua*, fol. 187v. See also Peyraut, *Summa de vitiis*, fol. 152r^b.

69. In "Learning from Shame," Strub draws on vernacular devotional literature and the history of emotions to develop the power of shame to teach and remake Will in this episode. Strub works almost exclusively with the B text. So does Wittig, who acknowledged some time ago the force of shame in Will's reform ("*Piers Plowman* B.," 248). See also Davlin, "Game of Heuene," 84; and Gallacher, "Imaginatif," 55–57.

70. Zeeman, "*Piers Plowman*," 217.

71. Bennett, *Preaching and Narrative*, chap. 4.

72. Langland, *"Piers Plowman": A Parallel-Text Edition*, vol. 2, Introduction, 615. Burrow traces the poem's concern with wasting words and time ("Wasting Time"). Wholesale revisions at the beginning of C 14 make Will's changed speech practices clearer than in the B text.

73. Smith, "Silence," 264.

74. In "Silence," Vance Smith finds love present even in the household and schoolroom of that pedagogue Dame Study.

75. *Vita Secundi philosophi*, ed. Perry, 92–93. This Latin translation by William Medicus of St. Denis survives in over one hundred manuscripts of the twelfth to fifteenth centuries and was adapted by English chroniclers like Roger Hoveden and Ranulph Higden and by the encyclopedist Vincent de Beauvais (38–39).

76. Steiner, *Reading "Piers Plowman,"* 112. Steiner develops several dimensions of the tension between "soffrance" and "lakking" in the B text, but silence is not among them.

77. In Nicolas de Byard's several divisions of taciturnity in his *Distinctiones theologicae*, the first of three modes of taciturnity in a life that gains benefits from others is "taciturnitas ... reuerentie et honestatis qua

quis doctorem vel predicatorem tacens audit pacifice sicut infirmus phisicum et peregrinus de patria sua rumorem. Sirach 32:[6]: 'Audi tacens, et pro reverentia accedet tibi bona gratia'" (fol. 161v^b). This *sententia* from Sirach, along with five ones from classical wise men and from Christian Fathers, authorizes Peyraut's reasoning about how one should listen in reverent silence to others rather than presuming to teach what one has not learned sufficiently (*Summa de vitiis*, fol. 96v^a).

78. Silence is associated with humility and openness to instruction in the Benedictine Rule and so more generally in Western monasticism, as MacCulloch notes in *Silence*, 92. Gehl gives a much fuller treatment of how silence as a normative practice was designed to further monks' and nuns' learning ("*Competens Silentium*").

POSTSCRIPT

1. Lawton, *Voice*, chap. 7; Craun, *Lies*, 198–212.

BIBLIOGRAPHY

PRINTED PRIMARY SOURCES

Albertano da Brescia. *De amore et dilectione Dei et proximi et aliarum rerum et de forma vitae*. The Latin Library. Accessed April 13, 2020. https://thelatinlibrary.com/albertanus/albertanus1.shtml.

———. *De arte loquendi et tacendi*. Edited by Thor Sundby. In *Brunetto Latinos Levenet og Skrifter*, 89–119. Copenhagen: J. Lund, 1869.

———. *Liber consolationis et consilii*. Edited by Thor Sundby. London: N. Trübner, 1873.

An Alphabet of Tales. Edited by Mary Macleod Banks. EETS, o.s., 126–27. London: Oxford University Press, 1904–5. Reprint, Millwood, NY: Kraus Reprint, 1975.

The Anglo-Latin "Gesta Romanorum." Edited and translated by Phillipa Bright, with Diane Speed and Juniata Ruys. Oxford, UK: Clarendon, 2019.

Aquinas, Thomas. *Catena in Matthaeum*. In *Catena Aurea in Quatuor Evangelia*, edited by A. Guarienti, 1:1–425. Rome: Marietti, 1953.

———. *Summa theologica*. Translated by Fathers of the English Dominican Province. New York: Benzinger Bros., 1947.

Arderne, John. *Treatises of Fistula in Ano*. Edited by D'Arcy Power. EETS, o.s., 139. London: Kegan Paul, Trench, Trübner, 1910.

Arnold of Liège. *Alphabetum narrationum*. Edited by Elissa Brilli. CCCM 160. Turnhout: Brepols, 2015.

Ashby, George. *George Ashby's Poems*. Edited by Mary Bateson. EETS, e.s., 76. London: Oxford University Press, 1899.

Benedict of Aniane. *Codex regularum*. PL 103, cols. 423–700.

Biblia Sacra Iuxta Vulgatum Clementinam. Edited by Alberto Colunga and Laurentio Turrado. 5th ed. Madrid: EDICA, 1977.

Bibliorum sacrorum cum glossa ordinaria. 6 vols. Venice, 1603.

Boethius, Anicius Manlius Severinus. *Philosophiae consolatio*. Edited by L. Bieler. CCSL 94. Turnhout: Brepols, 2015.

Book for a Simple and Devout Woman: A Late Middle English Adaptation of Peraldus's "Summa de vitiis et virtutibus" and Friar Laurent's "Somme le Roi." Edited by F. N. M. Diekstra. Groningen: Forsten, 1998.

The Book of Margery Kempe. Edited by Sanford Meech and Hope Emily Allen. EETS, o.s., 212. London: Oxford University Press, 1940.

The Book of Vices and Virtues. Edited by W. Nelson Francis. EETS, o.s., 217. London: Oxford University Press, 1942.

Bromyard, John. *Summa praedicantium*. 2 vols. Venice, 1586.

Carpenter, Alexander. *Destructorium viciorum*. Nuremberg: Koberger, 1496.

Cassian, John. *Collationes patrum XXIV*. Monumenta.ch. https://www.monumenta.ch/latein/text/php?tabelle.

Cassiodorus, Magnus. *Epistolae variae*. Intratext. https://intratext.com/IXT/LAT0253/_PSY.htm.

Caxton, William. *The Book of Good Manners*. Westminster, UK: Wynkyn de Worde, 1498.

———. *Caxton's Book of Curtesye*. Edited by Frederick J. Furnivall. EETS, e.s., 3. London: Trübner, 1868.

———. *The Game and Pleye of the Chesse.* Edited by Jenny Adams. Kalamazoo, MI: Medieval Institute Press, 2009.

Chaucer, Geoffrey. *The Riverside Chaucer.* Edited by Larry D. Benson et al. 3rd ed. New York: Houghton Mifflin, 1987.

The Chester Mystery Cycle. Vol. 1, *The Text.* Edited by Robert Lumiansky and David Mills. EETS, s.s., 3. London: Oxford University Press, 1974.

Cicero, Marcus Tullius. *De inventione.* In *On Invention; The Best Kind of Orator; Topics.* Translated by H. M. Hubbell. LCL 386. Cambridge: Harvard University Press, 1949.

———. *De officiis.* Edited by Jeffrey Henderson. Translated by Warren Miller. LCL 30. Cambridge: Harvard University Press, 1913

———. *Tusculan disputationes.* Edited by J. E. King. LCL 141. Cambridge: Harvard University Press, 1945.

"The Cok Hath Lowe Shoone." In *The Minor Poems of John Lydgate,* part 2, *Secular Poems,* edited by Henry Noble MacCracken, 813–18. EETS, o.s., 192. London: Oxford University Press, 1934.

Colonna, Egidio. *Egidius de regimine principum.* Venice: Bevilaqua, 1498.

"Consail and Teiching." In *Ratis Raving and Other Moral and Religious Pieces in Verse and Prose,* edited by T. Rawson Lumby, 90–103. EETS, o.s., 43. London: Trübner, 1870.

Corpus iuris canonici. Edited by A. Friedberg. 2 vols. Leipzig: Tauchnitz, 1879.

Cursor mundi. Vol. 2. Edited by Richard Morris. EETS, o.s., 59. London: Trübner, 1874.

De quadripartita regis specie. In *Four English Political Tracts of the Later Middle Ages,* edited by Jean-Philippe Genet, 22–39. London: Royal Historical Society, 1977.

Dicts and Sayings of the Old Philosophers. Edited by Curt F. Bühler. EETS, o.s., 211. London: Oxford University Press, 1942.

Disticha Catonis. Edited by Marcus Boas. 2nd ed., edited by Hendrik Botshuyver. Amsterdam: North-Holland, 1952.

The Early English Versions of the "Gesta Romanorum." Edited by Sidney J. H. Herrtage. EETS, e.s., 33. London: Trübner, 1879.

Fasciculus morum. Edited and translated by Siegfried Wenzel. University Park: Pennsylvania State University Press, 1989.

Flores philosophorum et poetarum. Edited by Irene Fernandez. Rome: Fédération Internationale des Instituts d'Études Médiévales, 2020.

The Governance of Kings and Princes: John Trevisa's Middle English Translation of the "De Regimine Principum" of Aegidius Romanus. Edited by David Fowler, Charles Briggs, and Paul Remley. New York: Garland, 1997.

Gower, John. *Confessio Amantis.* In *The English Works of John Gower,* edited by G. C. Macaulay, 1:1–456, 2:1–480. EETS, e.s., 81–82. Oxford: Oxford University Press, 1900–1901.

Gregory the Great. *Homiliae in Evangelia.* Edited by R. Était. CCSL 141. Turnhout: Brepols, 1999.

———. *Homiliae in Hiezechielem Prophetam.* Edited by Marc Adriaen. CCSL 142. Turnhout: Brepols, 1971.

———. *Liber regulae pastoralis.* PL 77, cols. 13–126. Bibliotheca Augustana.

———. *Moralia in Iob.* Edited by Marc Adriaen. 3 vols. CCSL 143. Turnhout: Brepols, 1979–85.

Heresy Trials in the Diocese of Norwich, 1428-31. Edited by Norman P. Tanner. Camden Fourth Series 20. London: Royal Historical Society, 1977.

"Heu! quanta desolatio Angliae praestatur." In *Political Poems and Songs Relating to English History: Composed During the Period from the Accession of Edw. III to That of Ric. III,* edited by Thomas Wright, 1:253–63. London: Longman, Green, Longman, and Roberts, 1859.

Hoccleve, Thomas. *"My Compleinte" and Other Poems*. Edited by Roger Ellis. Exeter: University of Exeter Press, 2001.

———. *The Regiment of Princes*. Edited by Charles R. Blyth. Kalamazoo, MI: Medieval Institute Publications, 1999.

———. *Thomas Hoccleve's Complaint and Dialogue*. Edited by J. A. Burrow. EETS 313. Oxford: Oxford University Press, 1999.

Holcot, Robert. *Super sapientiam Salomonis*. Paris: Wolf, 1489.

Hugues de Saint-Victor. *Didascalicon de studio legendi*. Edited by Charles H. Buttimer. Washington, DC: Catholic University Press, 1936.

Jacques de Vitry. *Exempla*. Edited by Thomas F. Crane. London: Nutt, 1890.

John of Wales. *Breviloquium de sapientia sanctorum*. In *Summa . . . de regimine vite humane seu Margarita Doctorum*, 232v–239v. Venice: Arrivabene, 1496.

———. *Compendiloquium*. In *Summa . . . de regimine vite humane seu Margarita Doctorum*, 170r–232r. Venice: Arrivabene, 1496.

———. *De vita religiosa*. In *Summa . . . de regimine vite humane seu Margarita Doctorum*, 260r–305v. Venice: Arrivabene, 1496.

Langland, William. *"Piers Plowman": The C-Text*. Edited by Derek Pearsall. Corrected ed. Exeter: University of Exeter Press, 1991.

———. *"Piers Plowman": A Parallel-Text Edition of the A, B, C, and Z Versions*. Vol. 1, *Text*. Edited by A. V. C. Schmidt. 2nd ed. Kalamazoo, MI: Medieval Institute Press, 2001.

———. *"Piers Plowman": A Parallel-Text Edition of the A, B, C, and Z Versions*. Vol. 2, *Introduction, Textual Notes, Commentary, Bibliography, and Indexical Glossary*. Edited by A. V. C. Schmidt. Rev. ed. Kalamazoo, MI: Medieval Institute Press, 2011.

A Late Fifteenth-Century Dominical Sermon Cycle. Edited by Stephen Morrison. 2 vols. EETS 337–38. Oxford: Oxford University Press, 2012.

Laurent d'Orléans. *La "Somme le roi" par Frère Laurent*. Edited by Édith Brayer and Anne-Françoise Leurquin-Labie. Paris: Société des Anciens Textes Français, 2008.

Liber pharetrae. The Digital *Liber pharetrae* Project. Accessed March 25, 2020. https://web.wlu.ca/history/cnighman/LP/index.html.

Liber regalis. In *English Coronation Records*, edited by Leopold George Wickham Legg, 81–131. London: Archibald Constable, 1901.

Lollard Sermons. Edited by Gloria Cigman. EETS 294. Oxford: Oxford University Press, 1989.

Lydgate, John. *The Fall of Princes*. Edited by Henry Bergen. 4 vols. Washington, DC: Carnegie Institute of Washington, 1923.

Lydgate, John, and Benedict Burgh. *Lydgate and Burgh's Secrees of Old Philisoffres*. Edited by Robert Steele. EETS, e.s., 66. London: Kegan Paul, Trench, Trübner, 1894.

Martin of Braga. *Formula honestae vitae*. In *Opera omnia*, edited by Claude W. Barlow, 236–50. New Haven, CT: Yale University Press, 1950.

Materials for the History of Thomas Beckett. Edited by James C. Robertson. 7 vols. Rerum Britannicarum Medii Aevi Scriptores 67. London: Longmans, 1875–85.

Matthew of Paris. *Historia Anglorum*. Edited by Frederic Madden. Rerum Britannicarum Medii Aevi Scriptores 46, part 3. London: Longmans, Green, 1869.

Memoriale credencium. Edited by T. H. L. Kengen. Nijmegen, the Netherlands: Katholieke Universiteit Nijmegen, 1979.

The Metrical Life of Christ. Edited by Walter Sauer. Heidelberg: Winter, 1977.

Millemete, Walter. *On the Nobility, Wisdom, and Prudence of Kings*. In *Political*

Thought in Early Fourteenth-Century England: Treatises by Walter of Millemete, William of Pagula, and William of Ockham, edited and translated by Cary J. Nederman, 24–61. Turnhout: Brepols, 2002.

Mum and the Sothsegger. In The "Piers Plowman" Tradition, edited by Helen Barr, 137–202, 291–368. London: Dent, 1993.

Mum and the Sothsegger. In Richard the Redeless and Mum and the Sothsegger, edited by James Dean, 75–169. Kalamazoo, MI: Medieval Institute Publications, 2000.

Mum and the Sothsegger. Edited by M. Day and R. Steele. EETS, o.s., 199. London: Oxford University Press, 1936.

"Eine Nordenglische Cato-Version." Edited by Max Förster. Englische Studien 36 (1906): 1–55.

The Northern Passion. Vol. 1. Edited F. A. Foster. EETS, o.s., 145. London: Trübner, 1913.

Ovid, Publius Naso. Ars amatoria. In Ovid: The Art of Love and Other Poems, rev. ed., edited by J. H. Mozley, 11–176. LCL 232. Cambridge: Harvard University Press, 1962.

Pamphilus de Amore. In "'Pamphilus, de Amore': An Introduction and Translation," edited and translated by Thomas J. Garbaty. Chaucer Review 2, no. 2 (1967): 108–34.

Peyraut, Guillaume. De eruditione principum. In Opera Omnia, by Thomas de Aquino, vol. 16. Parma: Fiaccadori, 1865. https://www.corpusthomisticum.org/xreo.html.

———. Summa de virtutibus. In Summa de virtutibus et vitiis. Basel: Amerbach, 1497.

Pierre le Chantre. Verbum abbreviatum: Textus prior. Edited by Monique Boutry. CCCM 196A. Turnhout: Brepols, 2011.

The Pilgrimage of the Lyf of Manhode. Vol. 1, Introduction and Text. Edited by Avril Henry. EETS 288. London: Oxford University Press, 1985.

Polythecum. Edited by A. P. Orban. CCCM 93. Turnhout: Brepols, 1990.

"The Prouerbis of Wysdom." Edited by J. Zupitza. Archiv für das Studium der neueren Sprachen und Literaturen 90 (1893): 241–68.

"The Proverbs of Alfred." In An Old English Miscellany, edited by Richard Morris, 102–39. EETS, o.s., 49. London: Trübner, 1872.

"The Proverbs of Salamon." Edited by Karl Brunner. Archiv für das Studium der neueren Sprachen und Literaturen 161 (1932): 191–95; 164 (1933): 178–91.

Ps.-Albertus Magnus. Paradisus animae sive libellus de virtutibus. In Alberti Magni opera omnia, edited by A. Borgnet, 37:447–512. Paris: Vives, 1898.

Ps.-Athanasius. Exhortatio ad monachos. PL 18, cols. 71–78.

Ps.-Caecilius Balbus. De nugis philosophorum. Edited by Eduard Woelfflin. Basel: Schweighauser, 1855.

Publilius Syrus. Sententiae. In Minor Latin Poets, edited by J. Wight Duff and Arnold M. Duff, rev. ed., 1:15–111. Reprint, Cambridge: Harvard University Press, 1982.

Secreta secretorum. In Opera hactenus inedita, by Roger Bacon, fasc. 5, edited by Karl Steele. Oxford, UK: Clarendon, 1920.

Seneca, Lucius Annaeus. Ad Lucilium epistulae morales. Edited by L. D. Reynolds. 2 vols. Oxford, UK: Clarendon, 1965.

Skelton, John. The Complete English Poems. Edited by John Scattergood. Rev. ed. Liverpool: Liverpool University Press, 2015.

Le Speculum laicorum. Edited by J. Th. Welter. Paris, 1914.

Speculum spiritualium. Paris: Wolfgang Hopyl, 1510.

Speculum vitae: A Reading Edition. Edited by Ralph Hanna. 2 vols. EETS 332. Oxford: Oxford University Press, 2008.

Summa fratris Alexandri. Edited by Brothers of the College of St. Bonaventura. 4 vols. Florence: Quaracchi, 1924–48.

The Testimony of William Thorpe. In *Two Wycliffite Texts*, edited by Anne Hudson, 24–93. EETS 301. Oxford: Oxford University Press, 1993.

"Think Before You Speak." In *Religious Lyrics of the Fifteenth Century*, edited by Carleton Brown, 280–82. London: Oxford University Press, 1939.

Thomas of Chobham. *Sermones.* Edited by Franco Morenzoni. CCCM 82A. Turnhout: Brepols, 1993.

Thomas of Ireland. *Manipulus florum.* The Electronic *Manipulus florum* Project. Edited by Chris Nighman, 2000–2013. https://manipulus-project.wlu.ca/MFedition/html.

The Towneley Plays. Vol. 1, *Introduction and Text.* Edited by Martin Stevens and A. C. Cawley. EETS, s.s., 13. Oxford: Oxford University Press, 1994.

"The Trial of Richard Wyche." Edited by F. D. Matthew. *English Historical Review* 5, no. 19 (1890): 530–44.

Valerius Maximus. *Memorable Doings and Sayings.* Edited and translated by J. Shackleton Bailey. 2 vols. LCL 492–93. Cambridge: Harvard University Press, 2000.

Vincent de Beauvais. *Speculum doctrinale.* Vol. 2 of *Speculum quadruplex.* Douai: Belleri, 1624. Reprint, Graz: Akademische Druck, 1964.

———. *Speculum historiale.* Vol. 4 of *Speculum quadruplex.* Douai: Belleri, 1624. Reprint, Graz: Akademische Druck, 1965.

Vita Secundi philosophi. In *Secundus the Silent Philosopher*, edited by Ben Edwin Perry, 92–100. London: William Colwes and Sons for the Philological Association, 1964.

Whiting, Bartlett J., and Helen W. Whiting. *Proverbs, Sentences, and Proverbial Phrases from English Writing Mainly Before 1500.* Cambridge: Harvard University Press, 1968.

Wyclif, John. *De veritate Sacrae Scripturae.* Vol. 1. Edited by Rudolph Buddensieg. London: Trübner, 1905.

———. *Sermones.* Vol. 2, *Super evangelica de sanctis.* Edited by Johann Loserth. London: Trübner, 1888.

———. *Tractatus de ecclesia.* Edited by Johann Loserth. London: Trübner, 1886.

———. *Tractatus de mandatis divinis.* Edited by Johann Loserth and F. D. Matthew. London: K. Paul, 1922.

The York Plays. Vol. 1, *The Text.* Edited by Richard Beadle. EETS, s.s., 23. Oxford: Oxford University Press, 2009.

The York Plays. Vol. 2, *Introduction, Commentary, Glossary.* Edited by Richard Beadle. EETS, s.s., 24. Oxford: Oxford University Press, 2013.

SECONDARY SOURCES

Adams, Robert. *The Poet and the Rokele Family: The Gentry Background to "Piers Plowman."* Dublin: Four Courts Press, 2013.

Aers, David. *Sanctifying Signs: Making Christian Tradition in Late Medieval England.* Notre Dame: University of Notre Dame Press, 2004.

Alford, John. "The Idea of Reason in *Piers Plowman.*" In *Middle English Studies Presented to George Kane*, edited by Edward D. Kennedy, Ronald Waldron, and Joseph S. Wittig, 199–215. Woodbridge, UK: D. S. Brewer, 1988.

———. *"Piers Plowman": A Guide to the Quotations.* Binghamton, NY: Center for Medieval and Renaissance Studies, 1992.

———. "The Role of Quotations in *Piers Plowman.*" *Speculum* 52, no. 1 (1977): 80–99.

Amsler, Mark. *The Medieval Life of Language: Grammar and Pragmatics from Bacon to Kempe.* Amsterdam: Amsterdam University Press, 2021.

Appleford, Amy. "The Sea Ground and the London Street." *Chaucer Review* 51, no. 1 (2016): 49–67.
Atkinson, Laurie. "'Why Þat Yee Meeued Been / Can I Nat Knowe': Autobiography, Convention, and Discerning 'Doublenesse' in Thomas Hoccleve's *The Series*." *Neophilologus* 101, no. 3 (2017): 479–94.
Barr, Helen. Introduction to *The "Piers Plowman" Tradition*, edited by Helen Barr, 1–58. London: Dent, 1993.
———. *Signes and Sothe: Language in the "Piers Plowman" Tradition*. Cambridge, UK: D. S. Brewer, 1994.
Barr, Helen, and Kate Ward-Perkins. "'Spekyng for One's Sustenance': The Rhetoric of Counsel in *Mum and the Sothsegger*, Skelton's *Bouge of Court*, and Elyot's *Pasquil the Playne*." In *The Long Fifteenth Century: Essays for Douglas Gray*, edited by Helen Cooper and Sally Mapstone, 249–72. Oxford: Oxford University Press, 1997.
Bataillon, Louis. "The Tradition of Nicholas de Biard's *Distinctiones*." *Viator* 25 (1994): 245–88.
Beadle, Richard. "Verbal Texture and Wordplay in the York Cycle." *Early Theatre* 3 (2000): 167–84.
Beckwith, Sarah. *Signifying God: Social Relation and Symbolic Act in the York Corpus Christi Plays*. Chicago: University of Chicago Press, 2001.
Bejczy, István. *The Cardinal Virtues in the Middle Ages: A Study of Moral Thought from the Fourth to the Fourteenth Centuries*. Leiden: Brill, 2011.
Benhabib, Seyla. *Situating the Self: Gender, Community, and Postmodernism in Contemporary Ethics*. New York: Routledge, 1992.
Bennett, Alastair. *Narrative and Preaching in "Piers Plowman."* Oxford: Oxford University Press, 2023. Oxford Scholarship Online Complete.
Billington, Sandra. *A Social History of the Fool*. New York: St. Martin's Press, 1984.
Blamires, Alcuin. *Chaucer, Ethics, and Gender*. Oxford: Oxford University Press, 2006.
Blenkinsop, Joseph. *Wisdom and Law in the Old Testament: The Ordering of Life in Israel and Early Judaism*. Oxford: Oxford University Press, 1983.
Bloomfield, Morton, et al. *Incipits of Latin Works on the Virtues and Vices, 1100–1500 A.D.* Cambridge, MA: Mediaeval Academy of America, 1979.
Breen, Katharine. *Machines of the Mind: Personification in Medieval Literature*. Chicago: University of Chicago Press, 2021.
Brilli, Elissa. Introduction to *Alphabetum narrationum*, edited by Elissa Brilli, i–cviii. CCCM 160. Turnhout: Brepols, 2015.
Burger, Glenn D., and Holly Crocker. Introduction to *Medieval Affect, Feeling, and Emotion*, edited by Burger and Crocker, 1–24. Cambridge: Cambridge University Press, 2019.
Burnley, J. D. *Chaucer's Language and the Philosophers' Tradition*. Cambridge, UK: D. S. Brewer, 1979.
Burrow, J. A. "Autobiographical Poetry in the Middles Ages: The Case of Thomas Hoccleve." In *Middle English Literature: British Academy Gollancz Lectures*, selected and introduced by J. A. Burrow, 223–46. Oxford: Oxford University Press, 1989.
———. Introduction to *Thomas Hoccleve's Complaint and Dialogue*, edited by J. A. Burrow, ix–lxv. EETS 313. Oxford: Oxford University Press, 1999.
———. "The Third Eye of Prudence." In *Medieval Futures: Attitudes to the Future in the Middle Ages*, edited by J. A. Burrow and Ian P. Wei, 37–48. Woodbridge, UK: Boydell, 2000.
———. *Thomas Hoccleve*. Aldershot, UK: Variorum, 1994.
———. "Wasting Time, Wasting Words in *Piers Plowman* B and C." *YLS* 17 (2003): 191–202.

Cannon, Christopher. *From Literacy to Literature: England, 1300–1400*. Oxford: Oxford University Press, 2016.

Carruthers, Mary. "Imaginatif, Memoria, and 'the Need for Critical Theory' in *Piers Plowman* Studies." *YLS* 9 (1995): 104–13.

Casagrande, Carla. "La *mala taciturnitas* tra il dovere della correzione et il piacere dell'affabilità." *Micrologus* 18 (2010): 225–39.

Casagrande, Carla, and Silvana Vecchio. *I peccati della lingua: Disciplina ed etica della parola nella cultura medievale*. Rome: Instituto della Enciclopedia Italiana, 1987.

Clopper, Lawrence. "Tyrants and Villains: Characterization in the Passion Sequences of the English Cycle Plays." *Modern Language Notes* 41 (1980): 3–20.

Cole, Andrew, and Andrew Galloway. "Christian Philosophy in *Piers Plowman*." In *The Cambridge Companion to "Piers Plowman,"* edited by Cole and Galloway, 136–59. Cambridge: Cambridge University Press, 2014.

Coley, David K. *The Wheel of Language: Representing Speech in Middle English Poetry, 1374–1422*. Syracuse: Syracuse University Press, 2012.

Craun, Edwin. "Aristotle's Biology and Pastoral Ethics: John of Wales's 'De Lingua' and British Pastoral Writings on the Tongue." *Traditio* 67 (2012): 277–302.

———. *Ethics and Power in Medieval English Reformist Writing*. Cambridge: Cambridge University Press, 2010.

———. "'It Is a Freletee of Flessh': Excuses for Sin, Pastoral Rhetoric, and Moral Agency." In *In the Garden of Evil: The Vices and Culture in the Middle Ages*, edited by Richard Newhauser, 170–92. Ithaca: Cornell University Press, 1997.

———. *Lies, Slander, and Obscenity: Pastoral Rhetoric and the Deviant Speaker*. Cambridge: Cambridge University Press, 1997.

Critten, Rory. *Author, Scribe, and Book in Late Medieval English Literature*. Cambridge, UK: D. S. Brewer, 2018.

Crocker, Holly A. "Engendering Affect in Hoccleve's *Series*." In *Medieval Affect*, edited by Glenn D. Burger and Crocker, 70–89. Cambridge: Cambridge University Press, 2019.

Dauenhauer, Richard. *Silence, the Phenomenon and Its Ontological Significance*. Bloomington: Indiana University Press, 1980.

Davidson, Clifford. *From Creation to Doom: The York Cycle of Mystery Plays*. New York: AMS Press, 1984.

Davis, Rebecca. *"Piers Plowman" and the Books of Nature*. Oxford: Oxford University Press, 2016.

Davlin, Mary Clemente, O.P. *"A Game of Heuene": Word Play and Meaning in "Piers Plowman" B*. Woodbridge, UK: D. S. Brewer, 1989.

———. "*Piers Plowman* and the Books of Wisdom." *YLS* 2 (1988): 22–33.

Dean, James. Introduction to *Mum and the Sothsegger*. In *Richard the Redeless and Mum and the Sothsegger*, edited by James Dean, 75–80. Kalamazoo, MI: Medieval Institute Publications, 2000.

Demarco, Patricia. "Violence, Law, and Ciceronian Ethics in Chaucer's *Tale of Melibee*." *SAC* 30 (2008): 125–69.

Devito, Joseph. "Silence and Paralanguage as Communication." *ETC: A Review of General Semantics* 74, no. 3 (2017): 482–87.

Fairclough, Norman. *Critical Discourse Analysis: The Critical Study of Language*. 2nd ed. London: Routledge, 2013.

Fenster, Thelma, and Daniel Smail, eds. *"Fama": The Politics of Talk and Reputation in Medieval Europe*. Ithaca: Cornell University Press, 2003.

Ferster, Judith. *Fictions of Advice: The Literature and Politics of Counsel in Late Medieval England*. Philadelphia:

University of Pennsylvania Press, 1996.
Forest-Hill, Lynn. *Transgressive Language in Medieval English Drama: Signs of Challenge and Change*. Aldershot, UK: Ashgate, 2000.
Gadamer, Hans-Georg. "Hermeneutics as Practical Philosophy." In *Reason in the Age of Science*, translated by Frederick G. Lawrence, 88–113. Cambridge: MIT Press, 1982.
———. *Truth and Method*. New York: Seabury Press, 1975.
Gallacher, Patrick. "Imaginatif and the *Sensus Communis*." *YLS* 6 (1992): 51–62.
Galloway, Andrew. "Parallel Lives: William Rokele and the Satirical Literacies of *Piers Plowman*." *SAC* 40 (2018): 43–111.
Gayk, Shannon. "The Form of Christ's Passion: Preaching the *Imitatio Passionis* in Late Medieval England." *YLS* 31 (2017): 232–56.
———. *Image, Text, and Religious Reform in Fifteenth-Century England*. Cambridge: Cambridge University Press, 2010.
Gehl, Paul. "*Competens Silentium*: Varieties of Monastic Silence in the Christian West." *Viator* 18 (1987): 126–40.
Giancarlo, Matthew. "Mirror, Mirror: Princely Hermeneutics, Practical Constitutionalism, and the Genres of the English *Fürstenspiegel*." *Exemplaria* 27, nos. 1–2 (2015): 35–54.
Glenn, Cheryl. *Unspoken: A Rhetoric of Silence*. Carbondale: University of Southern Illinois Press, 2004.
Goffman, Erving. *Forms of Talk*. Philadelphia: University of Pennsylvania Press, 1981.
Goldie, Matthew Boyd. "Psychosomatic Illness and Identity in London, 1416–1421: Hoccleve's *Complaint* and *Dialogue with a Friend*." *Exemplaria* 11, no. 1 (1998): 23–52.
Grady, Frank. "The Generation of 1399." In *The Letter of the Law: Legal Practice and Literary Production in Medieval England*, edited by Emily Steiner and Candace Barrington, 202–29. Ithaca: Cornell University Press, 2002.
Graham, Angus. "Albertanus of Brescia: A Supplementary Census of Latin Manuscripts." *Studi Medievali*, ser. 3, 41, no. 1 (2000): 429–44.
Green, Richard Firth. *A Crisis of Truth: Law and Literature in Ricardian England*. Philadelphia: University of Pennsylvania Press, 1999.
Green, Richard Firth, and Ethan Knapp. "Thomas Hoccleve's Seal." *Medium Aevum* 77, no. 2 (2008): 319–21.
Griffiths, Jane. "'In Bookes Thus Writen I Fynde': Hoccleve's Self-Glossing in the *Regiment of Princes* and the *Series*." *Medium Aevum* 86, no. 1 (2017): 91–107.
Grizzard, Carol. "The Scope of Theology in Wisdom Literature." In *An Introduction to Wisdom Literature and the Psalms: Festschrift Marvin E. Tate*, edited by H. Wayne Ballard Jr. and W. Dennis Tucker Jr., 195–214. Macon: Mercer University Press, 2001.
Hanna, Ralph, III. "Commonplaces of Late Medieval Patience Discussions." In *The Triumphs of Patience: Medieval and Renaissance Studies*, edited by Gerald J. Schiffhorst, 65–87. Orlando: University Presses of Florida, 1978.
———. "Langland's Ymaginatif: Images and the Limits of Poetry." In *Images, Idolatry, and Iconoclasm in Late Medieval England*, edited by Jeremy Dimmick, James Simpson, and Nicolette Zeeman, 81–94. Oxford: Oxford University Press, 2002.
———. *Patient Reading / Reading Patience*. Liverpool: Liverpool University Press, 2017.
———. "*Speculum vitae* and the Form of *Piers Plowman*." In *Answerable Style: The Idea of the Literary in Medieval England*, edited by Frank Grady and Andrew Galloway, 121–39. Columbus: Ohio State University Press, 2013.
Hazelton, Richard. "The Christianization of 'Cato': The *Disticha Catonis*

in the Light of Late Mediaeval Commentaries." *Mediaeval Studies* 19 (1957): 157–73.

Hickey, Helen. "Legal Personhood and the Inquisitions of Sanity in Thomas Hoccleve's *Series*." In *Theorizing Legal Personhood in Late Medieval England*, edited by Andreea D. Boboc, 192–217. Leiden: Brill, 2015.

Horobin, Simon. "The Dialect and Authorship of 'Richard the Redeless' and 'Mum and the Sothsegger.'" *YLS* 18 (2004): 133–52.

Hudson, Anne. Introduction to *Two Wycliffite Texts*, edited by Anne Hudson, xi–lxiii. EETS 301. Oxford: Oxford University Press, 1993.

———. *The Premature Reformation*. Oxford, UK: Clarendon, 1988.

Jaworski, Adam. *The Power of Silence: Social and Pragmatic Perspectives*. Newbury Park, CA: Sage, 1993.

Jensen, J. Vernon. "Communicative Functions of Silence." *ETC: A Review of General Semantics* 30, no. 3 (1973): 249–57.

Johannesen, Richard L. "The Functions of Silence: A Plea for Communication Research." *Western Speech* 38, no. 1 (1974): 25–35.

Johnson, Eleanor. *Practicing Literary Theory in the Middle Ages: Ethics and the Mixed Form in Chaucer, Gower, Usk, and Hoccleve*. Chicago: University of Chicago Press, 2013.

Johnson, Holly. *The Grammar of Good Friday: Macaronic Sermons from Late Medieval England*. Turnhout: Brepols, 2012.

Johnston, Alexandra. "'His Langage Is Lorne': The Silent Center of the York Cycle." *Early Theatre* 3 (2000): 185–95.

Johnston, Michael. "The Clerical Career of William Rokele." *YLS* 33 (2019): 111–25.

Jurkowski, Maureen. "The Arrest of William Thorpe in Shrewsbury and the Anti-Lollard Statute of 1406." *Historical Research* 75, no. 189 (2002): 273–95.

Kaeppeli, Thomas. *Scriptores Ordinis Praedicatorum Medii Aevi*. 4 vols. Rome: ad S. Sabinae, 1970–93.

Karnes, Michelle. *Imagination, Meditation, and Cognition in the Middle Ages*. Chicago: University of Chicago Press, 2011.

Kent, Bonnie. *Virtues of the Will: The Transformation of Ethics in the Late Fourteenth Century*. Washington, DC: Catholic University of America Press, 1995.

———. "Virtue Theory." In *The Cambridge History of Medieval Philosophy*, rev. ed., edited by Robert Pasnau and Christina Van Dyke, 1:493–505. Cambridge: Cambridge University Press, 2014.

Kerby-Fulton, Kathryn. *Books Under Suspicion: Censorship and Tolerance of Revelatory Writing in Late Medieval England*. Notre Dame: Notre Dame University Press, 2006.

———. *The Clerical Proletariat and the Resurgence of Medieval English Poetry*. Philadelphia: University of Pennsylvania Press, 2021.

———. "The Pedagogy of an Oppressed Text: The C Version of *Piers Plowman*." In *Approaches to Teaching Langland's "Piers Plowman,"* edited by Thomas Goodmann, 217–22. New York: Modern Language Association of America, 2018.

King, Pamela. "Medieval English Religious Plays as Early Fifteenth-Century Vernacular Theology: The Case Against." In *Devotional Culture in Late Medieval England and Europe*, edited by Stephen Kelly and Ryan Perry, 553–51. Turnhout: Brepols, 2014.

———. *The York Mystery Cycle and the Worship of the City*. Woodbridge, UK: D. S. Brewer, 2006.

Kirby, John. L. *Henry IV of England*. London: Constable, 1970.

Knapp, Ethan. *The Bureaucratic Muse: Thomas Hoccleve and the Literature of Late Medieval England*. University

Park: Pennsylvania State University Press, 2001.

Knuuttila, Simo. *Emotions in Ancient and Medieval Thought*. Oxford, UK: Clarendon, 2004.

Kolve, V. A. *The Play Called Corpus Christi*. Stanford: Stanford University Press, 1966.

Kruger, Stephen. "Mirrors and the Trajectories of Vision in *Piers Plowman*." *Speculum* 66, no. 1 (1991): 74–95.

Langdell, Sebastian James. "'What World Is This? How Vndirstande Am I?': A Reappraisal of Poetic Authority in Hoccleve's *Series*." *Medium Aevum* 78, no. 2 (2009): 281–99.

Lawes, Richard. "Psychological Disorder and the Autobiographical Impulse in Julian of Norwich, Margery Kempe, and Thomas Hoccleve." In *Writing Religious Women: Female Spiritual and Textual Practices in Late Medieval England*, edited by Dennis Reveney and Christina Whitehead, 217–43. Cardiff: University of Wales Press, 2000.

Lawton, David. *Voice in Later Medieval English Literature*. Oxford: Oxford University Press, 2017.

Lears, Adin. *World of Echo: Noise and Knowing in Late Medieval England*. Ithaca: Cornell University Press, 2020.

Lipton, Emma. *Cultures of Witnessing: Law and the York Plays*. Philadelphia: University of Pennsylvania Press, 2022.

Lochrie, Karma. *Covert Operations: The Medieval Uses of Secrecy*. Philadelphia: University of Pennsylvania Press, 1999.

MacCulloch, Diarmaid. *Silence: A Christian History*. London: Allen Lane, 2013.

Malo, Robyn. "Penitential Discourse in Hoccleve's *Series*." *SAC* 34 (2012): 277–92.

Meyer-Lee, Robert. *Poets and Power from Chaucer to Wyatt*. Cambridge: Cambridge University Press, 2007.

Middleton, Anne. "Narration and the Invention of Experience: Episodic Form in *Piers Plowman*." In *The Wisdom of Poetry: Essays on Early English Literature in Honor of Morton W. Bloomfield*, edited by Larry D. Benson and Siegfried Wenzel, 91–122. Kalamazoo, MI: Medieval Institute Publications, 1982.

———. "*Piers Plowman*, the Monsters and the Critics: Some Embarrassments of Literary History." In *The Morton Bloomfield Lectures, 1989–2005*, edited by Daniel Donoghue, James Simpson, and Nicholas Watson, 94–115. Cambridge: Harvard University Press, 2010.

Minnis, Alastair J. "The Poet's Imaginatif and Late-Medieval Theories of the Imagination." In *Comparative Criticism: A Yearbook*, edited by E. S. Shaffer, 3:79–92. Chicago: University of Chicago Press, 1981.

Mooney, Lynne. "Some New Light on Thomas Hoccleve." *SAC* 29 (2007): 293–340.

Morgan, Teresa. *Popular Morality in the Early Roman Empire*. Cambridge: Cambridge University Press, 2007.

Navone, Paola. "La doctrina loquendi et tacendi di Albertano da Brescia: Censimento dei Manoscritti." *Studi Medievali*, ser. 3, 35, no. 2 (1994): 895–930.

Nederman, Cary J. "Nature, Ethics, and the Doctrine of 'Habitus': Aristotelian Moral Psychology in the Twelfth Century." *Traditio* 45 (1990): 87–110.

Newhauser, Richard. "Augustinian *vitium curiositatis* and Its Reception." In *Saint Augustine and His Influence in the Middle Ages*, edited by Edward King and Jacqueline Schaefer, 99–124. Sewanee, TN: Press of the University of the South, 1988.

———. "Towards a History of Human Curiosity: A Prolegomenon to Its Medieval Phase." *Deutsche Vierteljahrsschrift für Literaturwissenschaft und Geistesgeschichte* 52 (1982): 569–95.

Newhauser, Richard, and István Bejczy. *A Supplement to Morton W. Bloomfield et al. "Incipits of Latin Works on the Virtues and Vices, 1000–1500 A.D."* Turnhout: Brepols, 2008.

Nuttall, Jenni. *The Creation of Lancastrian Kingship: Literature, Language, and Politics in Late Medieval England.* Cambridge: Cambridge University Press, 2007.

Orlemanski, Julie. *Symptomatic Subjects: Bodies, Medicine, and Causation in the Literature of Late Medieval England.* Philadelphia: University of Pennsylvania Press, 2019.

Orme, Nicholas. *Medieval Schools from Roman Britain to Renaissance England.* New Haven: Yale University Press, 2006.

Pasnau, Robert, and Christina Van Dyke, eds. *The Cambridge History of Medieval Philosophy.* Rev. ed. 2 vols. Cambridge: Cambridge University Press, 2014.

Pearsall, Derek. "Hoccleve's *Regiment of Princes*: The Poetics of Royal Self-Representation." *Speculum* 69, no. 2 (1994): 387–410.

———. "The Poetic Character of the C-Text of *Piers Plowman*." In *Medieval Alliterative Poetry: Essays in Honour of Thorlac Turville-Petre*, edited by John A. Burrow and Hoyt Duggan, 153–65. Dublin: Four Courts Press, 2010.

Perkins, Nicholas. *Hoccleve's "Regiment of Princes": Counsel and Constraint.* Cambridge, UK: Boydell and Brewer, 2001.

Perry, R. D. "Hoccleve and the Logic of Incompleteness." In *Thomas Hoccleve: New Approaches*, edited by Jenni Nuttall and David Watt, 65–84. Cambridge, UK: D. S. Brewer, 2022.

Porter, Jean. "Action and Intention." In *The Cambridge History of Medieval Philosophy*, rev. ed., edited by Robert Pasnau and Christina Van Dyke, 1:506–16. Cambridge: Cambridge University Press, 2014.

Powell, James M. *Albertanus of Brescia: The Pursuit of Happiness in the Thirteenth Century.* Philadelphia: University of Pennsylvania Press, 1992.

Raby, Michael. "Tasting Thomas Hoccleve: Discernment and the Ethics of Judgment in the *Series*." *Modern Philology* 114, no. 2 (2016): 195–218.

Raymo, Richard. "Works of Religious and Philosophical Instruction." In *A Manual of the Writings in Middle English*, edited by Albert Hartung, 7:2255–378. New Haven: Connecticut Academy of Arts and Sciences, 1986.

Revere, William. "Advise or Consent: Conscience and Power in *Mum and the Sothsegger*." *Exemplaria* 24 (2012): 127–42.

Robinson, J. W. "The Art of the York Realist." *Modern Philology* 60, no. 4 (1963): 241–51.

Rosenwein, Barbara. *Emotional Communities in the Early Middle Ages.* Ithaca: Cornell University Press, 2006.

———. *Generations of Feeling: A History of Emotions, 600–1700.* Cambridge: Cambridge University Press, 2016.

Rouse, Richard H., and Mary A. Rouse. *Preachers, Florilegia, and Sermons: Studies on the "Manipulus florum" of Thomas of Ireland.* Toronto: Pontifical Institute of Mediaeval Studies, 1979.

Saville-Troike, Muriel. "The Place of Silence in an Integrated Theory of Communication." In *Perspectives on Silence*, edited by Deborah Tannen and Saville-Troike, 3–18. Norwood, NJ: Ablex, 1985.

Scanlon, Larry. "The King's Two Voices: Narrative and Power in Hoccleve's *Regiment of Princes*." In *Literary Practice and Social Change in Britain, 1380–1530*, edited by Lee Patterson, 216–47. Berkeley: University of California Press, 1990.

Scase, Wendy. "'Heu! Quanta Desolatio Angliae Praestatur': A Wycliffite Libel and the Naming of Heretics, Oxford 1382." In *Lollards and Their*

Influence in Late Medieval England, edited by Fiona Somerset, Jill Havens, and Derrick Pitard, 19–36. Woodbridge, UK: Boydell, 2003.

———. *Literature and Complaint in England, 1272–1553*. Oxford: Oxford University Press, 2007.

Scattergood, John. "The Date and Composition of George Ashby's Poems." *Leeds Studies in English*, n.s., 21 (1990): 168–71.

———. "Insecurity in Skelton's *Bowge of Courte*." In *Genres, Themes, and Images in English Literature from the Fourteenth to the Fifteenth Century*, edited by Pietro Boitani and Anna Torti, 186–209. Tübingen: Gunter Narr Verlag, 1988.

Schieberle, Misty. "A New Hoccleve Literary Manuscript: The Trilingual Miscellany in London, British Library, MS Harley 319." *Review of English Studies* 70 (2019–21): 799–822.

Schiff, Randy. *Revivalist Fantasy: Alliterative Verse and Nationalist Literary History*. Columbus: Ohio State University Press, 2011.

Schirmer, Elizabeth. "William Thorpe's Narrative Theology." *SAC* 31 (2009): 267–99.

Seymour, M. C. "Manuscripts of Hoccleve's *Regiment of Princes*." *Edinburgh Bibliographic Transactions* 4, part 7 (1974): 253–97.

Sharpe, Richard. *A Handlist of the Latin Writers of Great Britain and Ireland before 1540*. 1997. Reprint, Turnhout: Brepols, 2001.

Simpson, James. *1350–1547: Reform and Cultural Revolution*. Vol. 2 of *The Oxford English Literary History*. Oxford: Oxford University Press, 2002.

Smith, D. Vance. "The Silence of Langland's Study: Matter, Invisibility, Instruction." In *Answerable Style: The Idea of the Literary in Medieval England*, edited by Frank Grady and Andrew Galloway, 263–83. Columbus: Ohio State University Press, 2013.

Smyth, Karen Elaine. *Imaginings of Time in Lydgate and Hoccleve's Verse*. Aldershot, UK: Ashgate, 2011.

Sobecki, Sebastian. "Authorized Realities: *The Gesta Romanorum* and Thomas Hoccleve's Poetics of Autobiography." *Speculum* 98, no. 2 (2023): 536–58.

———. *Last Words: The Public Self and the Social Author in Late Medieval England*. Oxford: Oxford University Press, 2019.

Somerset, Fiona. "Before and After Wyclif: Consent to Another's Sin in Medieval Europe." In *Europe After Wyclif*, edited by J. Patrick Hornbeck and Michael Van Dussen, 135–72. New York: Fordham University Press, 2017.

———. "Vernacular Argumentation in *The Testimony of William Thorpe*." *Mediaeval Studies* 58 (1996): 207–24.

Spearing, A. C., and R. Willian. *Medieval Autographies: The "I" of the Text*. Notre Dame: University of Notre Dame Press, 2012.

Steenbrugge, Charlotte. *Drama and Sermon in Late Medieval England: Performance, Authority, Devotion*. Kalamazoo, MI: Medieval Institute Publications, 2017.

Steiner, Emily. *Documentary Culture and the Making of English Literature*. Cambridge: Cambridge University Press, 2004.

———. *Reading "Piers Plowman"*. Cambridge: Cambridge University Press, 2013.

Strohm, Paul. *England's Empty Throne: Usurpation and the Language of Legitimation, 1399–1422*. New Haven: Yale University Press, 1996.

Strub, Spencer. "Hoccleve, Bursting and Swelling." In *Thomas Hoccleve: New Approaches*, edited by Jenni Nuttall and David Watt, 124–41. Cambridge, UK: D. S. Brewer, 2022.

———. "Learning from Shame." *YLS* 32 (2018): 37–75.

Suarez-Nani, Tiziana. "Faire parler le silence: À propos d'un paradoxe dans la pensée médiévale." In "Il silenzio." *Micrologus: Natura, scienze e società medievali* 18 (2010): 255–68.

Swanson, Jenny. *John of Wales: A Study of the Works and Ideas of a Thirteenth-Century Friar.* Cambridge: Cambridge University Press, 1989.

Tiner, Elza. "English Law in the York Trial Plays." In *The Dramatic Tradition of the Middle Ages*, edited by Clifford Davidson, 140–49. New York: AMS Press, 2005.

Tinkle, Theresa. "York's Jesus: Crowned King and Traitor." *Speculum* 94, no. 1 (2019): 96–137.

Tolmie, Sarah. "The Professional: Thomas Hoccleve." *SAC* 29 (2007): 341–73.

Turner, Wendy J. *Care and Custody of the Mentally Ill, Incompetent, and Disabled in Medieval England.* Turnhout: Brepols, 2013.

Walker, Greg. "The Cultural Work of Early Drama." In *The Cambridge Companion to Early English Theatre*, 2nd ed., edited by Richard Beadle, 75–98. Cambridge: Cambridge University Press, 2008.

———. "John Skelton and the Royal Court." In *Vernacular Literature and Current Affairs in the Early Sixteenth Century: France, England and Scotland*, edited by Jennifer Britnell and Richard Britnell, 1–15. Aldershot, UK: Ashgate, 2000.

Warner, Lawrence. *The Myth of "Piers Plowman": Constructing a Medieval Literary Archive.* Cambridge: Cambridge University Press, 2014.

Watt, David. *The Making of Thomas Hoccleve's "Series."* Liverpool: Liverpool University Press, 2013.

Wittig, Joseph. "*Piers Plowman* B. Passūs 11–12: Elements of the Inward Journey." *Traditio* 28 (1972): 211–80.

Wood, Sarah. *Conscience and the Composition of "Piers Plowman."* Oxford: Oxford University Press, 2012.

Wooffitt, Robin. *Conversation Analysis and Critical Discourse Analysis: A Comparative and Critical Introduction.* London: Sage, 2005.

Woolf, Rosemary. *The English Mystery Plays.* London: Routledge and Kegan Paul, 1972.

Wright, Claire. "Acoustic Tyranny: Metre, Alliteration and Voice in *Christ before Herod.*" *Medieval English Theatre* 34 (2012): 7–18.

Yeager, Stephen. *From Lawmen to Plowmen: Anglo-Saxon Legal Tradition and the School of Langland.* Toronto: University of Toronto Press, 2014.

Zeeman, Nicolette. *The Arts of Disruption: Allegory and "Piers Plowman."* Oxford: Oxford University Press, 2020.

———. "Pastoral Care by Debate: The Challenge of Lay Multiplicity." *Journal of Medieval and Early Modern Studies* 48, no. 3 (2018): 435–59.

———. *"Piers Plowman" and the Medieval Discourse of Desire.* Cambridge: Cambridge University Press, 2006.

INDEX

Endnotes are indicated by "n" followed by the endnote number.

Adams, Robert, 172n27
Aers, David, 97
affect. See feelings
Albertano da Brescia
　on benefits of silence, 10, 16
　on circumspect silence, 10, 18, 20–21, 111, 150
　on circumstances of speech, 17–18, 20, 21, 24
　De amore et dilectione Dei et proximi et aliarum rerum et de forma vitae, 156n9, 163n9
　De arte loquendi et tacendi, 10, 17, 20–21, 23, 33, 35, 136, 156n8
　on excessive speech, 20, 38
　Liber consolationi et consilii, 18, 20, 157n17
　on prudent speech, 18–20
　Senecan influences on, 18, 38
Alexander the Great, 32, 33, 35, 128–29
Alford, John, 136, 171n21, 174n61
Amsler, Mark, 94, 96, 167n71
Anna, in York cycle trial pageants, 3, 77, 81–83, 85, 87–89, 165n38, 166n48
Appleford, Amy, 168n18
Aquinas, Thomas, 159n13, 166n51
Arderne, John, 172n21
Aristotle
　Alexander the Great and, 32, 33, 35, 128–29
　biological writings of, 171n19
　Nicomachean Ethics, 32, 42
　Politics, 32, 42
Arnold of Liège: *Alphabetum narrationum*, 22, 124–25, 170–71n5
Arundel, Thomas, 3, 93–94, 96–97, 151
Ashby, George: *Active Policy of a Prince*, 42–43, 160n24, 160n28
Athanasius, 136, 173n42
Augustine (saint), 20, 23, 48, 157n19, 157–58n26, 162n35, 174n66

authoritative sayings. See *sententiae*

Bailey, John, 168n13
Barr, Helen, 45, 57, 160n2, 162nn39–42
Beadle, Richard, 77, 81, 165n35, 165n39, 166n46
Beckett, Thomas, 57
Beckwith, Sarah, 81, 93
Benedict of Aniane: *Codex regularum*, 173n42
Benhabib, Seyla, 5
Billington, Sandra, 84, 165n43
Blamires, Alcuin, 68
Boccaccio, Giovanni: *De casibus virorum illustrium*, 125
Boethius, Anicius Manlius Severinus
　Consolation of Philosophy, 117, 129–30, 141
　exhortation to practice silence, 16
　virtue as defined by, 156n2
Book for a Simple and Devout Woman, The, 28, 48, 136, 159n46
Book of Margery Kempe, The, 92–93
Book of Vices and Virtues, The, 26, 140, 157–58n26, 158n36
Bowet, Henry, 92
Breen, Katharine, 131
Bromyard, John, 25, 130, 140–41, 162n35, 174n61
Burnley, J. D., 8, 74
Burrow, J. A.
　on *Piers Plowman*, 174n72
　on *Regiment of Princes*, 159n2, 168n20
　on *Series* and "My Complaint," 120, 167n11, 168n13, 168n20, 170n55
　on third eye of prudence, 117, 170n47
　on urban companionship, 107

Caecilius Balbus, 16, 129, 155n14, 170n2, 171n18
Caesar, 75, 164n20
Caiaphas, in York cycle trial pageants, 3, 77, 80–85, 87–89, 165n38, 166n48
Cannon, Christopher, 163n47, 173n51

canon law
　clerical moral texts and, 23, 46
　on evil taciturnity, 52–54, 56–57, 59, 62–63
　fraternal correction and, 7–8, 46, 156n17
　Hoccleve's citations from, 52, 53, 152, 161n29
　priest's exclusive knowledge of, 61, 162n39
　on witchcraft and sorcery, 166n48
Casagrande, Carla, 49, 160n5
Cassian, John: *Collationes*, 127–28
Cassiodorus, Magnus, 102, 167n7
Catherine of Alexandria (saint), 92
Caxton, William
　The Book of Curtesye, 21
　Book of Good Manners, 21, 157n21
　The Game and Pleye of the Chesse, 42
　Woodville's *Dicts and Sayings* published by, 157n23
Chaucer, Geoffrey: *Canterbury Tales*
　Dame Prudence in, 18, 41, 164n24
　"General Prologue," 105, 168n21
　"The Manciple's Tale," 151
　"The Parson's Tale," 151, 163n9, 164n19
Chester cycle trial pageants, 77–78, 166n52
Cicero, Marcus Tullius
　on consistency, 164n17
　De officiis, 23, 158n28
　on emotions, 17, 157n11
　on fear vs. caution, 101–2
　on insults and injuries, 20
　patience as defined by, 73
　on prudence, 18, 23, 24, 34
　sententiae of, 126, 171n9
　Stoicism and, 16, 17, 101–2
　on suffering in silence, 28
　Tusculanae disputationes, 126
clerical moral texts
　audience for, 22–23
　on benefits of silence, 10, 17, 25, 28
　canon law and, 23, 46
　on circumstances of speech, 24–25, 29, 158n32
　ethical traditions and, 23, 68
　on evil taciturnity, 43–49, 53–55, 66, 161n14
　on excessive speech, 1–2, 10, 26–29, 38, 129
　Jewish wisdom literature and, 23, 28, 86, 116

"key of the tongue" image in, 109
on love, 7, 10, 23, 24, 102
as mirrors for princes, 27, 68
on patient silence, 75, 83
on political silence, 26, 66
on prudence, 10, 17, 23–24, 27
Roman popular morality and, 23, 46, 116, 129
on self-revelatory speech, 26–27
sententiae in, 23, 123, 159n6
on sorrow aggravated by silence, 12, 100, 114
Stoicism and, 23, 46, 116
on suffering in silence, 28–29
on untamable tongue, 26, 36, 159n15
See also specific authors and works
Clopper, Larry, 78
Cole, Andrew, 124
Coley, David K., 169n37
Colonna, Egidio: *De regimine principum*, 27–28, 32, 40, 42, 51, 160n26
complaint genre, 103–4, 113, 168n14
courtesy books, 21, 22
COVID-19 pandemic, 12
Critical Discourse Analysis, 94, 166–67n65
Critten, Rory, 116, 168n19
Crocker, Holly, 116
Cursor mundi, 86, 166n51

David (King of Israel), 29, 40–41, 75, 109, 159n48
Davidson, Clifford, 166n47
Davis, Rebecca, 133, 134
Day, M., 162n42
Dean, James, 57, 162n32
De lingua
　on deprivation of speech, 9
　on evil taciturnity, 46–47
　in library collections, 156n22
　on patient silence of Jesus, 75–76, 91
　on prudence in silence or speech, 24
　Psalms quoted in, 164n23
　on sins of the tongue, 8, 155n13
　on sorrow aggravated by silence, 114
　on transgressive speech, 155n13
　on virtuous speech, 8
Demarco, Patricia, 18
"Dialogue" (Hoccleve)
　on clipped and counterfeit coins, 112, 169n37
　fear in, 100, 103, 104, 116, 117

Friend in, 104, 112, 115–17, 122
on mental illness, 3, 103, 115–18
misconstruals of silence in, 3
on recognition of limits of life, 170n57
self-protective silence in, 101, 115
Dicts and Sayings of the Philosophers, 21, 157n23, 171n18
Diogenes: *Dicts and Sayings*, 171n18
Disce mori, 74–75, 164n19
Disticha Catonis
on harm avoidance, 7, 15–16, 46
Roman popular morality and, 15, 16, 54
sententiae in, 6, 7, 14–15, 58–59, 138
on virtue of silence, 14–15

education. *See* learning
Edward II (King of England), 22
Edward III (King of England), 27
Edward of Lancaster (Prince of Wales), 42
emotions
assessment of, 39, 112, 158n33
Cicero on, 17, 157n11
control of, 16, 29, 74, 98
conveyance through speech, 110
disclosure of, 3, 17, 26
disordered, 3, 112–14
distrust of, 10, 17, 41, 73, 116, 139
evil taciturnity and, 48, 49, 52
history of, 104, 174n69
in hybrid moral discourse, 152–53
impulsivity fueled by, 116
lack of restraint over, 10
medieval conceptualization of, 3, 155n5
perception by others, 106
power of, 74, 114, 143
role in assisting agents, 7, 156n16
shifts in, 3–4, 133, 153
social construction of, 5
violent, 17, 41, 43, 73, 125
See also fear; feelings
ethics
Aristotelian, 30, 35
cautionary, 7, 19, 123, 141
clerical moral texts and, 23, 68
ethical reflection, 3, 5, 8, 13, 138
of harm avoidance, 46
Jewish wisdom literature and, 18–19, 59–60
of language, 17
multiplicity and, 68, 138, 151–53
norms and, 46, 54

self-interested, 15
of silence, 3, 5–9, 23, 55, 58–59
of speech, 5–8, 55, 110, 147, 171n19
Stoic, 59–60
Étienne de Bourbon, 173n43
evil taciturnity (*mala taciturnitas*)
asymmetrical power relations and, 49
canon law on, 52–54, 56–57, 59, 62–63
in civil institutions, 61–62
clerical moral texts on, 43–49, 53–55, 66, 161n14
De lingua on, 46–47
emotions and, 48, 49, 52
ethical norms violated by, 54
excessive speech compared to, 49
fraternal correction and, 6, 46–50
ingratitude and, 119
John of Mirfield on, 6
in *Mum and the Sothsegger*, 11, 46, 54–66, 152
in *Regiment of Princes*, 10, 51–54, 59, 65, 152
in religious institutions, 60–61
as sin, 47–48, 160n5
Wyclif on, 11, 49–50, 58, 66, 152, 161n18, 161n20
excessive speech
clerical moral texts on, 1–2, 10, 26–29, 38, 129
dangers of, 20, 26–27, 37–38, 140
evil taciturnity compared to, 49
Jewish wisdom literature on, 37–38
off-putting nature of, 20, 28
in *Piers Plowman*, 135, 142, 145
Regiment of Princes on, 37–38, 160n18
restraint through prudence, 17
Exhortatio ad monachos, 173n42

fear
in *Bowge of Courte*, 111
cautionary view of, 102, 167n7
of confession to priests, 102
in "Dialogue," 100, 103, 104, 116, 117
evil taciturnity due to, 47–50, 52, 53, 59, 63, 64, 66
of inquisitors, 82, 98
of isolation, 12, 108, 113
in "My Complaint," 12, 100–101, 103–4, 108–11, 113, 121–22
silence and, 7, 9, 12–13, 101–3, 108–11, 113, 121–22, 124

fear (continued)
    of social rejection, 103, 113
    speech aiming to create, 79
    Stoic views of, 101–2, 167n2
feelings
    assessment of, 39
    disordered, 3, 109, 114
    distrust of, 10, 116, 150
    hiding through silence, 2, 59, 76
    in hybrid moral discourse, 152–53
    impulsivity fueled by, 116
    lack of restraint over, 10
    medieval conceptualization of, 155n5
    oppressive, 120
    perception by others, 106
    power of, 114, 132, 133
    provocation through silence, 3
    shifts in, 3–4, 70
    words as unstable vehicle for, 110
    See also emotions
Felton, John, 102–3, 167n9
Ferster, Judith, 33
Florilegium morale Oxoniensis, 16, 156n7, 156n15
Forest-Hill, Lynn, 165n32
fraternal correction
    canon law and, 7–8, 46, 156n17
    evil taciturnity and, 6, 46–50
    "Facientis" sententia and, 57, 162n35
    Gregory the Great on, 47–48
    Kempe's use of, 92, 93
    pastoral care and, 7, 24, 50
    privacy of, 58, 162n36
    Roger of Waltham on, 47–49
    "Tacere" extract on, 160–61n10
    Wyclif on, 49, 55, 161n20

Gadamer, Hans-Georg, 5
Galloway, Andrew, 124
Gawain-poet: *Patience*, 71, 163n3
Gayk, Shannon, 107, 167n66, 168n23
Gehl, Paul, 175n78
Geoffrey of Vinsauf: *Poetria nova*, 116–17
Gerson, Jean, 48
Gesta Romanorum, 104, 107–8, 162n35, 168n16, 168n26
Giancarlo, Matthew, 159n14
Glenn, Cheryl, 43, 150
Goffman, Erving, 2
Goldie, Matthew Boyd, 112, 168n18
Gower, John, 8

Gratian: *Decretals*, 47, 52, 57, 161n27
Green, Richard Firth, 159n17
Gregory I the Great (pope)
    Disticha Catonis and, 14
    on fraternal correction, 47–48
    Hoccleve on patient silence of, 40
    Homiliae in Evangelia, 157n19
    Liber regulae pastoralis, 114
    Moralia in Iob, 73
    on norms for silence, 6
    on pastoral care, 160n6
    on patience, 72–74, 82, 164n15
    sententiae of, 72–73
Gregory IX (pope), 161n27
Griffiths, Jane, 33
Grosseteste, Robert, 64
Guillaume de Deguileville, 70–73, 90, 94, 98

Hanna, Ralph, III, 73, 132, 137, 141, 163n7, 173n55
Hazelton, Richard, 15
Henry II (King of England), 57
Henry IV (King of England), 30, 31, 33, 45, 53–55, 57, 164n28
Henry V (King of England)
    avoidance of predecessor's mistakes, 159n17
    evil taciturnity as threat to, 43–44
    as exemplar for subjects' conduct, 33–34, 43, 67
    oaths and promises made by, 31, 35–37, 43, 109
    piety and orthodoxy of, 39
    prudent nature of, 31, 34–35
    public duties required of, 30
    reputation of, 10, 113
    See also *Regiment of Princes*
Herod, in York cycle trial pageants, 3, 69, 77, 79–86, 88–90, 165n32
Higden, Ranulph, 127, 158n39
Hippocrates, 127–28
Hoccleve, Thomas
    authority of, 32–33
    on circumspect silence, 151–52
    clerical training of, 161n29
    constraints on speech of, 30, 159n1
    destructive silence denounced by, 45
    Formulary, 104, 168n15
    Gesta Romanorum translations by, 104, 107–8, 168n26
    La male regle, 51, 103, 104, 116

L'epistre de Cupide, 104, 112–13, 169n39
  in Office of the Privy Seal, 30, 31, 103, 168n12
  as opponent of Wycliffites, 50, 161n23
  reception of poetry, 168n19
  textual self of, 99, 100, 167n1
  "To Sir John Oldcastle," 104, 161n23
  See also mental illness; *Regiment of Princes*; *Series*
Holcot, Robert, 23, 35, 127, 147, 171n12, 171n18
Horobin, Simon, 160n1
Hudson, Anne, 94, 97, 166n61
Hugues de Saint-Victor, 52, 128
humility, 47, 74, 82, 85, 127, 136, 148, 175n78

iconography, 71, 87, 166n47
inquisitions
  Chester cycle trial pageants, 77–78, 166n52
  of Jesus, 3, 69, 75, 77–91, 151, 165nn38–40
  of Kempe, 11, 92–93
  N-Town trial pageants, 77, 78
  silence generated by fear during, 9
  subversion through patient silence, 11
  of Thorpe, 3, 11, 92–99, 151
  Towneley cycle trial pageants, 77–78, 165n38, 165n41
  See also York cycle trial pageants
integrity, 2, 11, 37, 69, 73–75, 96–99, 126, 151
Isidore of Seville
  Disticha Catonis and, 14–15
  etymology from *sapor*, 171n12
  On Instruction for a Good Life, 76
  on patient silence of Jesus, 76, 91
  Synonyma, 120

Jacopo da Cessole: *Libellus de moribus hominum et de officiis nobilium super ludo scaccorum*, 32, 42, 51
Jacques de Vitry, 158n39
James (apostle), 6, 17, 26, 35, 37, 39
Jaworski, Adam, 4
Jerome (saint), 166n51
Jesus
  Beatitudes and, 65
  interrogation of, 3, 69, 75, 77–91, 151, 165nn38–40
  as lamb led to slaughter, 82, 165nn39–40, 165n42
  miracles performed by, 80, 87, 89, 166n48
  parentage and upbringing, 83, 88, 89, 165n41
  patient silence of, 11, 41, 69–72, 75–80, 82–92, 98–99, 164n24
  as Paulinian fool, 165n43
  physical stillness of, 69, 95–96
  sources of power, 78
  Wyclif on death of, 50
Jewish wisdom literature
  clerical moral texts and, 23, 28, 86, 116
  Disticha Catonis and, 15
  ethics and, 18–19, 59–60
  on excessive speech, 37–38
  injunctions to correct evils, 64
  on norms for silence, 6
  Piers Plowman and, 137–40, 172n38
  Roman popular morality and, 16
  self-protective view of silence and, 102
  sententiae and, 23, 39, 136
  value of counsel-giving in, 115
Johannesen, Richard L., 3
John of Mirfield
  on contentious speech, 136
  on evil taciturnity, 6
  Florarium Bartholomei, 1, 48, 155n1
  on taciturnity winning love, 28
  wise man in anecdote told by, 1–4, 6–7, 9, 155n14
John of Wales, 158n36, 171n9, 171n12
Johnson, Eleanor, 117
Johnston, Alexandra, 88, 166n46
John the Baptist, 49, 50
Jurkowski, Maureen, 166n61

Kempe, Margery, 11, 92–93
Kerby-Fulton, Kathryn, 131, 161n29, 174n61
King, Pamela, 87, 164n25, 164n28
Knapp, Ethan, 113, 168n18, 168n21, 169n40
Knuuttila, Simo, 101, 156n16
Kolve, V. A., 85
Kruger, Stephen, 172n37

Langdell, Sebastian James, 168n21
language
  body, 99, 113
  catechetical, 132
  cautionary, 117
  insulting, 134
  legal, 81, 95
  moral, 5, 17, 71
  power of, 17, 36

language (*continued*)
    theological, 95
    as tool for enforcing hierarchical rule, 11
    value as pedagogic resource, 49
    violent, 70, 87, 95
    See also speech
Lawes, Richard, 168n12
Lawton, David, 119, 151
learning
    cooperative, 132
    Latin, 173n51
    life of, 126, 132, 148
    listening and, 12, 128, 129, 145–48
    mirrors for princes and, 67
    silence and, 12, 124–32, 139, 146–48, 175n78
    social process of, 12, 124, 127, 138, 144
    student-teacher relations and, 96, 124, 127, 170n4
    verbal exchanges and, 9, 142–43
    wisdom, 12, 125–30, 139, 143
Lears, Adin: *World of Echo*, 172n28
Legrand, Jacques: *Livre de bonnes moeurs*, 157n21
Lipton, Emma, 81, 165n28
listening
    Ashby on, 42
    attentive, 12, 81, 145
    competence acquired through, 77
    to discern character and motives of speakers, 2
    learning and, 12, 128, 129, 145–48
    Paradisus animae on, 140
    wisdom and, 128, 129, 136
Lochrie, Karma, 129
loquacity. *See* excessive speech
Lorent d'Orléans: *Somme le roi*, 26, 140, 158n26, 173n45
love
    in acquisition of wisdom, 127, 147
    cardinal virtues and, 158n26
    clerical moral texts on, 7, 10, 23, 24, 102
    conventions in love complaint genre, 113
    as ground of theology and human action, 163n45
    martyrdom for love of God, 65
    for perpetrators of insults, 73
    prudence and, 10, 23, 24, 35, 147, 152
    worthiness for, 28
Lydgate, John
    on authority of learned monastic tradition, 159n1

"The Cok Hath Lowe Shoone," 102, 109, 111, 167n8
Fall of Princes, 125–26
Secrees of Old Philisoffres, 129
Temple of Glass, 103
on Zenocrates (Xenocrates), 125–26, 128, 149

MacCulloch, Diarmaid, 175n78
mala taciturnitas. *See* evil taciturnity
Malo, Robyn, 119
Martin of Braga
    Formula honestae vitae, 17, 18, 162n38
    on prudence's workings, 23
    works attributed to Seneca, 18, 23, 162n38
Matthew of Paris: *Historia Anglorum*, 64
Memoriale credencium, 75, 164n22
mental illness
    dating of Hoccleve's illness, 168n12
    "Dialogue" on, 3, 103, 115–18
    discernment of, 112, 169n36
    "My Complaint" on, 3, 11, 105–12, 118–21, 152
    as outside of social norms, 11, 99, 103
    recovery from, 101, 103, 105–7, 115, 117–22, 169n38, 170n53
    self-fragmentation and, 168n18
    temporal views of, 169n38
Metrical Life of Christ, The, 88, 90
Meyer-Lee, Robert, 159n1, 160n24
Middleton, Anne, 132, 172n29
Millemete, Walter: *On the Nobility, Wisdom, and Prudence of Kings*, 27
mirrors for princes
    Active Policy of a Prince, 42–43, 160n24, 160n28
    clerical moral texts as, 27, 68
    on education in governance, 67
    silence and, 5, 30–31, 39, 42
    See also Regiment of Princes
Mooney, Lynne, 168n12
morality. *See* ethics
Morgan, Teresa, 15
Mum and the Sothsegger
    in alliterative verse, 45, 54
    asymmetrical power relations in, 69
    authorship clues, 160n1
    cautionary silence in, 55, 58
    on clerical abuses, 60–61
    culpable silence in, 54, 62, 63
    dating of composition, 45

evil taciturnity in, 11, 46, 54–66, 152
fissures exposed by, 11, 55, 68
inconsistency in personification in, 63, 162n42
legal stratagems in, 61–62, 162n40
political silence in, 3, 46, 59, 60, 66
prudent silence in, 66
readership of, 162n32
Roman popular morality and, 11, 60, 152
as satire of bureaucratic and legal culture, 46, 160n4
sententiae in, 57–59, 64, 162n37
on truth-telling, 45–46, 54–56, 58, 62, 64–67, 163n46
Wycliffites and, 46, 54, 55, 58, 65–67, 160n2
"My Complaint" (Hoccleve)
as confession of faith, 12, 101, 119–21
dating of composition, 103, 168n13
fear in, 12, 100–101, 103–4, 108–11, 113, 121–22
on limitations of silence in social life, 12, 101
on mental illness, 3, 11, 105–12, 118–21, 152
mirror scene in, 113, 121, 168n23
misconstruals of silence in, 3, 12, 111–12, 152
patient silence in, 110, 120–22, 152
prologue to, 105–7, 109, 113–14, 168n21
on recognition of limits of life, 121
self-protective silence in, 101, 108–10, 121, 152
urban companionship in, 11, 99, 105, 107

Newhauser, Richard, 174n66
Nicolas de Byard, 48, 119, 148, 174–75n77
Nicolas de Lyre, 165n42
norms
clerical, 52
ethical/moral, 46, 54
oppressive, 99, 122
Roman popular morality and, 6, 15
for silence, 5–6, 30, 49, 103
social, 5–8, 11, 49, 99, 103, 122
for speech, 5–7, 29, 35, 49, 103
violation of, 9
N-Town trial pageants, 77, 78
Nuttall, Jenni, 55

Orlemanski, Julie, 112, 169n38
Ovid, Publius Naso

Ars amatoria, 14, 26, 156n2
exhortation to practice silence, 16

Paradisus animae, 140, 173n57
pastoral care, 7, 24, 50, 61, 114, 160n6, 172n30
patience
acquisition of, 75
Cicero on, 73
definitions of, 73, 163n7
Gawain-poet on, 71
Gregory the Great on, 72–74, 82, 164n15
paradoxes of, 70
Peyraut on, 73–74, 94
as remedy against wrath, 75, 164n19
as royal virtue, 32, 40, 43
sententiae on, 72–73, 137
value of, 85, 147
patient silence
of Caesar, 75, 164n20
clerical moral texts on, 75, 83
in COVID-19 pandemic, 12
Disce mori on, 74–75
of Gregory the Great, 40
of Jesus, 11, 41, 69–72, 75–80, 82–92, 98–99, 164n24
of Kempe, 11, 92–93
of King David, 29, 40–41, 75, 159n48
in "My Complaint," 110, 120–22, 152
as protective strategy, 94
in *Regiment of Princes*, 40–41, 43, 75, 105
as resistance, 11, 90, 94
of Socrates, 8, 40, 75
suffering and, 28–29, 71–74, 82, 89–90, 94–96, 114, 120
of Thorpe, 3, 11, 92–99, 167n66
as tool for evaluating opponents, 97
value of, 11, 78
in York cycle trial pageants, 11, 69, 77
Pearsall, Derek, 40, 137, 172n25, 172n35
Perkins, Nicholas, 32, 38
Perry, R. D., 104
Peyraut, Guillaume
De eruditione principum, 28
on excessive speech, 28, 140
on fear-based imaginings, 101
"key of the tongue" image used by, 109
on listening, 175n77
on patience, 73–74, 94
on sins of the tongue, 123, 136, 137
Summa de virtutibus, 95, 163n9
Summa de vitiis, 22, 123, 156–57n9, 165n39
on taciturnity winning love, 28

physiognomy, as means of discernment, 169n35
Pierre le Chantre
  on circumstances of speech, 24–25
  on evil taciturnity, 48, 49, 66
  Verbum abbreviatum, 143, 155–56n15, 164n23, 174n66
Piers Plowman
  Activa Vita in, 147
  in alliterative verse, 54
  authorship clues, 172n27
  Charity in, 146
  Clergy in, 130, 134, 141, 143, 145, 146
  Conscience in, 147
  conversionary potential of, 172n30
  Doctor of Divinity in, 146–47
  excessive speech in, 135, 142, 145
  Fortune in, 133, 135, 143
  Imaginitif in, 12, 123–24, 130–32, 139–48, 150, 173n41, 173n55, 174n61
  impulsive speech in, 12, 124
  Jewish wisdom literature and, 137–40, 172n38
  Kynde in, 130, 132, 134, 138, 144–46
  lack of attention to silence by modern readers, 3–4, 132
  Lady Holy Church in, 137
  Liberum Arbitrium in, 147
  moral discourse on silence in, 12, 132, 139, 149
  Patience, 146–47
  Pruyde of Parfit Lyuynge in, 143
  readership of, 162n32
  Reason in, 124, 130–44, 146, 148, 172n32, 172n36, 173n41, 173n55
  Recklessness in, 134–35, 137, 139, 144, 146, 172n35
  Roman popular morality and, 137, 138
  Scripture in, 130, 144
  sententiae in, 57, 123, 131–32, 136, 138, 140–41, 174n61
  shame in, 139, 144, 148, 174n69
  Study in, 130, 142
  Thought in, 130
  vision of "Mydelerthe" in, 130, 132–34, 137, 138, 141, 146
  Will the Dreamer in, 4, 12, 123–24, 130–49, 151, 172nn36–37, 173n41, 174n69, 174n72
  wise silence in, 12, 123–24, 131–32, 137–49
  Wit in, 130, 145
Pilate, in York cycle trial pageants, 3, 69, 77–82, 84–86, 88, 165n38
Pilgrimage of the Lyfe of the Manhode, The, 70–72, 83
political silence
  clerical moral texts on, 26, 66
  evil and corrupt, 46, 66
  in *Mum and the Sothsegger*, 3, 46, 59, 60, 66
  quality of counsel and, 27–28
  Regiment of Princes on, 4, 10, 31, 35, 39, 43, 45, 104
  self-interested and self-protective, 12
Powell, James, 17, 18
power
  absolute, 79
  abuses of, 60
  affective, 114, 132, 133
  asymmetrical, 9, 49, 69, 124, 127
  coercive, 9, 69, 85
  cognitive, 102
  creative, 131, 139
  of emotions, 74, 114, 143
  of God, 107, 117–19, 121, 122
  institutionalized, 49, 82, 88, 98
  of language, 17, 36
  oppressive, 11, 99, 151
  of prudence, 43
  secular, 54, 57
  of silence, 11, 28, 60, 144, 150–51
  sources of, 78, 80, 81
  textual basis of, 33
  transcendent, 120, 122
pride, 80, 82, 142–43, 174n64, 174n66
prodigality, 53, 161n28
Proverbs, book of, 15, 19, 28, 38, 74, 140, 158n36
prudence
  Cicero on, 18, 23, 24, 34
  clerical moral texts on, 10, 17, 23–24, 27
  elements of, 23, 158n27
  foresight and, 23, 36–37, 101, 117
  love and, 10, 23, 24, 35, 147, 152
  reasoning and, 14, 46, 54
  as royal virtue, 9, 34–35, 43, 159n13
  silence and, 4, 9–10, 16–17, 23–24, 27, 30–31, 53, 66–67
  speech and, 18–20, 24
  third eye of, 117, 170n47
  wisdom and, 126, 127
Psalms, book of, 37, 75, 76, 95, 108, 164n23

public silence. *See* silence
Publilius Syrus, 6, 16, 127
Pythagoras, 128, 129, 171n15

Raby, Michael, 169n35
Regiment of Princes (Hoccleve)
   asymmetrical power relations in, 69
   cautionary silence in, 10, 30, 39–41, 43
   culpable silence in, 52, 54
   dating of composition, 31, 159n2
   on emotions and feelings, 39, 43
   evil taciturnity in, 10, 51–54, 59, 65, 152
   on excessive speech, 37–38, 160n18
   on oaths and promises, 31, 35–37, 43
   pastoral sensibility in, 161n29
   patient silence in, 40–41, 43, 75, 105
   political silence in, 4, 10, 31, 35, 39, 43, 45, 104
   prudent silence in, 4, 10, 30–31, 35, 67
   royal silence in, 30–31, 35, 37–43, 109
   sententiae in, 39, 109, 159n6
   sources for, 27, 30, 32, 42, 51
   surviving manuscripts, 159n2
   on treatment of veterans, 108, 168–69n27
   on untamable tongue, 35–37
   on virtues, 31–35, 39–43, 67, 68
Richard II (King of England), 31, 33, 34, 53, 62, 93, 105, 159n17
Robinson, J. W., 77
Roger of Waltham
   Compendium morale de virtutibus, 22, 126–27, 157n25, 173–74n60
   on defending the truth, 47, 161n21
   on excessive speech, 28, 129
   on fraternal correction, 47–49
   on prudence's workings, 23–24
   on self-revelatory speech, 26–27
   on suffering in silence, 28–29
Rokele, William, 172n27
Rolle, Richard: *Melos amoris*, 166n57
Roman popular morality
   clerical moral texts and, 23, 46, 116, 129
   Disticha Catonis and, 15, 16, 54
   on harm avoidance through silence, 15
   Mum and the Sothsegger and, 11, 60, 152
   on norms for silence, 6
   on outcomes from opposite courses, 37
   Piers Plowman and, 137, 138
   sententiae and, 23, 123, 129
Rosenwein, Barbara, 48, 101, 156n16, 157n11, 164n17

Scanlon, Larry, 34, 36, 39
Scase, Wendy, 64, 104, 174n61
Scattergood, John, 160n24, 160n28, 169n32
Schieberle, Misty, 168n26
Schirmer, Elizabeth, 94
Schmidt, A. V. C., 142, 145
Scrope, Stephen, 157n23
Secreta secretorum, 32, 33, 42, 128–29
Secundus, 148
Seneca, Lucius Annaeus (Seneca the Younger)
   fear as conceptualized by, 101
   as influence on Albertano da Brescia, 18, 38
   Martin of Braga's works attributed to, 18, 23, 162n38
   Stoicism and, 16, 59, 73, 101, 126–27
sententiae (authoritative sayings)
   of Cicero, 126, 171n9
   in clerical moral texts, 23, 123, 159n6
   in *Compendium morale de virtutibus*, 173–74n60
   in *Disticha Catonis*, 6, 7, 14–15, 58–59, 138
   "Facientis," 57, 162n35
   of Gregory the Great, 72–73
   Jewish wisdom literature and, 23, 39, 136
   in *Manipulus florum*, 72, 155n15, 157n19, 157n26, 161n26, 162n35
   in *Mum and the Sothsegger*, 57–59, 64, 162n37
   on patience, 72–73, 137
   patristic, 6, 159n6
   in *Piers Plowman*, 57, 123, 131–32, 136, 138, 140–41, 174n61
   of Publilius Syrus, 6, 16, 127
   in *Regiment of Princes*, 39, 109, 159n6
   Roman popular morality and, 23, 123, 129
   self-protective view of silence and, 102
   of Solomon, 6, 20, 65, 136
   in *Summa de vitiis*, 123
   in *Tractatus de mandatis divinis*, 49
   on wise silence, 123
   of Xenocrates, 124–25
Series (Hoccleve)
   dating of composition, 168n13
   holograph of, 167–68n11
   power of disordered affect and emotions in, 114
   reenvisioning of penitential discourse in, 119

Series (Hoccleve) (*continued*)
   textual self of Hoccleve in, 99, 100, 167n1
   translations of *Gesta Romanorum* in, 104, 107–8, 168n26
   See also "Dialogue"; "My Complaint"
Servasanta da Faenza, 128
Seymour, M. C., 159n2
Sidrach, 59, 64
silence
   cautionary, 10, 30, 39–41, 43, 55, 58, 122, 144
   circumspect, 10, 15, 18, 20–21, 43, 55, 61, 111, 150–52, 157n24
   culpable, 12, 47–50, 52, 54, 62, 63, 160n7
   destructive, 12, 45, 53, 114, 152
   ethics of, 3, 5–9, 23, 55, 58–59
   evaluation of, 4–5, 7–8, 156n18
   fearful, 7, 9, 12–13, 101–3, 108–11, 113, 121–22, 124
   functions and meanings of, 2–4
   learning and, 12, 124–32, 139, 146–48, 175n78
   limitations in social life, 12, 101
   mirrors for princes and, 5, 30–31, 39, 42
   misconstruals of, 1–4, 12, 78, 87–89, 98, 111–13, 152
   moral discourse on, 12, 82, 124, 132, 139, 149, 151–53
   norms for, 5–6, 30, 49, 103
   performative nature of, 5, 155n10
   power of, 11, 28, 60, 144, 150–51
   in prevention of violence, 10, 15, 20, 28
   prudent, 4, 9–10, 16–17, 23–24, 27, 30–31, 53, 66–67
   as resistance, 9, 11, 90, 94
   royal, 30–31, 35, 37–43, 109
   self-interested, 11, 12, 16, 45–46, 51, 59
   self-protective, 12, 99–102, 108–11, 115, 121, 152
   sorrow aggravated by, 12, 100, 114
   suffering in, 28–29, 71–74, 82, 89–90, 94–96, 114, 120
   sustained, 10, 19, 31, 43, 67, 88, 91, 109, 150–51
   value of, 2–4, 11, 25, 28, 78, 100, 124, 126, 129, 131
   wisdom and, 2, 9, 12, 19, 108, 123–32, 137–49, 171–72n21, 174n60
   See also evil taciturnity; listening; patient silence; political silence
Simon of Boraston, 27, 127, 160n8
sins of the tongue, 8, 47, 123, 136–37, 142, 155n13, 174n64
Sirach (Ben Sira), 6, 19–20, 28, 37–38, 136, 148, 172n39, 175n77
Skelton, John: *Bowge of Courte*, 110–11, 169n32
Smith, Vance, 146, 174n74
Smyth, Karen Elaine, 169n38
Sobecki, Sebastian, 167n1, 168n13, 168n26
Socrates, 8–9, 40, 75
Solomon, 6, 19, 20, 26, 28, 65, 136
Somerset, Fiona, 94, 161n27
Spearing, A. C., 168n18
Speculum laicorum, 22, 25, 26, 102, 159n48, 164n23
Speculum spiritualium, 164n19, 164n23
Speculum vitae, 137, 140, 142, 159n47, 173n45, 174n66
speech
   abusive, 69–72, 74–76, 85, 89, 95, 96
   circumstances of, 17–18, 20–22, 24–25, 29, 158n32
   clerical discourse on, 25–26
   coercive, 90, 98
   constraints on, 30, 38, 159n1
   contentious, 20, 135–37, 149, 172n39
   deprivation of, 9, 88, 89
   destructive, 17, 26, 36, 49, 125, 139
   deviant, 13, 137, 142
   emotions conveyed through, 110
   ethics of, 5–8, 55, 110, 147, 171n19
   genres of, 11, 75, 78, 83, 87, 93, 95
   God-given functions of, 136, 173n43
   hasty/rash, 10, 17, 20, 28, 41–43, 109, 142, 147
   impulsive, 12, 124
   Jesus's discourse on, 86–87, 166n46
   limitations of, 108, 110
   moral discourse on, 136, 142
   norms for, 5–7, 29, 35, 49, 103
   prudent, 18–20, 24
   reckless, 135, 140, 151
   retaliatory, 11, 76, 83, 85, 95, 110
   self-revelatory, 26–27
   shifts in, 3–5, 155n11
   silence as influence on, 2, 4, 5
   sins of the tongue, 8, 47, 123, 136–37, 142, 155n13, 174n64
   as source of violence, 10, 20, 26
   as tool of amusement at expense of others, 85

transgressive, 37, 155n13
  value of, 29, 47
  See also excessive speech
Steele, R., 162n42
Steiner, Emily, 132, 148, 174n76
Stoics and Stoicism
  Cicero and, 16, 17, 101–2
  clerical moral texts and, 23, 46, 116
  distrust of violent emotions and, 17, 41
  ethics and, 59–60
  on fear, 101–2, 167n2
  injunctions to correct evils, 64
  on norms for silence, 6
  Seneca and, 16, 59, 73, 101, 126–27
  on wisdom, 126–27
Strohm, Paul, 33
Strub, Spencer, 105, 114, 174n69
Styron, William, 103, 168n12
Suarez-Nani, Tiziana, 4
Suese, Heinrich, 104
Summa fratris Alexandri, 47, 160n6

"Tacere" extract (*Pera peregrini*), 24, 155n14, 160–61n10
taciturnity. *See* evil taciturnity; silence
Testimony of William Thorpe, The, 92–99, 166n61, 167n65
textual self, 99, 100, 167n1
Thomas of Chobham, 142
Thomas of Ireland: *Manipulus florum*
  on elements of prudence, 158n27
  on Isidore of Seville's etymology from *sapor*, 171n12
  on Pythagoras's practice of learning, 128
  on Seneca's conceptualization of fear, 101
  sententiae in, 72, 155n15, 157n19, 157n26, 161n26, 162n35
Thorpe, William, 3, 11, 92–99, 151, 166n61, 167nn65–66, 167n71
Tiner, Elza, 166n48
Tinkle, Theresa, 165n38
Towneley cycle trial pageants, 77–78, 165n38, 165n41
Trevisa, John, 27–28, 40, 51
Trump, Donald, first impeachment trial of, 12
truth-telling, 45–46, 54–56, 58, 62, 64–67, 163n46
Turner, Wendy J., 169n36

Valerius Maximus: *Facta et dicta memorabilia*, 16, 125, 155n14
Vecchio, Silvana, 49
verbal abuse, 69–72, 74–76, 85, 89, 95, 96
Vincent of Beauvais
  Speculum doctrinale, 171n9
  Speculum historiale, 178n3
violence
  capacity for, 63
  of emotions, 17, 41, 43, 73, 125
  silence in prevention of, 10, 15, 20, 28
  speech as source of, 10, 20, 26
  threats of, 78–80, 98
  torture of Jesus, 80, 85, 89, 91
virtues
  advocacy for pursuit of, 16
  cardinal, 15, 34, 158nn26–27
  for consistency in conduct, 8, 9
  as defined by Boethius, 156n2
  Disticha Catonis on, 14–15
  magnificencia (greatness of character), 22, 29
  Regiment of Princes on, 31–35, 39–43, 67, 68
  royal, 9, 32, 34–35, 39–43, 47, 159n13
  See also humility; patience; prudence; silence

Walker, Greg, 91, 164–65n28, 169n32
Ward-Perkins, Kate, 45
Warner, Lawrence, 132, 162n32, 172n27
Watt, David, 120, 168n19
Whiting, Bartlett and Helen, 169nn33–34
William of Nottingham, 166n51
William of Ockham: *Dialogus*, 57, 162n35
Willian, R., 168n18
wisdom
  evil taciturnity and, 56
  folk, 109, 111, 138
  foresight and, 15, 116
  of God, 165n43
  learning, 12, 125–30, 139, 143
  listening and, 128, 129, 136
  love in acquisition of, 127, 147
  philosophers as sources of, 124–30
  pragmatic, 108
  prudence and, 126, 127
  silence and, 2, 9, 12, 19, 108, 123–32, 137–49, 171–72n21, 174n60
  Stoics on, 126–27
  See also Jewish wisdom literature

witchcraft, 87–88, 166n48
Wittig, Joseph, 174n69
Woodville, Anthony, 157n23
Woolf, Rosemary, 78, 91
Wright, Claire, 79
Wyche, Richard, 96, 97
Wyclif, John and Wycliffites
  on clerical abuses, 60–61
  condemnation of institutional enforcers, 93
  on defending the truth, 50, 161n21
  De veritate Sacrae Scripturae, 50, 161n18
  on evil taciturnity, 11, 49–50, 58, 66, 152, 161n18, 161n20
  on fear of confession, 102
  on fraternal correction, 49, 55, 161n20
  Good Friday sermon and, 85, 165–66n44, 167n66
  Hoccleve as opponent of, 50, 161n23
  martyrological rhetoric of, 46, 50
  Mum and the Sothsegger and, 46, 54, 55, 58, 65–67, 160n2
  patient silence as protective strategy for, 94
  Tractatus de ecclesia, 161n18
  Tractatus de mandatis divinis, 49, 161n19

Xenocrates, 124–26, 128, 129, 131, 149, 155n14, 170n2

York cycle trial pageants
  abusive speech in, 69, 85, 89
  Anna in, 3, 77, 81–83, 85, 87–89, 165n38, 166n48
  audience response to, 77, 78, 87, 164–65n28, 165n32, 165n38, 166n47
  Caiaphas in, 3, 77, 80–85, 87–89, 165n38, 166n48
  Christ Before Annas and Caiaphas, 77, 82
  Christ Before Herod, 77, 85–86
  Christ Before Pilate I: The Dream of Pilate's Wife, 77
  Christ Before Pilate II: The Judgement, 77, 86, 99
  discourse on speech by Jesus in, 86–87, 166n46
  genres of speech employed by antagonists, 11, 78, 83, 87
  Herod in, 3, 69, 77, 79–86, 88–90, 165n32
  interpretations of Jesus's silence in, 3, 85, 87–89
  opening monologues of, 78–80, 83
  patient silence of Jesus in, 11, 69, 77–80, 82–91
  physical stillness of Jesus in, 69, 95–96
  Pilate in, 3, 69, 77–82, 84–86, 88, 165n38
  shared characteristics of, 77–79
  torture of Jesus in, 80, 85, 89, 91
  in York Register, 164n25

Zeeman, Nicolette, 133–34, 138, 139, 144, 172n30
Zenocrates. *See* Xenocrates

www.ingramcontent.com/pod-product-compliance
Lightning Source LLC
Chambersburg PA
CBHW032337300426
44109CB00041B/1117